WITHDRAWN

The moving finger writes,
and having writ

Moves on; nor all your
piety nor wit

Shall lure it back to cancel
half a line

Nor all your tears wash
out a word of it.

Stanza 71
The Rubaiyat of
Omar Khayyam

JOHNS HOPKINS UNIVERSITY STUDIES

IN

HISTORICAL AND POLITICAL SCIENCE

HERBERT B. ADAMS, EDITOR

History is past Politics and Politics present History—*Freeman*

EXTRA VOLUME

X

SPANISH INSTITUTIONS

OF THE

SOUTHWEST

By **FRANK W. BLACKMAR, Ph. D.** *(Johns Hopkins University)*

Professor of History and Sociology in the Kansas State University

The Rio Grande Press, Inc.

GLORIETA, NEW MEXICO · 87535

First edition from which this
edition was reproduced was
supplied by
T. N. LUTHER, Books,
P. O. Box 6083
Shawnee Mission, Ks. 66206

Library of Congress Cataloging in Publication Data

Blackmar, Frank Wilson, 1854-1931.
   Spanish institutions of the Southeast.

(A Rio Grande classic)
   Reprint with new introd., of the 1891 ed.
published by Johns Hopkins Press, Baltimore, which
was issued as extra v. 10 of the Johns Hopkins University studies in historical and political science.
   Bibliography: p.
   1. Southwest, New--History--To 1848. 2. Spain-
-Colonies--North America--Southwest, New.
4. Missions--Southwest, New. I. Title. II. Series: Johns Hopkins University. Studies in historical and political science : Extra volumes ; 10.
F799.B62 1976   979'.01   76-48197
ISBN 0-87380-117-2

A RIO GRANDE CLASSIC
First published in 1891

First Printing 1976

The Rio Grande Press, Inc.

GLORIETA, NEW MEXICO · 87535

Publisher's Preface

Years ago, when we published *The Coronado Expedition* (translated from the Spanish of Castaneda in 1891 by George Parker Winship), we were taken to task by some of our erudite and scholarly friends. Do you not know, they would ask, that the Winship has been long outdated by newer translations? And moreover, much, much more has been discovered about Coronado since 1895?

Well, sure, we knew that. Nevertheless, we reminded our friendly critics, no student or scholar or historian or researcher could study the Spanish in the American Southwest and *ignore* the Winship. It was, for all practical purposes, the *starting point* for historical research. Wherever one went in the end, bibliographically speaking, one *started* with Winship. We also mentioned, in passing, that we did not conceive it to be within our purvue, or scope of publishing (so to speak), to bring reprints ". . . up to date" with deep scholarly research and annotations. We were pursuing the goal of making fine old books available again for the current and future generations; we felt then, as we do now, that a facsimile reprint of a first or early edition with a new scholarly *Introduction,* a new index if appropriate, a germane map or chart, or contemporary photographs that illustrate the original text in some meaningful way, was and is our field of endeavor. We've stuck pretty close to that idea since founding The Rio Grande Press in 1962.

Now comes time to present Frank W. Blackmar's fine classic study *Spanish Institutions of the Southwest.* Of course we know that many studies of the Spanish institutions of the Southwest have been made and published since Dr. Blackmar published his work in 1891. But we have found that the first edition, wherever it can be found in locked cases, is still very much in research demand; and why not? It is a *starting point,* an early but very good study well worth putting back onto circulating shelves of libraries. Our price for this beautiful Rio Grande Classic may seem big, but compared to the cost of a first edition, our price is quite modest. Any library—public, institutional or private, can now afford our edition which is, of course, a somewhat emended facsimile copy of a first edition. Thus the first editions can be kept and guarded in locked cases for future generations, assuming there will be a constant flow. Our edition is made to be used, and used, and used . . . and we hope it is.

We thank our friend T. N. Luther, who sells rare and out of print books out of Shawnee Mission, Kans., for supplying the first edition from which this edition was reproduced.

We have not emended this title as much as we have most of our others. The index in the first edition was quite adequate, and we have retained it in our edition. The author included a lot of photographs of the California missions as they were in the late 19th century, but we felt he slighted the Spanish missions of Texas, New Mexico and Arizona. We have, therefore, added on the endpapers our own 1976 photograph (in color) of the "White Dove of the Desert", the beautiful mission church of San Xavier at Tucson, Ariz.

We invited Dr. Michael Cox of the Museum of New Mexico in Santa Fe to write a scholarly introduction here, and he did so with grace and felicity. His words follow ours, and the reader who passes them up will miss a better understanding of the honored place this title holds in the bibliography of Western Americana.

No doubt we should mention, in passing, our inclusion on the very first page of this book a nicely printed copy of the 71st stanza of the *Rubaiyat of Omar Khayyam.* One of the many sons of a rich Arabian tentmaker, young Omar nine centuries ago had a superb contemporary education combined with what has since become notable for its absence in many young people—common sense. Modern youth tends to sneer at *any* aphorisms these days, new *or* old. What is worse, so do some of their addlepated elders. What is truth, anyway? The ancient Greek philosophers drove each other up the wall, we are told, trying to analyze this cryptoaphorism:

"If a man says of himself, I lie, he tells the truth; if he says of himself, I tell the truth, he tells a lie."

Those old Greeks were dust for some eleven centuries before young Omar Khayyam rhymed an eternal verity as immutable as the orbits of the planets, and even more so, for the planets *can* perhaps some day change but the thought expressed in this particular aphorism of the poet cannot.

Think about this: what is past, is past. What has been done, has been done. What has been written cannot, to coin a word, be unwritten. The world has been imperfect since there have been people with the perception to perceive the imperfection, and for eons before that. The world will *always* be imperfect, and so will the people in it. And what has happened—history—cannot be "unhappened". The scribe who writes history as he wishes it might have been writes fiction. The wise man recognizes that even as one cannot unscramble an egg, one cannot change things that were, and things that never were.

This title is the 106th beautiful Rio Grande Classic.

Robert B. McCoy

La Casa Escuela
Glorieta, New Mexico 87535
October 1976

BLACKMAR, Frank Wilson, univ. prof.; b. W. Springfield, Pa., Nov. 3, 1854; s. John S. and Rebecca (Mershon) B.; Ph.B., U. of the Pacific, 1881, A.M., 1884; prof. mathematics, U. of the Pacific, 1882-86; grad. student and fellow, Johns Hopkins, 1886-89, Ph.D., 1889; LL.D., U. of Southern Calif., 1921, Coll. of Pacific, 1924, Baker Univ., Baldwin, Kan., 1929; m. Mary S. Bowman, June 25, 1885 (died Mar. 4, 1892); m. 2d, Kate Nicholson, July 26, 1900; children—Winifred Margaret, Mrs. Cora Gertrude Geisler, Howard Bowman, Dorothy Leoti. Prof. history and sociology, 1889-99, sociology and economics, 1899-1912, sociology, 1912—; dean Grad. Sch., 1896-1922, U. of Kan. Pres. Kan. Conf. Social Work, 1900-02. Elector Hall of Fame. Author: Federal and State Aid to Higher Education in the United States, 1890; Spanish Colonization, 1890; Spanish Institutions in the Southwest, 1891; The Study of History and Sociology, 1890; The Story of Human Progress, 1896; Economics, 1907; History of Higher Education in Kansas, 1900; Charles Robinson, The Free State Governor of Kansas, 1900; Life of Charles Robinson, The First Governor of Kansas, 1902; The Elements of Sociology, 1905; Economics for High Schools, 1907; Editor Cyclopedia of History of Kansas, 1912; Outlines of Sociology, 1914,23; History of Kansas State Council of Defense, 1921; Justifiable Individualism, 1922. History of Human Society, 1926. Home: Lawrence, Kan. Died Mar. 30, 1931.

—*Who Was Who 1897-1942*
Pp. 102

Foreword

As a new field of consideration, the study of Southwest history was only beginning to bud when Dr. Frank Blackmar began his classical work on Spanish institutions in the Southwest. Blackmar was thus handicapped by a lack of bibliographic guides to primary sources and by a lack of substantial work in the various areas he attempts to consider. Bolton, Chapman, Haring and Scholes were still years away, and yet with this lack of material Blackmar was still able to produce a work which must be referred to by anyone in the field of Borderlands history.

Dr. Blackmar sets the tone for the entire volume in the first two paragraphs of Chapter One. He claims that the results of Spain's occupation were mournful, that Spaniards are slow to accept improvements in living and that the Spanish soldier was more cruel than the savage he conquered. From this point, the author attempts to demonstrate the truthfulness of these assertions by studying the governmental and religious institutions of the Southwest. Comparing Roman institutions of war and conquest with Teutonic institutions of freedom, Blackmar concludes that because certain Spanish institutions found their origins in similar Roman systems, they were inherently inferior to those imported to Britain by the Saxons. The author further states that the inferior institutions had little effect on America and were replaced in the Southwest by superior angloteutonic customs. Here the author is guilty of committing the most common error committed by scholars of the Southwest. For nearly 250 years, the area of California, Arizona, New Mexico and Texas was the northern frontier of New Spain and Mexico. The institutions of the area came north from Mexico. Those imposed by conquering armies from the East were not readily accepted nor did they seem to change basic custom or traditions in many areas of the Southwest. Indeed the institutions of Mexico have had as great effect on the Southwest as have those of the United States.

Perhaps the most valuable portion of the entire work is the second chapter. By describing and tracing in detail the Roman institutions transferred to Spain by the armies of Rome, the author provides the reader with indepth information on Roman government in Spain and allows the reader to compare Roman institutions with those which evolved under the Christian rulers of Medieval Spain. Unfortunately there is very little consideration of the Gothic and Moorish influences on Spanish institutions.

After discussing the condition of Spain on the eve of conquest of New Spain by Spanish conquistadores, Blackmar begins his indepth analysis of Spanish institutions. It is in the ensuing chapters that the reader finds both the value and the weakness of Dr. Blackmar's work. Beginning with the Mission system as it functioned in California, he presumes to praise the missionaries for their patience, bravery and long suffering and at the same time recounts their cruelty to Indian neophytes, their greed for land and their interference with governmental systems. In fact, he suggests that their prime function was to act in the name of the king as agent for the crown. Herbert E. Bolton disagrees not only with the greedy, cruel characterization, but also points out that religion was the first matter of business for the hundreds of pioneer missionaries in the Borderlands frontier. If the missionary assisted the state in subduing the Indians and colonizing the frontier, it was incidental to the religious cause they served. To doubt the religious fervor and commitment of the missionary, Bolton suggests, "is to confess complete and disqualifying ignorance of the great mass of existing missionary correspondence . . . so fraught with unmistakable proofs of the religious zeal and devotion of the vast majority of the missionaries."

The mission as reported by Blackmar acted in conjunction with the encomienda, but there were others in New Mexico and Texas that had no relation to the encomienda. Missions in New Mexico for example had very little in common with those of California or elsewhere in the Frontier. Instead of nomadic Indians, the missionaries found well organized villages complete with local governments. Instead of building a mission church and then a settlement to house Indians, the clergy were forced to build on the edge of the pueblo village. Instead of introducing the natives to the benefits of a sedentary life, the religious pioneers were forced to live with a strict social system based on a strong religion. Because the mission system was different in New Mexico it also affected the architecture of the mission complex. Unlike the large structures of California, Sonora, Arizona and Texas the pueblo missions were smaller buildings built only to accommodate the residents of the pueblo. These buildings were often served by an itinerant circuit missionary system rather than the sedentary resident clerical system of other areas on the frontier.

Using California as his only source for the study of the presidial system, the author totally ignores the use and value of the presidio throughout the southwest. Studies by Moorhead, Gerald, Thomas, Garcia Navarro and others have shown the importance of the presidio in protecting settlements throughout the Borderlands frontier. Unlike the spiritless and unwarlike Indians Blackmar refers to, the Apache, Comanche, Ute and Navajo Indians were highly skilled in the arts of war, and posed formidable barriers to the Spanish "leather jacket." The presidio's importance to physical occupation of the frontier cannot be denied, nor can the bravery of the agrarian soldier who served to guard the frontier. Their uniforms of cloth and leather, rather than Quixotic as Blackmar describes them, were extremely practical in warding off Indian arrows and yet were light weight and much cooler than heavy armor.

The physical possession of the land exemplified by the frontier presidio must have created a certain abstract feeling of security. It was the existence of these presidios that insured conquest. As long as they remained, the frontier empire remained. Should they fall to the native population then the entire empire felt threatened as occurred during the Pueblo Revolt of 1680. Outlying settlements might come and go as they often did, but if the presidio was lost it must be regained or the frontier in that area was abandoned. The importance of the presidio as a symbol of the Spanish empire is not adequately dealt with by Blackmar but is discussed by Moorehead.

Although troubled by numerous minor factual and typographical errors, the chapter dealing with settlement of Arizona, New Mexico and Texas provides basic information as it was then available. However one point which might lead to certain amount of confusion is the discussion of the founding of the village of Santa Cruz de la Cañada. The author indicates that Santa Cruz was founded during the period 1680-95 by seventy-five Spaniards. During the initial insurrection of 1680 the entire Spanish population was expelled from New Mexico and did not return until the reconquest by DeVargas in 1690-92. Thus settlement of Santa Cruz was not 1680-95 but instead occurred in 1695. It is unfortunate that Blackmar was unable to consult the work of Charles W. Hackett which provided much of the documentation on the revolt and its causes. The Pueblo Revolt caused a major shift in policy resulting in the abolishment of the encomienda system in New Mexico and establishing better working relations between church and state. Relations which in fact made continued occupation possible.

Dr. Blackmar fails completely when discussing the social conditions of the Indians. The chapter does not relate to his overall theme and the author obviously had little understanding of the people he described. His statements regarding the primitive nature of pueblo religion are particularly unfortunate because more accurate information was available at the time. Pueblo religion was not based on sun worship or on anything relating to worship of Montezuma. Discussion of pueblo religion and society as well as other Indian groups is a lengthy and very detailed topic not in the scope of either the book or the foreword.

The lack of available source material is again made evident in Chapter XIII dealing with the social and political life of the colonists. Here the author uses life in California as the prototype for all of the Southwest. His judgments regarding the lazy character of California's ranchers belies the prejudice seen elsewhere within the work. Unfortunately, Dr. Blackmar failed to indicate the nature of social and political life in areas other than California. New Mexico had a socially and politically more active life than that of California. For example New Mexico was able to elect and send to Spain, Pedro Bautista Pino as a member of the Royal Cortez. The distinction between Spanish and Mexican heritage was also of less importance in other areas of the Borderlands than evidenced in California. While blood lines were important in determining social position, the New Mexico frontier seems to have been somewhat democratic, using wealth, political activity and military success as more important indicators of social status.

On the whole the work is a classic which must be referred to by any serious student of the Spanish Southwest. It is the first attempt to synthesize the history of Spanish institutions in the Southwest and at the same time provide information relating to old world antecedents to those institutions. Dr. Blackmar's study is also a classic because it is so demonstrative of its times. The author's enthusiasm for things Anglo was typical of American scholarship at the turn of the century. America had spanned the continent and had conquered;all Protestant religious ethics dominated American thought. Anglo superiority had been proved. Dr. Blackmar consciously or unconsciously attempts to validate these beliefs in every chapter of his work. Therefore *Spanish Institutions of the Southwest* is not only a classic in the study of the Southwest but also a classic in the historical study of the late 19th century.

Scholars in both fields will be pleased that the book is now available in this reprint edition and Rio Grande Publishers should be acclaimed for assisting the study of history by making such volumes once again available to the public.

Michael Cox

Santa Fe, N.M.
October 1976

som. Photo.

MONTEREY, FROM THE FORT.

SPANISH INSTITUTIONS

OF THE

SOUTHWEST

By **FRANK W. BLACKMAR, Ph. D.** (*Johns Hopkins University*)

Professor of History and Sociology in the Kansas State University

———————

BALTIMORE

THE JOHNS HOPKINS PRESS

1891

JOHN MURPHY & CO., PRINTERS.

BALTIMORE.

PREFACE.

The present work was suggested to the writer while a student at the Johns Hopkins University. There coming in contact with the large amount of work which has been done in the study of Teutonic institutions as represented in England, Germany, and America, it seemed to him that Spanish-American institutions were also worthy of investigation and especially interesting in comparison with Anglo-American institutions as developed in the colonies of the Atlantic coast. A former residence of a number of years in California, where certain forms of the old civilization still remain, served to heighten the writer's interest in the subject. Its study has been profitable and interesting to the writer, though carried on during a busy university life. To the latter fact may be attributed, in part, many of the imperfections of the book, which is far removed from the author's ideal. However, it is hoped that this volume will at least awaken a deeper interest in a long neglected part of American history.

The Southwest is a comparatively new field for the study of the history of institutions. As it did not figure in our early colonial life and later national development, it cannot claim as great importance in nation-building as other parts of our country. Its contributions to our national life have necessarily been meagre; for, during the formative period of our nation the country was long under the rule of foreign powers. There was a great break in the continuity of its colonial life owing to conquest and immigration. Therefore but few institutions were transmitted after contact with that sturdy race which carries its own institutions with it when going out to conquer. But the growing importance of the Southwest, as a component part of the great American Commonwealth, renders its early history very important and interesting, not only to those who live in that section but also to students, scholars, and historians.

This volume is not intended to be a history of the Spanish conquest of America. It is simply a study in Spanish-American institutions. However, in the process of representing social and political institutions the best part of the story of the conquest is told; for, indeed, the description of the social and political institutions of a country is an epitome of its history. As the study of institutions treats of the forms and functions of government and of the customs and life of organic society, expeditions, wars, intrigues, and the deeds of great men are of value only in so far as they assist to a better understanding of institutions. In such a study chronological perspective should be used, but no attempt should be made to tell stories for their own sake nor fully to relate historic events. In the present work only sufficient descriptive history has been given to illustrate the social and political life of the people and to show to what extent and in what manner the laws and forms of government have been applied in practical life. On this account many of the subjects treated appear to be incomplete and fragmentary, so far as full descriptive history is concerned, but they serve the purpose intended in the presentation of the development of institutions. To those who desire the whole story of Spanish conquest and occupation the writer would recommend the great work of Hubert Howe Bancroft. It is a rich mine of historical wealth. The writer has consulted, cited, and quoted it frequently in this work as an authority on difficult points.

The objective field of research covers the period from the conquest and settlement of New Mexico in the sixteenth century to 1846, the date of the American conquest. But the student of institutions claims all times for his own and uses material that best subserves his purpose. The times of Cortes must be referred to in order to discover what institutions of old Spain were transmitted to the colonies, and the institutions of old Spain must be investigated to understand the nature of those transmitted. Turning from the Teutonic institutions, which have been studied with great care by scholars, and from the Germanic political atmosphere with which our institutions are surrounded, the student is impressed with the striking contrast which Spanish-American institutions present. The key to that difference is found in the Roman influence on the development of Spanish institutions. Therefore the writer makes no apology for showing the Roman origin of Spanish institutions, nor for presenting the nature of those that were transmitted to America; for these matters are of vital importance. No attempt has been made to represent modern institutions in the Southwest but the author has frequently mentioned phases of government and events occurring after the establishment of American rule. There is much in modern life relating to old Spanish life and institutions which has not been described.

The illustrations have been chosen with a view of showing more clearly the nature of the ancient civilization described in the text and to preserve representations of ruins which cannot retain their forms much longer in the presence of the rapid changes going on in the country.

FRANK W. BLACKMAR.

UNIVERSITY OF KANSAS,
    June 3, 1891.

CONTENTS.

Contents.

CHAPTER VI. THE FIRST SETTLEMENTS IN ALTA CALIFORNIA:

Chapter VIII. Spanish Colonial Municipalities:

xvi *Contents.*

AUTHORITIES CONSULTED.

ALBERT, LIEUT. Description of a Pueblo. Executive Document, No. 41. First Sess., 30th Cong., 1848, p. 462.

ADAM, REV. J. Padre Junipero Serra. San Francisco, 1884.

ARNOLD, W. T. Roman Provincial Administration. London, 1879.

BALLOU, M. M. Aztec Land. New York, 1890.

BANDALIER, A. F. The Delight Makers. New York, 1890.

BAEGERT, JACOB. An Account of the Aboriginal Inhabitants of the California Peninsula. Smithsonian Report, 1863-4.

BANCROFT, H. H. Native Races. 5 vols. San Francisco, 1882-3.

BANCROFT, H. H. History of the North Mexican States. 3 vols. San Francisco, 1884-89.

BANCROFT, H. H. History of California. 7 vols. San Francisco, 1884-90.

BANCROFT, H. H. California Pastoral. San Francisco, 1888.

BANCROFT, H. H. History of Mexico. 6 vols. San Francisco, 1883-88.

BANCROFT, H. H. Arizona and New Mexico. San Francisco, 1889.

BARTLETT, J. R. Personal Narrative, New Mexico, Texas and California. 2 vols. New York, 1854.

BEECHY, FRED. W. Narrative of a voyage (1836-42) to the Pacific Coast and Behring Strait. 2 vols. London, 1843.

BEGERT, JACOB. Nachrichten der Americanischen Halbinsel California. Manheim, 1772.

BOSCANA, JERONIMO. Chinigchinich. New York, 1846. (Robinson.)

BROWN, ALEXANDER. The Genesis of the United States. 2 vols., 8vo. Boston, 1890.

BRYANT, E. What I saw in California. New York, 1849.

BURKE, EDMUND. An Account of European Settlement in America. 2 vols. London, 1808.

CABEZA DE VACA. Relation of, Terneaux-Compans. Paris, 1838.

CABEZA DE VACA. Commentaries, Terneaux-Compans. Paris, 1838.

CALIFORNIA, Debates in Convention of, on the Formation of the State Constitution, 1849. Washington, 1850.

CAPRON, E. S. History of California. Boston, 1854.

CASTANEDA, PEDRO DE. Relation, Terneaux-Compans, vol. IX, p. 138. Paris, 1838.

COPPEE, HENRY. The Conquest of Spain, by the Arab-Moors. 2 vols. Boston, 1881.

COXE, WILLIAM. Memoirs of the King of Spain, of the House of Bourbon. London, 1813.

CRESPI, JUAN. Viage de la expedicion de terra de San Diego a Monterey. Doc. History of Mexico, tome VI.

CRONISE, T. F. Natural Wealth of California. San Francisco, 1868.

DANA, R. H. Two Years before the Mast. New York, 1886.

DAVIS, W. W. H. El Gringo. New York, 1857.

DAVIS, W. W. H. The Spanish Conquest of Mexico. Doylestown, Pa., 1869.

DE MOFRAS, DUFLOT. Explorations de l'Oregon, des Californias. Paris, 1844.

DOYLE, JOHN T. The Pious Fund. Cal. Hist. Soc., vol. I.

DUNHAM, S. A. History of Spain and Portugal. 5 vols. London, 1833.

DURUY, VICTOR. History of Rome, 8 vols. New York, 1884.

DWINELLE, JOHN W. Colonial History of San Francisco. San Francisco, 1863.

ENCYCLOPAEDIA BRIT. Spanish-American Colonies.

EVANS, R. S. Cabrillo's Voyage. U. S. Geolog. Survey, vol. VII, 1879, Archaeology.

FARNHAM, THOS. J. Life and Adventures in California. New York, 1846.

FERRELO, BARTOLOME. Cabrillo's Voyage. U. S. Geolog. Survey, vol. VII, 1879, Archaeology.

FORBES, A. History of California. London, 1839.

FOOTE, MARY HALLOCK. The Cascarone Ball. Century, Aug., 1879.

GAYARRÉ, CHARLES. Philip II, of Spain.

GREISINGER, THEODORE. The Jesuits. 2 vols. Putnam, 1883.

GWIN, W. M. Private Land Titles in the State of California. Speeches in the Senate. Washington, 1851.

GIBBON, EDWARD. History of the Decline and Fall of the Roman Empire.

HAKLUYT'S VOYAGES. The Principal Navigators. Sir Francis Drake. 3 vols. London.

HALE, E. E. The Name of California. Atlantic Monthly, Vol. XIII.

HALL, FREDERIC. History of San José. San Francisco, 1871.

HALLECK, H. W. Report on Land Titles in California.

HALLECK, H. W. Report 133, Correspondence of Sec. of State 1846–8 in California and New Mexico, Mes. and Doc., 1850.

HARRIS, J. M. Paper on California. 1855.

HARRISON, J. A. History of Spain.

HELPS, SIR ARTHUR. The Spanish Conquest of America. 4 vols. New York, 1868.

HEEREN, A. H. L. Historical Researches, etc. Oxford, 6 vols., 1833.

HITTELL, J. S. History of the City of San Francisco. San Francisco, 1878.

HOLLEY, MRS. M. A. Texas. Lexington, Ky., 1836.

HUGHES, MRS. ELIZ. The California of the Padres. San Francisco, 1875.

HUMBOLDT, ALEX. VON. The Kingdom of New Spain. London, 1811.

HUMBOLDT, ALEX. VON. Ensayo Politico sobre Nueva Espana. 5 vols.
Paris, 1856.

ICAZBALCETA, JUAN G. Documentos para la historia de Mexico. 1853-7.

IHNE, WILLIAM. History of Rome. 5 vols. London, 1871-82.

INGERSOLL, ERNEST. In a Redwood Logging Camp. Harper's Mag.
LXVI., p. 144.

JACKSON, H. H. A Century of Dishonor. Boston, 1886.

JACKSON, H. H. Father Junipero and his Work. Century Mag., Vol. 26.
Present Condition of the Mission Indians. Century Mag., Vol. 26.

JONES, W. C. Report on Land Titles in California ; The Pueblo Question
Solved. Washington, 1850.

JONES, THOS. C. Agresion en Californias, 27c, 3s, H. ex. Doc., 166.

KING, T. B. Report on California. Washington, 1852.

KINNEY, ABBOTT. Report to Commissioner of Indian Offices.

KOTSEBUE, OTTO VON. Voyages.

LA FUENTA, MODESTO. Los Reyes Católicas. Selection from Historia de
España.

LA FUENTA, MODESTO. Historia general de España. Madrid, 1850-67.

LOCKMAN, JOHN. Travels of the Jesuits into various parts of the World.
London, 1762.

LANGDORFF, GEO. H. VON. Voyages in various parts of the world (1803-7).
London, 1813-4.

LA PEROUSE, J. F. G. DE. Relation Abrégée du Voyage de La Perouse.
Leipzig, 1799.

LA PEROUSE, J. F. G. DE. Voyage around the World. London, 1798.

LEX MALAGA. Edited by Mommsen.

LEX SALPENSA. Edited by Mommsen.

MARQUARDT, JOACHIM. Römische Staatsverwaltung. 2 vols. Leipsic,
1873.

MARCOU, JULES. Notes on the First Discovery of California and Origin of
the Name. Government Doc., 1878.

MAYER, B. Mexico, with Notes on California. 1853.

MERIVALE, H. Colonization and Colonies. London, 1861.

MOMMSEN, THEODORE. The History of Rome. 4 vols. New York, 1889.

MOMMSEN, THEODORE. Staatsrechte der Lateinischen Germinden Salpensa
und Malaca in der Provinz Baetica.

MOMMSEN, THEODORE. The Provinces of the Roman Empire. 2 vols.
London, 1886.

MORGAN, LEWIS H. Systems of Consanguinity and Affinity of the Human
Race. Smithsonian Con., vol. XVII, 218.

MOSES, BERNARD. Data of Mexican and United States History. Cal.
Hist. Assoc., Vol. I.

MOSES, BERNARD. The Establishment of Municipal Government in San Francisco. Johns Hopkins University Studies, Series VII.

MOTLEY, J. L. Rise of the Dutch Republic. New York, 1880.

MOTLEY, J. L. United Netherlands. New York, 1880.

MORGAN, LEWIS. Houses and House-life of the American Aborigines. Contributions to American Ethnology, Vol. IV. Washington, 1881.

MURPHY, JAMES CAVANAUGH. The Arabian Antiquities of Spain. London, 1813.

NEVE, PHILIP DE. Regulations for the Government of the Province of California. San Carlos, 1779. (Rockwell, 445.)

OBER, FREDERICK A. Travels in Mexico. Boston, 1884.

PALOU, FRANCISCO. Relacion de la Vida del Padre Junipero Serra. Mexico, 1787.

PALOU, FRANCISCO. Noticias de la California. Hist. Doc., Tomes VI–VII.

PALOU, FRANCISCO. Magazine of American History, IV. Letter, 1783.

POWERS, STEPHEN. Aborigines of California. U. S. Geolog. Survey. J. W. Powell, 1888.

PRESCOTT, W. H. History of the Conquest of Mexico. Philadelphia, 1890.

PRESCOTT, W. H. Ferdinand and Isabella. Philadelphia, 1890.

PRESCOTT, W. H. Philip the Second. Philadelphia, 1890.

PRINCE, L. B. History of New Mexico. Kansas City, 1883.

PRIVATE LAND CLAIMS. Report of Committee. San Francisco, 1852.

RECOPILACION de Leyes de los Reynos de las Indias. Madrid, 1774.

ROBERTSON, W. Charles V. of Spain. Philadelphia, 1873 (Prescott).

ROBERTSON, W. History of America. London, 1778.

ROBINSON, A. Life in California. New York, 1846.

ROYCE, JOSIAH. California. Boston, 1888.

ROCKWELL, JOHN A. A Compilation of Spanish and Mexican Law. New York, 1851.

SCHMIDT, GUSTAVUS. The Civil Law of Spain and Mexico. New Orleans, 1851.

SCHUMACHER, PAUL. Aborigines of California. Popular Science Monthly, 1887, p. 253.

SCHUBERT, F. W. Verfassungs Urkunden. 2 vols.

SHEA, J. G. History of Catholic Missions in the U. S. New York, 1855.

SHINN, C. H. Mining Camps. 1886.

SHINN, C. H. Pioneer Spanish Families in California. Century, Vol. 41.

SMITH, ADAM. Wealth of Nations. Book IV., Chap. 7.

SOULE, FRANK. Annals of San Francisco. New York, 1885.

TORQUEMADA, JUAN DE. Monarquia Indiana. Madrid, 1723.

TUTHILL, FRANKLIN. History of California. San Francisco, 1866.

UNITED STATES Government Documents.

VALENCIA. Noticias de la Provincias de las Californias, 1794.

VANCOUVER, GEO.   Voyage of Discovery to the Pacific Ocean.   London, 1798.

VANCOUVER, GEO.   Voyage de Decouvers a l'Ocean Pacifique.   Paris, 1798.

VENEGAS, MIGUEL.   Noticias de la California.   Madrid, 1757.

VENEGAS, MIGUEL.   Natural and Political History of California.   2 vols. London, 1759.

WHEELER, G. M.   U. S. Geolog. Survey, 1878, Vol. VII.

WHITNEY, J. D.   Geolog. Survey of California.   6 vols.

WARNER, WIDNEY AND HAYES.   An Historical Sketch of Los Angeles, Cal.   Los Angeles, 1876.

WILKES, CHARLES.   U. S. Explor. Expedition, Vol. V.   Phil., 1845.

WILLEY, H. S.   An Historical Paper relating to Santa Cruz, Cal.   San Francisco, 1876.

WILSON, HON. B. D.   Report to the Interior Department, 1853.

WINSOR, JUSTIN.   Narrative and Critical History of America.   8 vols.

WELLS, DAVID.   A Study of Mexico.   New York, 1888.

ILLUSTRATIONS.

SPANISH INSTITUTIONS OF THE SOUTHWEST.

CHAPTER I.

INTRODUCTION.

The student of history and politics finds the deepest interest and the greatest profit in the social and political institutions of a people; for in these are represented the first life of a nation. Whether he study the tribal life of the Iroquois, the politics of Greece and Rome, the colonial life of New England, the municipality of Spain, or even the problems of modern political administration, it is the same humanity which he studies, every part of which bears its own lesson. And it is not infrequent that the field of history which is the least promising reveals the greatest truth. In its larger sense there is but one history, and that is the history of humanity; the past and present are one; time alone is old. Greece and Rome were young; immediately about us are the oldest institutions. It only remains to choose what part of this great domain shall be first investigated, even as one would choose which of the colonial elements of our great nation should be first studied.

Of the four great nations of the Old World, which, through war and diplomacy, competed for supremacy on the Western continent, none has left a more interesting record than that of Spain. Mournful as were the results of her enterprises, her history is everywhere tinged with colors of romance; for

1

the exploration and conquest of the Spaniard bordered on the marvelous. There were excitement, adventure, and old-time glory in every exploit which has exhibited on plain, mountain, or in forest, the characteristics of Spanish national life. This life, to the casual observer, is a series of paradoxes; to the thoughtful a natural outcome. The Spanish explorer, apparently as devout as a monk, was frequently more cruel than the savage whom he conquered. A liberty-loving people, the Spanish have produced the worst types of absolutism; possessed of an active and progressive spirit, they have been slow to grasp and hold the vital elements of permanent improvement; and while in the very act of inaugurating a reform, they have sown the seeds of anarchy and oppression. Popular representation and individual rights, the flowers of early independence, were crushed by the ruthless hand of tyranny and despotism. Abounding in magnificent opportunities for gaining and holding power, the Spanish people were again and again forced to yield to foreign oppression.

The prestige of Spain in the New World was great, and in the Old World her power was supreme. It is well to remember that the discovery of America was accomplished under the patronage of Spain, and that priority of discovery and exploration gave her the first right to the soil; that the first adventurers and explorers that over-ran the New World were Spaniards, a fact that strengthened her claim to the newly discovered territory; and that in the century following the discovery, Spain had become the foremost nation of all Europe; consequently the right of might was in her favor. In addition to this, Pope Alexander VI., by an assumed divine right, bequeathed to Spain nearly the whole of the newly discovered continent.[1] With these advantages the opportunities of Spain were great. Indeed it may be said that, among the modern nations of Europe, no other had such great opportunities of extending territory and of building and establishing a great

---

[1] Robertson, *History of America*, I, 113.

empire as Spain; no other nation had such opportunities to develop and perpetuate civil liberty. Yet with all this prestige and power, Spain yielded her territory in the New World step by step, and lost her proud position in the front rank of the nations of the Old. The result of this withdrawal was that the permanent institutions of North America have been established by other nationalities. Remnants of laws, customs, and institutions, and influences of the same, are all that we see to-day of an empire once magnificent in extent. The work of building the American Republic was performed by another nation.

It is generally recognized that our American political life is Teutonic in its origin and fundamental characteristics, and that the germs of American institutions have been derived directly from England. So marked are these phases of historical truth, that a celebrated historian has written of "The English people in their three Homes,"[1] the Old, the Middle, and the New England; the continental, the island, and the trans-continental homes. Nor is this a sentimental or visionary conception. It is historical; for in these three homes are people of a common stock, whose early institutions were the same; though now differentiated, on account of environments, until the three vary in customs, laws, and social life. But the liberty of which they speak, and the progress of which they boast, originated in a common birth-right, and descended through a common lineage. It may be justly claimed that in this same source the element of modern civilization may be found. And since the life and spirit of modern progress flow largely from Teutonic sources, our laws, forms of local government, education, and social life, have a direct continuity with these early institutions; wherever we find the vitalizing process of modern civilization, there we recognize the effects of the "liberty born in a German forest;"[2] and we may trace

---

[1] E. A. Freeman.
[2] Montesquieu.

the germs of American institutions in the customs of the "generous barbarians." [1]

But in conceding that the vital forces of history, especially those that appeal most directly to the interests of human society, are of Teutonic origin, it must be remembered that the "generous barbarians" and their worthy descendants owe much for forms of government and administration as well as for processes of law, to the Roman civilization that preceded their own; and that wherever the Romans and their direct descendants have gone, they have carried with them their institutions, which will continue to be an element of all history, and an ever fruitful source of study.   Spain's chief contributions to the New World consist of these surviving Romanized institutions, and within the territory of the American Republic they continue until this day.   Yet it is not surprising that the study of Teutonic institutions as they have come to us through England, has ever been more attractive to students of history than the fragmentary results of Spanish occupation in the New World; for the living issues of a progressive people are more interesting and more useful than those of a people whose power has declined on account of inherent characteristics and peculiar conditions.   And, moreover, the history of the institutions of our own stock must always ·invite greater attention than those of a people of foreign race.   Consequently the investigation of our rich heritage of Teutonic institutions, of the colonies of the Atlantic sea-board, has been extensive and thorough and productive of the best results.   However, of late, these more remote elements of civilization in our country have been receiving greater attention; for they represent a part of our colonial life, and have contributed to our national existence.   Now all parts of the historical drama played upon this continent are considered essential parts of American history.   Intense, noble, and useful as the life of the English colonies on the

---

[1] Hume.

Atlantic coast has been, powerful as has been its influence in nation-building, the far west and south presents its claim as a historical factor in the great drama; and to this extent is entitled to the consideration of the true scholar. As history continues to be studied for the truth it reveals, every branch of organic society will become the legitimate field of the historian; for each part throws some light upon the general whole of human development. But at any event, the student should not pause at the boundary of that which is uninviting; for indeed the highest civilization is characterized by forms of enlightenment and shades of moral barbarism; and while our boasted civilization may exalt the former, it cannot escape the latter. The causes that prevent national development and eminent success, bring their own valuable and peculiar lessons. The relics of departed greatness, the broken fragments of institutions, and the maladies that consume nations, are the rightful subjects of the student of history; as well as are the full flush of victory, the permanency of development, and the glorious life-forces of modern progress. Nor should the student shrink from entering this field; for the adage of Goethe, " Wer fremde Sprachen nicht kennt, weiss nichts von seiner eigenen," may apply with equal force to history; for indeed, he that knows not the history of other countries, knows not the history of his own. The power of contrast and comparison is the strength of the study of history; and in this respect it includes all nations and societies in its scope, and has for its interests the development of each separate society, and the welfare of humanity at large. On this account the study of Spanish American institutions claims our attention; not only because of contrast, but especially because they have to do with the development of our nation.

The southwest represents the connection of a great closed circuit of the world's civilization, whose first foundations were laid in the early institutions of Roman and Teuton. Here two great streams of civilization have met; the one Romance, the other Teutonic. The former, moving first and more rapidly, having passed from Rome to old Spain, and thence to Mexico and the lands of the north, awaited the coming of the latter, moving from the northwest through Old England and New, and thence across the continent. As the latter has ever been characterized by thorough conquest and complete reduction of the resources of nature, and the former by loose and extended occupation of territory, the result of this meeting is easily determined by the general judgments of history. Descending like an avalanche from the northwest, the sturdy Anglo-Saxons overpowered and dominated the Spanish people, who long before migrated from the mother country; and now within the boundaries of the United States are slowly absorbing or crushing the last remnants of the institutions of this romance people. To-day the Anglo-Saxon exults in the strength of a predominant and united nation, while the Spanish-American yet within our borders deplores the failure of his people, and reflects on the "buenos tiempos" of the Spanish occupation.

The points of contact of these two systems of colonization, where traces of the old institutions of Spain yet exist, are easily pointed out; for their line of demarkation is very distinct. Florida, Louisiana, Texas, New Mexico, Arizona, and California, represent the field of early Spanish occupation, and the territory where are found the remains of old Spanish institutions. I say *old Spanish* institutions; for it is the fate of colonies to preserve the older institutions of a nation, while the national character may be subject to greater changes. At present the influence on American institutions of this early occupation is very slight; in the older states quite obliterated; on the Mexican frontier and in the newer states quite distinct; while in Mexico we find the old forms of life and government crystallized through long inactivity. But even here the modern industrial revolution is making great inroads upon old customs; and we shall soon hail the new Republic, the republic of railroads and engines, of arts, industries, and education. In Florida, a few buildings with the traces of early Spanish architecture, a few Spanish names of places, growing comparatively less by the constant addition of English names, and a small Spanish population, recruited by reason of the contact with Cuba and the surrounding Spanish speaking countries, are all that is left of the Spanish domination of Florida for a period of over three centuries. Perhaps the greatest effect of this domination is seen in the slow development of the country in educational and administrative lines. 'For in the Spanish colonial possession, but little systematized effort was expended in behalf of education.

In Louisiana, a country of Spanish exploration and later domination, we find that Spanish laws are on the statute books, that the Spanish system of administration has had its influence upon the present system of government, and that Spanish blood flows in the veins of many of the inhabitants. Though the later Spanish rule was of short duration in Louisiana, it was distinctively the key to the Spanish occupations in the present territory of the United States. It was a hopeless case for Spain in America, when Louisiana was given over to a foreign power. Here American life predominates, as do American laws and systems of administration.

In Texas, once a part of Mexico and subsequently an independent republic, we should naturally look for the most lasting effects of Spanish institutions; but here as elsewhere there are but few traces. A few laws, mostly obsolete, are printed on the statute-books; a few towns that retain traits of the old Spanish life, the ruins of the missions and buildings of the early padres, a few half civilized Indians as the result of their teaching, and the use of the language on the frontier, are the chief characteristics of this former Mexican province. The language spoken is largely Mexican, as the old Castilian does not count for much in Texas. A few families of noble blood still trace their lineage to the early Spanish colonists.

Turning now to New Mexico, we find, in spite of the rapid transformation of the past few years, more distinct traces of

the early colonial life. For over three centuries the Spanish
people dominated this country.   Here the language is spoken
to a considerable extent by Spaniards, Mexicans, Americans,
and Indians.   Some of the towns have yet the appearance
that they wore a century ago, while under the Spanish rule.
The old adobe buildings, the form of the town, and its general appearance and improvements, all speak of the Spanish
life on the frontier.   The work of the missionaries is clearly
visible, not only in the remnants of the buildings that they
constructed, in the predominance of the religion which
they taught, but in the effects upon the Indians whom they
instructed.   The natives speak the Spanish language, in many
instances worship according to the Spanish faith, and have a
civilization somewhat different from that which their fathers
possessed prior to the conquest.   Their religion is semi-pagan
and semi-Christian ; a mixture of the old Indian superstition
and the Christian faith; and may, perhaps, be a grade better
than the old, though no one knows.   The method of worship
of an Indian is his own property, whatever he may say or do;
and frequently the converted have only exchanged unorganized
for organized superstition.   In New Mexico are evidences of the
old Spanish grants and laws of settlement as well as traces of
municipal life, both in the Spanish population and their early
subjects, the Indians.   Here too are practical results of the
Spanish domination observed in the endless litigation concerning the land titles to much of the territory.   Another marked
feature is the Spanish names of towns and rivers, and the words
of common speech that have been Anglicised, as well as the
continued use of the Spanish language.   In New Mexico the
line must be carefully drawn between the language of the old
Castilian families, and the common speech ; that is, between
Spanish and Mexican.

In Arizona but little is to be noticed of Spanish rule beyond
the work of the missionaries in early times.   There are only
two remnants of churches ; one a ruin, and the other a grand
example of the early achievements of the fathers.   Arizona

was the field of the early explorers; but the Spanish institutions did not take so firm a hold in this territory as in others. Many of the modern towns have a Spanish population of a late immigration; and one may hear the soft, fluent language spoken to a considerable extent.

The last trace of a vast colonization plan of the Spanish people was in the occupation and settlement of California. Centuries after the occupation of the New World was begun under the reign of Ferdinand and Isabella, the Spanish nation made its last great effort to extend its territory in the New World. The history of this attempt is the history of the Spanish occupation of California, which really closed, so far as institutions are concerned, with the American conquest of California in 1845. The relics of this occupation have been prominent, although they are now fast fading away before the onward march of the invincible American. The nomenclature of the country, the few remaining Castilian families,[1] the rapidly declining Mexican population, the scattered natives still reciting the story of their wrongs, the old missions with their characteristic architecture rapidly crumbling to ruins, the schools and colleges that have been their natural successors, laws relating to the holding of lands and the legislation concerning the original grants, the early records of towns and town life;—these are the chief remaining points to remind us of the previous existence of a civilization crushed by its own weight. The period of the civilization falls within a century; but let us not look upon it lightly, though it has proved a failure; for beneath the shadow of romance, under the surface of petty and ineffectual political management, lies the

---

[1] "The great families of the Spanish pioneer period have mostly representatives at the present day; some of them have retained wealth and influence, especially in the southern counties . . . Most of the old families sank into obscurity, and it is now difficult to trace their connections. Only about thirty Spanish families of California have retained any wealth or influence."—*Pioneer Spanish families in California*, Century Magazine, January, '91, Charles Howard Shinn.

unmistakable grandeur of a great pioneer work. Slow and uncertain as the work of colonizing California may now seem to us, the Spanish settlers broke the virgin soil, faced the perils and dangers of the wilderness, and prepared the way for a newer and broader civilization. With great hardihood and great bravery, these early founders pushed into the frontier countries, and exhibited characteristics which are truly heroic. If the colonies lacked in thrift and vigor and established a system that ended in failure, let us consider on the other hand the almost insurmountable difficulties that they had to face in this new land, and the impracticality of the home government, still more detrimental to their interests. Certainly we must acknowledge that this early colonial life had a heroic beginning, though we must record for it a gloomy and humiliating end.

When we contrast the vigor of the New England colonies on the Atlantic sea-board, when we consider their thrift, the completeness of their conquest, their steady and sturdy growth to wealth and power, their development of liberty and local government, when all these points and more are compared with the lack of these sterling qualities in the Spanish colonies of the Pacific coast, we shall have little reason to wonder at the results of such dissimilar conditions. With its qualities of bravery and hardihood in enduring dangers, we must look to other things besides the Spanish character to account for the wide difference in these two groups of settlers. The causes of their failure are inherent in the nature of the conditions under which the colonies were established. Their institutions could not have been otherwise than evanescent, while those of the English were destined by their very nature to become permanent. The Spaniards brought the natives into a semi-civilized state; they taught them agriculture and other arts and industries; they instructed them in the tenets of religion, and brought them under the influence of the rudiments of learning; they maintained themselves in this country for nearly a century, and were bringing the country slowly

but surely under the influences of civilization. In view of
all of these facts, though there is a wide difference between
the English and the Spanish people, we must accredit their
failure more to the conditions under which they labored, and
the nature of their institutions and laws, than to the character
of the Spanish colonists. It is true that the elements of the
Spanish nation were such that it might have been an easy
matter to predict in a general way the temperament of the
Spaniard of the sixteenth century, and to set his possibilities
and limitations. But no one could predict that there would
be imposed upon this liberty-loving people an abnormal government. No one could see, until it was effected, that the
illegitimate government, the absolute rule of princes, would
so soon extend its blighting influences to every foot of Spanish
soil, and permeate the whole Spanish nation.

While Spain was developing absolutism and the inquisition
with one hand and suppressing the liberty of the people with
the other, England was developing constitutional liberty and
establishing the natural rights of the people. The Spanish
colonies were the direct outcome of the life of Old Spain,
characterized by the suppression of permanent advancement;
and they were tainted everywhere with the evils of the mother
country. On the other hand, at the time of the planting of
the New England colonies, England had entered into the era
of the Puritan revolution, and her colonists carried with them
the foremost ideas of liberty then existing in the world; and
in addition, sterling characters formed in actual struggle. They
had all of the advantages of the Puritan spirit and character.
The attitude of England toward her colonies was not at all
beneficent. She cared nothing for them, or only so far as they
helped her. Her motto was to force the colonies to help
themselves, to fight their own battles, and then to assist her.
But with all of this, her treatment was more favorable to
growth than that of Spain. The attitude of Spain in regard to
her colonies in respect to the aid they were to give the mother-
country was similar to that of England; but the process

of obtaining this end was entirely different. Spain dealt paternally with her colonies, incorporated them and their territory into the government and the territory of the crown, and for fear of not governing enough she governed too much. The result was that, with no chance for self-development, the colonies became very dependent. Thus living under the protection of the mother-country, curbed in every desire for self-government, crippled in trade and commerce, and suppressed in individual growth, the colonies had ever before them an unproductive life and a dismal future, and failed ultimately in performing that for which they were created.

The contrast between the Spanish and the English colonies in regard to the development of civilized life in America has been great. Long before the first permanent English settlement had been made on the Atlantic coast, the Spanish conquerors had explored the continent from ocean to ocean ; and before the first permanent settlement at Jamestown, they had established permanent colonies in New Mexico. While we realize that their methods were not calculated to establish permanency of development in the new territory, we can not fail to admire those daring explorers who traversed so far the unknown wilds of American deserts and forests, planting with such zeal the missions and colonies that floated the Spanish flag over so many lands. But the accompanying picture is not the less startling ; that while the English colonies were fighting for independence and were so far advanced as to form a separate and independent nation, the Spaniards were trying to extend their conquests and settlements on the Pacific coast, in order to prevent the encroachment of foreigners. Even while the representatives were assembled in the old "State House" at Philadelphia to sign the declaration which called into existence a free and independent people, a little company of pioneers were waiting at the entrance of the Golden Gate to found a town. That town was founded on the site of the city that now guards the western entrance to our nation, three thousand miles from the nation's birth-place.

At this time Spain owned the whole of the territory west of the Mississippi except Oregon and Washington; and doubtless had a rightful claim to these—a territory comprising more than two-thirds of our present domain. Three-quarters of a century after this, Spain claimed not a foot of soil on the continent, while the United States extended from ocean to ocean. The rapid decline of one power and the rise of the other involve many interesting questions in the making of nations.

The history of the English colonies and of our own national development has been followed with such care and skill on the part of the historian and the student, that it remains only to present the other side of the contrast. It is necessary to enter at once upon a careful analysis of the origin and development of Spanish institutions, their establishment and their decline in America. The institutions of other countries will be used only as auxiliary to the accomplishment of this purpose. The development of the Spanish people in a portion of the territory of the United States, their social and political institutions, their early triumphs, and their later decline, are the themes before us. To accomplish this purpose it will be necessary to consider the nature of the Spanish institutions of the Old World before making a study of them as they are found transplanted into the colonies. In ascertaining the true nature of the Spanish institutions, it seems necessary to refer to the Roman institutions which have done so much to shape and develop Spanish administration, government, and law.

CHAPTER II.

THE ROMAN ORIGIN OF SPANISH INSTITUTIONS.

The mixture of races in Spain would necessarily lead to the development of original political and social institutions. Yet the constant changes wrought through repeated conquests by the people of different nationalities leaves room for the predominant influences of the institutions which were strongest in constitution and most practical in their use. Of the dissimilar social elements which have at different times dominated Spain, each has left its mark upon the character, life, and institutions of this ancient country. As wave after wave of conquest rolled over the Iberian peninsula, each failed to obliterate entirely the institutions of its predecessor. Even the ancient Iberians, mingling with the Celts, contributed to the vivacity and life of the people; and in remote districts left distinct traces of their institutions.

The Phoenicians and the Carthaginians, who conquered the southern parts of the peninsula, had at least a slight influence upon the customs and laws of that portion of the territory occupied. The trading stations which they established on the coast later developed into thriving cities, and long retained their original customs. The Roman domination which followed was complete; and the distinctive marks of the earlier civilization became traceable only under the administration of the laws and government of the "Eternal City." The invasion of the Teutonic races brought with it customs and laws of a different nature, which existed side by side in the

14

new Gothic Kingdom. On the same soil Teuton and Roman commingled; and the higher system of laws finally prevailed, while every institution was permeated for a time with the spirit of German freedom and lawlessness. After an existence of nearly three hundred years, the Gothic kingdom went down before the standard of the Arab-Moor; and consequently the religion, laws, and customs of this oriental people prevailed for several centuries in the fairest portion of the peninsula. But with all of their learning and practice in the arts and sciences, and in spite of their wise and subtle character, they were reconquered in the name of Christianity and through a rising national life, by the same people whom they had formerly subdued. These are the sources, so diverse in race, language, customs, and laws, out of which arose the spirit that remodelled and amalgamated dissimilar elements to form the modern Spanish nation.

When all of these combined influences are recognized, it must be affirmed that there has been a direct continuity of Roman institutions in Spain from the time when the first colonies were planted in the peninsula to the present. Although the spirit of the German, in its persistent declaration for liberty and against despotism and oppression, has had great influence in making the Spanish nation, the Roman law, government, and system of administration, as well as the Roman municipality and religion, have been the predominating influences which have shaped the national polity. It is to the Roman civilization that we must look for form and manner of procedure; and in no other institution is this more evident than in the methods of colonization at home and abroad, adopted by both peoples.

In order to show that the continuity of Roman law and custom may be traced to the Spanish institutions of the present day, it will be well first to consider what kind of institutions Rome carried into Spain, to what extent they obtained, and how long they continued. It is to be observed that Spain was the first province of the empire to be completely Romanized.   The method of extending the Roman civilization was by colonization, voluntary immigration, and the extension of the provincial administration.   By these processes a country was soon transformed in government, law, language, customs, and frequently in religion.   Immigration began very early in Spain ; and many followed in the wake of the army, either for the purposes of trade, or for permanent settlement.   In the period immediately following the conquest by Scipio, from the year 196 to 169 B. C., more than 140,000 Italians entered the province of Spain.[1]   This aided greatly the infusion of the language, customs, and institutions of the Romans.   Along the Mediterranean coast, the indigenous population and that of the Phoenicians was made to conform, under the republic, to the customs of the ruling people.[2] Under imperial reign, through colonization, and the extension of the municipal system throughout the peninsula, Spain was completely Romanized.   Under the rule of Augustus, there were in all Spain fifty communities with full citizenship ; nearly fifty others up to this time had received Latin rights, and were in their internal organization equal to burgess communities.[3]   Some of the earlier towns adopted Roman civilization long before ; thus the towns of Baetica in the time of Strabo were Roman in custom and speech.   On the occasion of the imperial census instituted in 74 A. D., the Emperor Vespasian introduced the Latin municipal organization into the remaining towns of Spain.[4]

But it was through colonization that the Roman institutions were introduced into new provinces.   In all colonization it was the fundamental idea that the territory colonized must become a part of the empire and be subject to the government of Rome.   Whatever laws were established or forms of government granted, they must emanate from the central authority at Rome.   The colonies were sent as the offspring of the parent

[1] Duruy, II, 217.   [2] Mommsen, *Roman Provinces*, I, 68.
[3] Mommsen, *Roman Provinces*, I, 68.   [4] Marquardt, IV, 258.

government, and were to retain their filial relation indefinitely. Included within the general purpose of the extension of territory, there were in the Roman policy four distinct objects of colonization ; usually one of the four objects predominated, but all four might be entertained in the planting of a single colony.   These objects were, (1) to people a province with persons of Roman blood ; (2) to guard and control a conquered province ; (3) to dispose of the surplus population of a city ; and (4) to settle the veteran soldiery whom Rome paid in lands.   But in all these methods of settlement one idea was never lost, the idea of guarding the frontier.[1]   The earliest colonies of Rome were purely military garrisons sent out to occupy the territory, to keep it in subjection, and to guard the frontier against invasion.   Cicero terms the Roman colony of this class, *Specula populi Romani ac propugnaculum.*[2]   Colonies of this nature were at first few in number, and confined to the colonies of the Sabines and to Latium ; but they soon extended over all Italy, as there was need, continually growing in size and importance.   As an example of this class, there were six thousand men settled in Beneventum to guard Campania.[3]   These military colonies developed into cities where Roman laws and customs prevailed.

As Rome continued her conquests beyond the limits of the peninsula, it became necessary to plant colonies for the sake of retaining her sovereignty over partially subdued countries. In the Province of Spain there was founded at Italica (Old Seville), by Scipio's veterans, a military colony which developed at a later date into a flourishing city, the birth-place of Trajan, Hadrian, and Theodosius.   Somewhat later, in 171 B. C., another colony of the same nature was established at Carteia ; but as the colony was formed of families of a mixed race, it had Latin right only.[4]   The Senate had not yet sent citizens

---

[1] Arnold, *Roman Provincial Administration*, 218.

[2] Cicero, *Pro M. Fonteio*, I, 33.

[3] Duruy, *History of Rome*, I, 490.   [4] Duruy, *History of Rome*, II, 217.

to settle in the provinces, and it was not until after the passage of the law of Gracchus (lex Sempronia agraria), which had for its chief object the relief of over-populated Rome and the provision of land for the poor, that any move was made to form colonies of citizens in the provinces.[1] The plan of Caius Gracchus for trans-marine colonies failed during his lifetime ; but in after years it was carried out with good results. In 122 B. C., he set out with 6,000 colonists to found a colony at Carthage, which he called Junonia.[2] A burgess town with full Roman rights was established; but during the absence of Caius, his enemies brought influences to bear which caused the repeal of the land-law during the following year, and the new colony was without the support of the central government. The colonists, though disfranchised, continued to claim their holdings ; and in later years the colony was in a flourishing condition. This was the first burgess town founded as a colony outside of Italy, although others were begun before this became firmly established. In 118 B. C., the "Colonie Narbo Martius," called Narbonensis, was permanently established in Gaul. In nature and object it partook more of the form of a military out-post than of a civic colony ; but it had a burgess population with full Roman rights.[3]

In the latter part of the first century before Christ, foreign colonization was carried on extensively. At this period Cæsar founded many colonies, and established not less than 80,000 citizens in the different colonies outside of Rome, many of whom were sent to Spain and Gaul.[4] Augustus continued the colonization so vigorously prosecuted by Cæsar ; the majority

[1] Marquardt, *Römische Staatsverwaltung, Handbuch der römischen Alterthümer*, IV, 106.

[2] Mommsen, *History of Rome*, III, 110, 133; Plutarch, IV, 542; Ihne, IV, 456, 473–4.

[3] Marquardt, *Römische Staatsverwaltung, Handbuch der römischen Alterthümer*, IV, 262.

[4] Arnold, *Roman Provincial Administration*, 218.

of the colonies founded by him were of a military nature and created for the purpose of disposing of the army veterans.[1] Frequently other colonies were formed than those sent out by Rome, by admitting the towns of the province to the rights and privileges of the colonies; although sometimes the inhabitants of the towns were expelled to give room to Roman colonists. And again Roman colonists would be added to the already existing population, and the town would thus receive the rank of colony.[2] When this was the case, dissensions often arose, which led to a struggle for supremacy; and this usually ended in giving to the original inhabitants larger privileges, though sometimes it produced results just the opposite.

But wherever Romans went, there went the Roman government, and the Roman law and system of administration; and as far as possible, the recognition of the provincial towns as parts of Rome seems to have been a distinct policy. Whether the town was formed on a civil or military basis, it was still a type of old Rome, an integral part of the empire. Even in the founding of the town, Rome was imitated; and municipal life and municipal custom, as well as municipal law and administration, were taken directly from the parent city.[3] From the moment of the conquest, the Romans appropriated all of the royal domain and frequently part of the common lands; and in some instances they appropriated the whole territory of the conquered, which thus at once became Roman domain. The inhabitants were allowed to hold these lands as tenants of the state, and were obliged to pay taxes (one-tenth) on the land, a personal tax, duties and royalties, and were also required to furnish requisitions when demanded.[4] On the other hand, the colonists were Roman citizens, and might if they desired, go to Rome and exercise their rights as such. They were also free from the tribute on land, but must fill all requisitions made by the central government in time of

---

[1] Marquardt, IV, 118.   [2] Arnold, 218.
[3] Arnold, 220.   [4] Duruy, II, 239.

war. Though the colonists were Roman citizens, they could
not own the land which they occupied, but held it as a fief
from the state. When the officer (*agrimensor*) appointed for
the purpose led out a colony, he chose a tract of land, divided
it into squares (*centuriae*) of two hundred acres each,[1] which
were again subdivided into smaller ones (*sortes*), and apportioned with the houses to the colonists according to rank, to
be held as above stated. Thus the inequalities of old Rome
were transferred to the colonies. At first the method of distribution varied; but it is held that Cæsar established a norm
for the apportionment on lands in the several colonies. As to
the internal workings of the colony, the Roman right, or the
Latin right, was a meagre affair as far as an independent
organization of the municipium was concerned. It received
its municipal law from the Roman senate, and its whole form
and process of administration were derived from the mother
country. There were senators, or *decuriones*, consuls called
duumvirs, and censors, or *duumviri quinquennales*.[2] But with
all of this, a certain amount of civil and military power was
delegated to local authority, and as the central power at Rome
declined, the towns tended to develop some originality in government.

There is one class of Roman towns, formed by the establishment of garrisons throughout the provinces for the sake
of guarding the frontiers, which are of such historic interest
as to deserve special attention, although they have been
already alluded to. This class is represented by the line of
forts on the mark, or boundary of a nation, which became
frontier cities, and frequently the foremost of the land. We
shall find Spain following the same policy in the nineteenth
century. Whenever it became necessary for the protection of
the Roman interests or the repression of a warlike people, a
chain of fortresses was established along the frontier or in

---

[1] Arnold, 219.   [2] Arnold, 223 *et seq.*

the heart of the territory of the offending people.[1] But whether planted on the boundary line of the Roman possessions or in the midst of a disaffected people, the primary object of these garrisons was to protect Rome. Examples of these garrisoned towns are those military settlements founded among the Silures in Britain, and the later colonies established by Agricola.[2] Another notable example is the line of fortresses established by Cæsar in Gaul on the boundary of the Narbonensis;[3] other familiar examples are the line of presidia in Spain, and the forts along the Danube. The development of towns from these military centres must have been very gradual; the military camp changing first into a village, and then into a municipium or a colony.[4] There is but little distinction between these terms; in a general sense they may be used interchangeably, although the colony was of a higher order than the municipium,[5] having been sent out by Rome, and having been granted full civil privileges from the start. However, a municipium might become a colony; and in fact a town might partake of the nature of the municipium and of a colony at the same time.[6] It was customary for the campfollowers, such as sutlers, settlers, and merchants, to pitch their tents outside of the ramparts, where thus a small community, more or less united, sprang up. If the camp remained in one place for a long time, as was frequently the case, the village grew rapidly, and finally became a Roman town with all the rights, duties, and privileges of Roman citizenship attached. The soldiers usually intermarried with the surrounding people and became attached to the soil, or they brought their families with them and thus became permanent settlers. There were other species of military colonies: first, those that were established by Rome from the beginning, as when a whole army

---

[1] Londinium, Tacitus, *Annals*, XIV, 33.

[2] Merivale, *History of Rome*, VI, 30–31.

[3] *De Bello Gallico*, VII, 8.   [4] Arnold, 206.

[5] Aulus Gellius, *Noctes, Atticae*, XVI, 13.

[6] Duruy, *History of Rome*, II, 242.

was retired to subdue the country; and second, the colonies formed by retired veterans who were given lands in payment for services, or as pensions, and were paid according to their rank.   The nature of these colonies differed chiefly as to the process of formation; although the ceremonies in the distribution of the land at the founding of a colony were uniform in all cases.   But it is not possible to pursue this part of the subject further than barely to indicate the Roman method of colonization.

The provincial system of administration in the Roman government had during its organization under the Republic, many marks of excellence.   It was the policy of the Roman Senate never to destroy people, cities, and institutions, unless it was deemed necessary for the present or future safety of the Republic.   The policy was economic rather than humane; for a depopulated town pays no tribute, and furnishes no recruits.   The people conquered were, as a rule, allowed to retain their own religion, their laws, their magistrates, and their public assemblies.[1]   They were left in possession of a part of their lands and revenues.   When the country first submitted to Rome, a constitution was given to the people, fixing the amount of tribute to be paid and defining their obligations to the new government; and that order might be the sooner restored, the people were given a new civil code, which retained as far as possible the old forms of municipal government.[2]   By degrees the territory, its laws and people, were Romanized.   The governor was the chief ruler in the province; municipal authority, except in cases of towns granted special privileges, was reduced to a minimum, and the vestiges of a provincial assembly were removed by the policy of "divide et impera."[3]

The Roman provinces in Spain were of rather a loose organization, and it seems that there was no connecting link

---

[1] Duruy, II, 227; Tacitus, *Annals*, III, 60–63.
[2] Duruy, II, 229.   [3] Arnold, 17.

between the imperial power represented by officers sent out from Rome, and the local government of towns. Except in form, no representative body of the province existed; consequently the power of the governor, who was called either proconsul or praetor, was almost absolute.[1] He was appointed at first by the senate, later by the Emperor of Rome; and fulfilled his duties as an agent of the Roman government. As the power of the home government declined, the imperial officers became more and more independent, and the government of the provinces was more absolute than the home government. The governors were in the position of monarchs. The officers that were appointed to assist the governor were also of the home government. The policy was to extend the rule of the City over the whole empire; consequently every new territory conquered was considered a part of the Roman Empire or Republic. But though the whole province or country conquered was considered as belonging to Rome, not all of the lands were confiscated by the conquerors. As a rule the public lands of conquered peoples became Roman Lands, and the private lands of public enemies of Rome were also confiscated. All other lands were subject to taxation, except in the cases of free or privileged towns. This Roman domination of civil law and administration rapidly transformed the simple customs and laws of the people to the more dignified administration of the Roman government, whose influence on political life was strong and uncompromising.

But there were other methods used in Romanizing Spain. Peaceful intercourse carried on what war and politics had begun.[2] The intercourse of the Italians with the Spaniards in trade and commerce, brought into the province Roman money and Roman Language. There was a constant influx of the Italian nations which continued to transform manners, customs, and laws. Even the habits of dress and modes of life followed

---

[1] Arnold, 48.

[2] Mommsen, *The Provinces of the Roman Empire*, I, 70, 73.

the Roman methods. The introduction of the Italian municipal law, one of the most enduring monuments of Rome, helped
to complete this transformation; for the old towns were then
admitted to the Roman rights with the usage of the Roman
law, and the new towns and colonies were formed after the
Roman model.

But nowhere is the transformation of Spain more marked
than in the spread of the Christian religion.[1] In the study
of mediaeval institutions in any part of Europe, the student
must not overlook the effects of religion. They are seen
everywhere; in the modification of the old laws, and in the
construction of the new ones; in the influence on the moral
and religious conduct of individuals, and in the effects of the
establishment of justice. The priest, posing as a scribe in
compiling laws, was educated under the influence of Rome,
and not infrequently modified these laws to conform to the
Roman type. And again, as the church posed as a tribunal
to try offenders against the moral law, its officers came in
direct contact with the civil law and its administration; consequently the powerful organization of the church had great
influence in shaping public affairs. By degrees the religion
of the indigenous population was replaced almost entirely by
the Christian religion, which gave it great importance in the
development of society.

Thus in language, literature, religion, law, administration,
municipality, customs of dress, and habits of life, trade, commerce, and organization, Spain became Romanized. During
the Roman domination it is evident that almost the entire
province yielded to the civilization of the conquered. It can
be conclusively shown that this Roman life continued with
slight modifications down to the time of establishment of the
modern nation, and even to the organization of the Spanish
colonies of America. Not only was there a continuity of

---

[1] Guizot, *History of Civilization*, II, 55 *et seq.*; Dunham, *History of Spain and Portugal*, I, 196.

Roman institutions, but they were essential to the foundation of the Spanish monarchy. The Spanish people, naturally conservative, retained their adopted language, customs, laws, and administration, notwithstanding the rude shock of Saracen and Teutonic invasion, and the wasting influences of time. At least, these elements furnished the material for the new structures.

Spain is noted for the number and variety of its codes of law.[1] So regularly have these compilations been made, and with such thoroughness, that it may be said that they represent the best part of the history of the Spanish people. When the Goths conquered the province in the fifth century, they brought with them customs and ideas of government which were anti-Roman in every respect. The old spirit of Teutonic freedom was manifested in them, and the right of choice in the selection of a king still prevailed. They also practiced the system of individualistic government so common to all Germanic tribes. No sooner were the Goths well established in their new home than there began a struggle for predominance of institutions, the Teutonic and the Roman; and this struggle resulted in the toleration for a long time of both systems of law, one for each people, dwelling side by side.

The first code of laws in Spain after the decline of the Roman supremacy was that of Euric (466–483), supposed to have been compiled during the latter part of the fifth century. It was a compilation of the ancient customs of the Goths, and for nearly two hundred years had an important function in the government. Alaric, the successor of Euric, who was killed by Clovis, collected and published the laws of the Romans, as then practiced in Spain and Gaul, in a code called the Breviarium.[2] Thus the law of the barbarians and the law of the Romans were entirely distinct; and each people was governed by its own law. At the middle of the seventh cen-

---

[1] Dunham, *History of Spain and Portugal*, IV, 71.

[2] Guizot, *History of Civilization*, II, 218 (Breviarium Alaricianum or Lex Romana Visigothorum).

tury, at the time when the Goths were driven out of France, their King, Chindasunithe (642–701), united the two codes in one, by which the entire people were governed. This remarkable code was published under the title of "Forum Judicum," appeared later as the "Liber Judicum," and is commonly known as the "Fuero Juzgo." It is said by jurists to be the source of Spanish jurisprudence.[1] This code was based upon the Roman law, the constitutional fueros of the kings and lords, and their decrees respecting civil and criminal laws and the rights and the administration of municipalities. It represented the power of the Gothic monarchy and the usefulness of Roman jurisprudence. The "Forum Judicum" was the result of the councils of Toledo in which the interests of the whole country—the clergy, the lay aristocracy, royalty, and the people were represented.[2] In this fact is illustrated the power of the clergy; for at the councils of Toledo, as well as throughout Spain, at this period, all other classes were grouped about the clergy. The councils were national assemblies in which the affairs of the country were debated and laws were readjusted. "What the field of Mars or May was to the Franks," says Guizot, "what the Wittenagemote to the Anglo-Saxons, and what the general assembly of Pavia was to the Lombards, such were the councils of Toledo to the Visigoths of Spain."[3] The Fuero Juzgo, formed by the amalgamation of the Gothic and Roman laws, represented the rights of humanity, the duties of government, and the interests of the people; but it was without the ordinary checks on authority. In it the traces of Teutonic society have disappeared and the Roman principles predominate.

This close union of the Gothic and the Roman codes has resulted in a vast system of administration, "semi-ecclesiastical and semi-imperial," dominating all society, and forming the

---

[1] Rockwell, *Spanish and Mexican Law*, 9.

[2] Guizot, *History of Civilization*, II, 219.

[3] Guizot, *History of Civilization*, II, 219.

main support of a Gothic monarchy that grows daily more absolute. From this time forth, religious and civil imperialism was the characteristic mark of the Spanish government. The whole of the code has never been repealed ; and notwithstanding frequent compilations, it still remains the corner-stone of Spanish jurisprudence. The domination of the Arab-Moors failed to obliterate it ; and, in truth, its principles prevailed throughout the entire legal history of the nation. It must not be inferred that, because the Roman principle predominated in early codes, the Teutonic life ceased to have influence. " Fourteen centuries of revolutions and changes of every kind, so common to the government of this peninsula," says Sempere, " have not yet entirely extinguished the spirit which the founders of the Gothic monarchy imparted to its inhabitants. Many of the usages and customs introduced by the barbarians are still preserved." [1] Yet it must be maintained that their most enduring work is seen in the formulation and use of the Roman law as the foundation of Spanish jurisprudence. However, side by side with these principles, are recorded the old constitutional rights of the Teuton. Law second of the preliminary title asserts, " Thou shalt be king if thou doest right, and if thou doest not right thou shalt not be king." [2] The Cortes of Spain attempted to formulate this same principle in the constitution of 1812.

It is not necessary to discuss the numerous legal codes of Spain which appeared from time to time, mostly in the form of compilations or fueros of the king. Those of the latter class were frequent, and of almost every description. The term *fuero* has various significations in both ancient and modern jurisprudence. [3] It may mean a decree, a law, a charter, or a code granted by the sovereign. Used in its specific sense, it represented the documents granted by a lord

---

[1] *Hist. del Derecho Español*, 35 (Quoted by Schmidt in Civil Law of Spain and Mexico, 21).

[2] Schmidt, 34.   [3] Schmidt, *Civil Law of Spain and Mexico*, 64.

or a king to a municipality, securing to it certain rights and privileges conformable to the constitution.[1] The *fueros* were a fruitful source of law, and represented the principal addition for many centuries after the formation of the Fuero Juzgo. But each new law or decree represented only an addition to the general code. Among the more important codes of this general nature were the Fuero Viejo de Castilla, and the Fuero Real. These were all granted prior to the famous Siete Partidas of the thirteenth century, and represent the growth of the power of the Spanish monarchy. The old imperialism of Rome was fast changing the Teutonic elective king into a hereditary monarch with unlimited authority. Of the early legislation, the Siete Partidas was the last formal act of the incorporation of the Roman law into the laws of Spain. It was proposed by Alfonso the Wise, who collected or caused to be collected the laws of Spain from many sources. It has been asserted that this code was similar in arrangement to the Pandects of Justinian; and this is easily accounted for when we consider that the compilers were the learned scholars of Salamanca. Alfonso X. began a reform by encouraging the study of Roman law at the University of Salamanca, where he created three chairs for its instruction, and caused several manuals to be compiled for the students. The Roman law was found favorable to the unity of the country and to absolute monarchy; and it was his purpose to make a general use of its most favorable parts to strengthen the government of his kingdom. Consequently, the Siete Partidas did not neglect to make free use of the Pandects. It was formed from (*a*) the ancient customs of Spain, (*b*) the Roman laws, (*c*) the canon law, and (*d*) the writings of the fathers and quotations from various sages.[2] The law was promulgated in the year 1263; but was not formally adopted until 1348, during the reign of Alonzo XI, when it was sanctioned by the

---

[1] Rockwell, *Spanish and Mexican Law*, 9.   [2] Rockwell, 12.

Cortes held at Alcalá de Henares.[1] From time to time it was recognized by the Cortes, and by the authors of various compilations that followed, as the standard law of the land. The Siete Partidas (seven parts), is a thorough and philosophical treatise; and although it did not occupy the highest legal position, it remained the authority to which cases not covered by special legislation were referred. During the domination of the Moors, the laws of Spain remained in force in most instances, although interrupted in their action by the tribal bands that held sway over the land. And it may be said that the Teutonic customs grew to have less and less influence in law, and the Roman law more, as the kings continued to issue their decrees for the control of the people. The feudal system, which prevailed to a considerable extent at first, did not strengthen royalty; but in the final settlement of power it increased imperialism in law and government. Thus the Roman law prevailed until long after the setting forth of the laws of the Visigoths, and then coalesced with the latter. There were added to this portions of canon and feudal laws, and the municipal decrees; from all of these sources arose the actual jurisprudence of Spain.[2] Notwithstanding its various modifications, the direct influence of the Roman law never ceased, even in modern jurisprudence.

But the municipal system was to Spain, as well as to other European nations, the great legacy bequeathed by Rome. Amidst all the changes to which mediæval institutions were subjected, the Roman municipality was continuous. It has been shown above that the municipal system was carried into Spain at an early date, and that municipal law prevailed there quite extensively. There was little direct evidence of the real nature of this municipal law, beyond that it was Roman, until the recent discovery (1857) of the tablets containing the constitutions of the towns of Malaga and Salpensa in the ancient province of Baetica. These tablets have done much

---

[1] Schmidt, 74.   [2] Schmidt, 10, 11.

to clarify the ideas already existing concerning the provincial administration. The municipal charters were granted in the time of Hadrian, and represent the full Roman rights granted to the burghers of the towns. The provincial Roman towns had the curia, decuriones, duumvirs, and aediles; and these officers corresponded to those of the central city.[1] Each corporation regulated its internal affairs through officers elected by the citizens of the town.[2] Consequently, the municipalities, while in a measure subordinate to Rome, were within certain limits self-governing bodies. The citizens elected the magistrates of whom the senate was composed, but had no further control over it. This body was composed of one hundred decuriones, who had more power and less responsibility than the members of a modern town council.[3] As the senate was formed from the six chief magistrates, ex-officers, old senators, and those persons having sufficient property to qualify them for the office of decurion, it must, of necessity, have been aristocratic in its nature. The government was based upon the personal right of a superior magistrate rather than upon representative authority as in case of the modern municipality. The senate, or town council, represented the executive body, from which the magistrates received their orders, and with whom they often consulted.[4] Thus we find that in municipal organization, the provincial towns of old Spain were smaller types of old Rome; and that the same privileges were extended to citizens in the former as in the latter.

These municipalities continued to exist in Spain after the decline of the Roman Empire. They continued long after the invasion of the Goths; and during the period of the overlordship of the Arab-Moors, the cities of Spain were permitted to carry on their own government. Even the Goths, who at first contact with the Romans did not care for cities,

---

[1] Lex Malacitana, Art. 54.   [2] Lex Malacitana, Art. 52.
[3] Arnold, *Roman Provincial Administration*, 232.   [4] Arnold, 234.

soon learned to build their own or occupy those already built. In this and in other things, we find the strong influence of Roman institutions, and their persistant continuance during rapid and radical changes. During the domination of the Arab-Moors, a few of the conquered Spaniards fled to the mountainous districts of Asturias, where they established a small kingdom that continued to increase rapidly in power and extent. These people, who sought to escape servitude to the Moslem, carried with them their own laws and customs, which laid the foundations of the new empire. From this nucleus of freedom there sprang up several small kingdoms which began to reconquer the territory. This was the beginning of modern or Christian Spain, and was the occasion of founding the modern Spanish municipalities.

From the mountain districts of Asturias began the re-conquest of Spain, which recovered all the territory that had hitherto fallen into the hands of the Moors. At this period the feudal system prevailed to a considerable extent, but was never quite so complete in Spain as in France and Germany. Of the reconquered territory, the usual portions went to the followers of the king who led the victorious forces. This gave the nobles great power, which the king attempted to offset. To accomplish this, he granted municipal charters to colonies that settled on the territory made vacant by the expulsion of the Moors from Spanish territory. These municipal grants represent the revived Roman municipal charters; and the process of colonizing these waste places resembles in a measure the practice of the Romans at a much earlier date. There was a show of liberty, but little more; because of the arrogance of the feudal nobility and the principles of municipal organization. During the re-conquest, the Spanish people had received assistance from the adjoining Franks; and it is supposed that municipal organization received some influence from this source. But whatever appearance of liberty there might have been in the formation of these first modern municipalities, it was theoretical rather than practical. It is true that the municipality had changed in its fundamental idea, as its governing body was now representative rather than personal; but the interference of feudalism made this more frequently a theoretical right than a practical exercise of the liberties of the people. The transition period from the ancient form of the aristocratic municipality to the modern democratic one, was of long duration. If rights and prerogatives were secured against the encroachments of the feudal nobility, the king eventually usurped them.

All grants to free communities were given in such a manner that they tended to strengthen royalty. Indeed, nearly all of the privileges granted to towns and to their popular representation in the Cortes were attended with such restrictive measures as to favor the central government—that is, the king. In the charters granted to the people, it was clearly stated of what class the town should be; it was granted fixed limits and boundaries, and to its citizens were guaranteed common wood-land and common water privileges. Alfonso established that no colony or community could be formed without the consent and approval of the king, and that the acts of the town councils must be approved by royal mandamus before they could become laws. From this time the struggle between the Teutonic and the Roman elements of law was on. The result was that the Teutonic spirit was crushed, and Spain returned to the principles of Rome. Spain became as if no Teutons had ever conquered and settled and held sway for three centuries in her territory. The old principles that had been working in government and administration, even through the Gothic reign and the Moorish predominance, came to the front and maintained themselves until not even a vestige of the popular government and spirit of freedom which characterizes Teutonic customs was left.

Popular representation in Spain began at an early date through the instrumentality of the independent towns. But this representation was never universal or regular. These towns by their charters claimed certain rights; and yet at no one time were all of the towns represented in the Cortes. These popular representations were in vogue for a time, but gradually died out; and under the Bourbon monarchs the ancient liberties were entirely suppressed. Under the reign of Ferdinand and Isabella, the Cortes were seldom called; and when they were, it was for the advantage of the sovereigns rather than for the advantage of the people. The familiar act of voting supplies to the central government was their only privilege. Although the spirit of freedom still slumbered on among the people, as it always has done and does now, it must be maintained that popular representation in Spain was something of a formality; similar no doubt to the representation of the people in the English Parliament in the thirteenth century. It remained for the successors of Ferdinand and Isabella only to make complete that which had already been begun. The Roman Imperialism predominated. The system of ruling provinces was Roman. The plan of magnifying central government through the appointment of royal officers was after the old Roman type. Whatever institutions flowed from old Spain from this time on, were Roman in their nature. The Germanic elements were crushed out save in a few local institutions. But, whether of colonization or of municipal government or of national or provincial administration, the predominating characteristics were Roman. The Christian church aided greatly this Romanizing process. The Hierarchy was absolute. The church had inherited the Roman forms of government, and her methods of procedure were Roman. The Pope was the natural successor of the Emperor in Imperial affairs. He posed as the universal spiritual and temporal arbiter for the world. The empire was his own. The Christian religion took a strong hold in Spain; and it went so far as to attempt to maintain its own authority against the papal authority, through the emperors and kings. When Spain projected her system upon other countries, it was a type of old Rome that she represented.

3

In administration the modern Spanish nation resembled the Roman. When the Moors were expelled step by step, it was by the force of predatory warfare incident to feudalism. It was in most instances a local rather than a national triumph, until after the union of Castile and Leon and the conquest of Grenada. Ferdinand III. of the two former kingdoms, endeavored to establish unity by translating and enforcing the old laws; and tried to improve his administration by replacing the governors of the provinces by royal officers (adelantados majores) who were directly responsible to the crown. Once begun, the return to the imperial system as used in the empire and practiced by Charlemagne was rapid, until all parts of administration centered in the king, and each part of the government was a check on every other part.

In the planting of the early colonies in Spain, the Roman system of forming the laws and of granting privileges to the inhabitants was followed. These colonies were formed for the purpose of re-peopling the waste territory and of guarding the frontier—two of the special purposes in the Roman plan. For these purposes, as well as to counteract the influences of the feudal nobility, they were granted charters.

The English colonies from the start rested on a different basis, as did all English institutions. However great the influences of the Roman law and the Roman system of administration may have been upon the progress of the English government, the Teutonic life always predominated in its institutions. This is true in the colonies; for into these the ancient laws and customs were transplanted. The Roman method of treating the public land prevailed to a great extent in Spain, and consequently in the Spanish colonies. The laws regulating right and titles to land, and the laws of estates, were derived directly from Roman code. Thus in law, in municipal organization, in administration, and in methods of colonization, the Roman influence predominated. But this influence was modified in many ways by the development of

Spain. The new national life, and the changing policy of different rulers, brought about many new phases of government consequent upon national development. It will, therefore, in order to understand the nature of the institutions which were transplanted to the American colonies, be necessary to consider more fully the condition of Spain at the time of the conquest and settlement of America.

CHAPTER III.

The Condition of Spain during the Conquest and Settlement of America.

Despite the show of freedom in the communities of Spain, and the representation in the Cortes of privileged towns by deputies, feudalism finally obtained complete domination, and prevailed during and after the rise of Christian Spain through the successful struggle against the Saracens. But the tide of centralization set in as the people began to fight a common enemy and to espouse the cause of a universal religion. Out of the many kingdoms of Spain there came finally, by a series of progressive changes, one that was stronger and better than the rest; and it formed a nucleus for the foundation of the nation. The reign of Ferdinand and Isabella marks the origin of the modern nation, and the first part of a period of centralized government. It was during this period that feudalism declined, and the old absolutism of the central power was revived.[1] Prior to this, the time-honored rights of the people had mostly disappeared; and the whole Spanish nation lapsed into lords and vassals. If a town occasionally retained its early rights, they were so overshadowed by the forms of feudal society that they amounted to a mere show of civil liberty. Through the union of Castile and Leon by a fortuitous marriage and the inheritance of Aragon, the Spanish sovereigns became possessed of a large territory; and this was extended by the conquest of the Saracens. By this con-

---

[1] Dunham, IV, 173.

quest, patriotism and religious zeal tended to cement the old kingdoms into a national unity. But the internal disorders were not easily disposed of. The long sway of rapacious nobles had broken down the courts of justice, and had quenched the flame of liberty that occasionally flashed in the gloom. The judges of the courts were intimidated by the armed lords, and their decisions set aside by the power of the sword.

Ferdinand and Isabella attempted to restore the judicial rights of the people, and to suppress the power of the nobility.[1] Their success was only partial; and in gaining this they introduced measures, which, used by designing men, led to oppression greater than that of the nobles had been. There was first instituted a body of superior judges (corregidores), whose duty it was to visit the local judges, to inspect their work, to force them to do their duty, and to hold court, if necessary, in their several jurisdictions. This body gradually obtained increased powers, and a new constitution was created defining these powers. The body (Santa Hermandad), consisted of two thousand horse and two thousand foot with their laws and judges, who directed their authority toward the severe administration of justice and the repression of the power of the feudal lords.[2] If the powers of this body had ceased here, the wrongs of the people might have been suppressed and justice enthroned; but their activities were further directed against those who had offended in religious belief. They set up a special tribunal in Seville to try offenders and apostates: the three judges of this tribunal were instructed to search diligently for evidence against those who neglected religious worship, and after trial to hand them over to the civil authorities for punishment. This process, sanctioned by the Pope and enforced by the zealous sovereigns, developed into the inquisition. It was vain for the pious sovereigns to unite diverse states, conquer

[1] Dunham, IV, 174.   [2] Dunham, II, 271.

and disperse the Saracens, establish civil justice, repress the power of the nobles, and consider the rights of the people, while they sowed the germs of disease which was eventually to prove the ruin of the nation.   All the attempts to secure enlightened political development, territorial extension, and national unity, were accompanied by the blighting influences of bigotry and oppression.

The church and the state were united in administration as well as in conquest.   Wherever floated the banners of Spain, there was planted the cross of Christ; wherever went the judges of civil justice, there went the tribunals of the church. The religious zeal thus inaugurated by kings developed into fanaticism and religious disease; the inquisition was introduced and henceforth was to be a. vulture tearing at the vitals of every attempted social, political, or religious reform. Underneath a surprising intelligence there lurked a fatal stupidity; for the short-sighted policy of Isabella could discern no such results as were finally wrought by the inquisition.   As Lafuente well says, " Without doubt she desired to make with judicious care a benign institution for establishing the unity of religion, and reared, contrary to her intention, a tribunal of extermination." [1]   Under the management of Torquemada, this " benign institution " became a monstrosity of injustice and a terror.   But the instrument of torture fell heaviest upon the Saracens and the Jews.   These two classes included some of the best artisans and laborers of Spain; consequently the inquisition fell most heavily upon the bread earners and producers.

The close of the reign of Ferdinand was marked by many troubles arising from the mistaken policy.   The power of the church had grown to great proportions; and the power of the nobles, though somewhat curtailed, had increased on account of the immunities granted them and the course of feudal war-

---

[1] Lafuente, *Los Reyes Católicos*, 8.

fare.[1]   When Charles I., better known as Emperor Charles V., came to the throne, he inaugurated the most brilliant epoch that Spain has ever known.   In this golden age of political supremacy, no other nation of Europe could equal Spain. By direct inheritance, fortunate marriages, and political successes, Charles became the ruler of half of Europe.   To maintain these possessions he inaugurated a brilliant war policy accompanied by a strong personal administration.   His treatment of Spain was upon the basis of his own convenience; but that convenience meant the increased political power of the nation.   He sought to make Spain the foremost nation of Europe, and to establish and maintain the power of the Catholic faith.[2]   To accomplish these designs he combined the shrewdness of an astute politician with the piety of a monk.   If necessary, everything else was to be sacrificed to these two ideas, of which the former was the more important. In the extension of this policy the monarchy passed into a state of extreme absolutism.[3]   Had this absolutism been enlightened, there would have been laid the foundations of a strong government based upon enduring principles.

But to carry out the policy inaugurated the voice of the people was hushed and their wants passed by unheeded.   The power of the Cortes, a time-honored institution, which was suppressed in the time of Enrique and nominally revived under Ferdinand, was effectually taken away by Charles. The nobles, so long dominant, remained in power, although the new system of administration and the new laws had a tendency to weaken them.   They rested their claims on the old Visigothic laws; and these were favorable to the feudal society.   Later usages were framed on the basis of a growing feudalism.   We find that all venerable rights of the people were crushed out; their constitutional privileges were abro-

[1] Prescott, *Ferdinand and Isabella*, II, 533, 537.

[2] Robertson, *Charles V.;* Dunham, *History of Spain.*

[3] Coxe, *Memoirs of the Kings of Spain*, I, 419.

gated, and their free institutions absorbed by the central authority. The Cortes remonstrated that they were not well used, and the result was that Charles granted them their desires; but the next time the Cortes were called, but few cities were represented, and this representation was only for the purpose of levying taxes and supplies. The representatives were not allowed to sit with the royal officers, and knew but little of the deliberations of the government. To carry on the brilliant war policy, it was necessary to tax the people to such a great extent that their burdens in this respect were unbearable.

Two other political events had great economic influence upon the nation; the expulsion of the Moors, and of the Jews. The former were conquered by Ferdinand, partially expelled by Charles, and finally driven from the country by Philip and his successors. The unity of Spain was established by a continuous warfare on those who were foreign in blood and in religion, but the economic effects of this policy were wholly evil. The Moors were among the best artisans and the most intelligent producers of Spain, and their loss was seriously felt. Every nation that has driven from its midst intelligent skilled labor, has felt the loss. The Jews were wealthy, and were valuable as wealth producers, wealth accumulators, and money loaners. From a country like Spain it was poor policy to drive out the bankers. Philip followed on the footsteps of his father, and carried out with even more rigor the national policy of Spain.

But it was not until the close of Philip's reign that the fallacy of his father's policy began to be seen. The gold of America and the high prices paid for the products of home industry upheld the government for a time; but in the midst of strength there were maladies ready to appear at the first hour of weakness. Philip was a cold, cruel monster; a commander of a system of spies; he could calculate with exactness the political results of the death of his enemy, and consequently the inquisition suited his temperament.[1]   With one hand he patronized learning and intellectual activity; with the other he stifled every attempt leading toward independent thought. While he planned to send the dagger to the heart of the victim over-watched by spies, he was a most devout catholic—a most pious king.   Piety, religious fanaticism, and diabolical cruelty were among his chief characteristics.[2]

There was never before such great power given to an individual nation to accomplish good as that given to Spain.   There never was a better opportunity given to a nation for advancing liberal government and elevating humanity by an enlightened policy of rulers than the one given in the political supremacy of Spain.   It was the dawn of the new era, the era of discovery, exploration, and commercial activity.   The spirit of reform had already been moving among the people and was soon to produce lasting effects.   The political and religious forces needed the direction of men of power; but at the same time everything seemed to call for new methods of government. But blinded by the two-fold idea of religious and political absolutism, Spain lost her opportunities, and permitted the government to be narrowed to the measure of royalty and bigotry.   This policy that culminated in the reign of Philip sealed the possibilities of the nation for centuries to come, and its evil effects were felt in the rapid decline of national power in the succeeding reigns.   When the government based on the absolutism of the monarch passed into the hands of weak rulers, they were unable to support the system.   Consequently, while other nations were laying the permanent foundations of political, industrial, and economic life, the ephemeral glory of Spain was waning.   While nations like England and the Netherlands were developing constitutional liberty and political power, and were promoting home industries and foreign commerce, Spain was losing or crushing the very safeguards to national life.

---

[1] Prescott, *Philip II.*, III, bk. VI.   [2] Gayarré, *Philip II.*, Chapter I.

A more careful analysis of the economic condition of Spain will assist in determining her true position and reveal many reasons for her rapid political decline.   In the first place the process of obtaining power was by force of arms and reliance upon the money that flowed from other nations.   It was largely a repetition of the old theory of the Romans, that of getting rich by the exploitation of other countries rather than by the natural development of home resources.   As has been stated, the Moriscoes, who were conquered by Isabella and dispersed by her religious zeal, persecuted by Philip II. and the Inquisition, and driven out by the stupid bigotry of Philip III., were among the most valuable inhabitants of the realm.[1]   They were agricultural laborers, skilled artisans and manufacturers; and had given great attention to science and literature.   When nearly eight hundred thousand of these toilers were thrust out of the kingdom, there were no producers to take their place.   The government was removing the wealth producing elements of the nation.   Further, the Jews were the native bankers and traders of the country; and they also were robbed, persecuted, and banished.   The great loss to productive industry was enhanced by the destructive influences of the Inquisition, which nearly always fell upon the toiling part of humanity.

But the discouragement given to productive industry was even more fatal in its influence.   While everything militated against honest labor, there was being educated a race of cavaliers and a dissolute nobility, that despised all labor as ignoble and all peasants because they were laborers.   Not only did all labor become dishonorable, but all home production unprofitable.   Manufacturers could not sustain themselves and pay the taxes.   They were hampered on account of a lack of laborers, and their factories were eventually closed on account of a lack of profits.   Those engaged in agricultural pursuits

---

[1] From 600,000 to 800,000 of these toilers were thrust out of the country and there were no laborers to take their place.

found it impossible to pay the taxes imposed by the government, although the price of products was high; consequently the soil went out of cultivation. There were few native capitalists in Spain; and the middle class in general was poorly represented. As the artisans were too poor to carry on their work unaided, shops were closed, and all trading was soon carried on by others. The people of Spain soon found themselves living on the products of foreign industries at the expense of their own prosperity. Not only did the manufactures pass to other lands, but soon nearly all of the foreign and domestic trade was in the hands of foreigners.[1] The English, French, Dutch, German, and Italian traders and manufacturers hastened to profit by the situation.[2]

To add to the burdens of the people, the taxes were enormous; and they fell, as is generally the case under such circumstances, upon the few who were the least able to bear them. It seems almost incredible that the rulers should have levied such an exorbitant taxation upon the declining industries of a nation. It seemed that absolutism had exceeded its profitable bounds of bigotry and oppression. The Cortes remonstrated; but the remonstrance was of no avail. Embodied in their complaint of 1594 is the statement that the sale of food was taxed fourteen per cent.; that merchants had to pay a tax of three hundred ducats on every one thousand ducats of property—a tax of thirty per cent.;[3] that taxes exceeded the income of estates, and that no tenant farmer could maintain himself, however low his rent might be. But the rich nobles and owners of feudal estates were exempt from taxation, as was also the church. Exempt from the whole taxable list the vast wealth of the church and the revenues of the estates, then consider the great number of idlers and vagabonds which in some districts equalled the number of laborers,

---

[1] Coxe, *Memoirs of the Kings of Spain*, III, 517.   [2] Dunham, V, 265.
[3] Harrison, *History of Spain*, 542.

and it is at once seen that the number of tax-payers was comparatively small.

Meanwhile the church flourished, and gained in wealth and
power constantly, until in the reign of Ferdinand VI. (1746–
1759) it reached the culminating point, owning at this time
one-fifth of all of the land and great possessions besides.   In
the year 1749, the income of the church was equal to the
entire revenue of the state, about 341,000,000 reals.[1]   Freed
from the burdens of taxation, and with this large income, is
it any wonder that the church flourished?   Is it any wonder
that a government which limited the burdens to a few persons
and exempted the remainder, should make a failure?   Is it
surprising that the church as an organization continued to
grow in wealth and power while the nation's temporal prosperity declined?   The church grew strong because it was a
government within a government, and bore none of the re-
sponsibilities of the political organization.   It was an equal
partner in the idea of absolutism, but it also had the strength
of a close corporation.   The inquisition could be urged on by
the church ; but the state must bear the terrible responsibility
of its results, and be held the perpetrator of the crimes which
were enacted by this instrument of extermination.   Thus it
was that while the state was declining the church was growing in temporal power and wealth.   Its spirituality necessarily
declined, but its organizing power went on increasing.

Religious orders swarmed, and the membership of the
church increased.   If the term " priest-ridden " could ever
be applied fittingly to a country, it was certainly applicable to
Spain at this period.   It became the policy of every family
to have at least one representative in one of the religious
orders, for the sake of the benefits derived from alms ; and
by distributing members of the family among different orders,
it was possible to make it a paying business.   Thus, fostered
by an inquisition that cut off all opposition, and by the favors

---

[1] Dunham, V, 282.

of the government respecting taxes and benefits, as well as by government recognition of its power, the church continued to grow and increase in apparent strength. While the ancient Castilian was remarkable for his independent resistance to Papal encroachments, he was subjected at home to excessive ecclesiastical influence arising from the situation. The church, by urging the inquisition, was preparing for a time when all freedom of thought should be stifled, and when all attempted reforms would be silenced. But it cannot be held that the church was wholly responsible for all of the ills of the country at this time; for a careful inquiry will show that the lands rented by the church were better tilled, and that the renter fared better than did the tenant of any other class of lands. There was something vitally wrong at the centre of administration. It was either a lack of the knowledge of government, or an entire disregard of the sources of national prosperity. The government, artificial, wrong in principle, and false in execution, could not restore declining prosperity. There was a lack in industry and a lack in trade, consequently the economic conditions of the country were continually made worse by every new legislative act. The vast sums of gold that came from America raised prices, but did not stimulate industry. It passed through Spain to pay the debts of foreign wars or else to pay for the industrial product consumed by the Spanish people. It is estimated that of the $70,000,000 which came from the colonies to Spain in the year 1595, not a dollar was to be found in Castile in the following year. Spain had the reputation of being wealthy, while in truth the nation was poor. The government and the power might be maintained for a while under the influence of such powerful monarchs as Charles and Philip, but a relaxation of the skill of such rulers long at a time no nation could endure. The decline in prosperity was as rapid as the rise. The laws and customs of the Spanish nation at this time were modified to a great extent by the arbitrary usage of the monarchs. The age of feudalism was past, although

there were some remnants of the system still existing.
The power of the feudal lords had never been quite suppressed; but when a monarch of so much power as Philip
ascended the throne, they were compelled of necessity to gather
under his banner and to be pensioners upon his bounty, receiving power and position from him. Consequently there was
created a dissolute nobility and a hierarchy of grandees as an
expensive appendage to the national administration.

In Aragon and Castile, before their union, there was a spirit
of popular liberty evinced in their constitution that could come
only from the ancient Teutonic polity. It outlived the conquest of the Moors and the shock of the feudal system. The
old principles regulating the election of the kings and limiting
the royal prerogative appear in their strongest forms. The
dignity and independence of the nobles was remarkable, and
the rights of the people to a seat in the Cortes were empha-
sized. In Aragon an officer called the *justiza* was elected,
who was a supreme guardian of the law and of the acts of the
king. Speaking in behalf of the sovereign barons, this officer
addressed the king in the language of the following oath of
allegiance taken by all subjects : " We who are each of us as
good, and who are altogether more powerful than you, promise
obedience to your government, if you maintain our rights and
liberties : but if not, not." [1]

In Castile the Cortes included the nobles, the ecclesiastics,
and the representatives of the cities. The duties of this
assembly were to take action respecting public revenues, the
redressing of grievances, and the presentation for the sanction
of the king of new measures favoring the people. Although
the reign of Ferdinand and Isabella tended to repress the power
of the nobles and to administer a better justice throughout the
realm, the royal prerogative was much curtailed throughout
the reign of Ferdinand, and for a long time in the reign of
Charles V. The remnants of feudalism long remained in

---

[1] Robertson, *Charles V.*, I, 178.

Spain, although in the time of Charles V. the power of the monarch was greatly increased. The traditional free government of the people, dating back to the time of the reign of the Goths and Vandals, dwindled away and became little more than a farce. But this spirit of freedom has shown itself at every possible turn throughout the history of Spain; and even to this day there are those who, recognizing the ancient rights of the people, look forward to a time that shall give them full expression. The administration became gradually absorbed by the king and the king's officers, and the government, becoming more imperial, was carried on without consulting the interests or opinions of the people of any class. Such was the condition of Spain at the time of the disclosure of the New World to the gaze of the European. These conditions modified to a great extent the explorations and settlements of the New World. Many of the institutions of Spain were transmitted bodily to the colonies, and the same spirit of legislation and government that existed in the mother country followed the adventurers wherever they went.

It is now proper to enquire into the nature of Spanish colonization, and to observe what was the character of the institutions transplanted to the New World and the effects of the same on the policy of colonial life and government.

CHAPTER IV.

Spanish Colonization.

Colonies of every class have repeated the types of institutions existing in the mother country. The ancient Greek colonies carried with them the institutions and characteristics of the states from which they sprung. The colonies were formed on account of internal disorders in the city, or in consequence of overpopulation.[1] They had their own constitution, usually patterned after those of their respective parental cities, with independent governments, having as far as political organization was concerned, no relation to the mother cities.[2] The migrations were generally undertaken with the approval and encouragement of the cities from which they issued, and particularly under the favorable auspices of the oracles. Once established, there was no feeling of dependence on the part of the colony, nor any claim of authority on the part of the parent city, although there was a bond of union arising from kinship. This moral sentiment was sufficiently strong to call mother and child to each other's defense in time of war; but it was not infrequently that they were found fighting on opposite sides. The colonization was a natural outflow, and its chief support was an active trade and commerce with other colonies and nations. The English colonies resembled, in a great measure, the Grecian. This is especially true in their inception, when they sought a new life in a new land on account of dissatisfaction at home. The resemblance would

---

[1] Heeren, *Ancient History*, 156.   [2] *Ibid.*, 157.

48

have been still more marked, had it not been for the commercial monopoly that later interfered with the natural course of events in the control of the English colonies of America.

But it must be borne in mind that, in all methods of modern colonization, the prime object sought was the direct benefit of the mother country. Colonization was instituted to relieve overpopulation, to develop commerce, to extend the dominion of the home government, or to guard the frontier. In every case the home governments sought their own welfare rather than the prosperity of the colonists. Among all of the above reasons for the establishment of colonies, none was more potent in modern times than the desire to establish stations for forwarding the interests of commerce. But the colonies of each nation had their own distinctive features, differing in many ways according to the objects, methods, and results of the enterprise. Thus England desired the colonies to produce raw materials for home manufactures; and endeavored to stimulate home industries by purchasing these materials in gold, and then returning manufactured articles in trade. To facilitate this, England granted great monopolies to companies such as the East India Company and the Hudson Bay Company. Spain, on the contrary, tried by legislation to keep all of the gold within the country; but succeeded instead in letting it all out because there were no home industries to employ it. Spain tried to create a government monopoly instead of granting a monopoly to companies.

The relation of the Spanish colonies to the central government was similar, in many respects, to the relation of the Roman colonies in her provinces to Rome. Spain desired to people the new territory and guard the frontier; in other words, to extend the dominion of the crown; consequently the Spaniards considered the lands colonized as part of the territory of the parent country, and the government of the country an integral part of the central government. Spain's policy was either to incorporate the natives into the colony, or to displace them by the new colonists. Rome practiced the

4

same method. However, it may be asserted that wherever Rome found an existing organization, its institutions were permitted to be retained by the people, if they did not seriously interfere with the government of the ruling power. On the other hand, the Spaniards considered no existing institutions worthy of recognition; intolerance in religion and absolutism in royal authority could recognize no good unless it flowed from supreme rulers. The result was a universal system of slavery introduced by the system of Spanish colonization.

Likewise we find, following Roman methods, the Spaniards sending out the military colony, and establishing the praesidium on the frontier of the royal domain. In many instances the colonies of Spain were filled with army veterans. The civil communities were also created by the central body, and sent by the parent country to become a part of the realm. Their laws were made by the central government, and their officers appointed by the same power. Every colony was made after the same plan, under the same law. The self-government of colonies was in great part suppressed, and the power of the home government was continually augmented. Of the one hundred and seventy Viceroys of the department of Buenos Ayres, four were Americans, and the remainder were Spaniards sent from the home government. Of the six hundred and ten captains-general and governors, only fourteen were Americans. Nearly all of these offices were sold in Madrid to the highest bidder.[1] In the department of Neuva España, the offices were filled by those needing positions, and not infrequently the office was created for the man. The Spanish provinces were ruled with consummate skill as regards the control of royal officers: one part of the government was set to watch another part; and the system of espionage was maintained in order to acquaint the home government with the exact state of affairs as well as to prevent

---

[1] Merivale, *Colonies and Colonization*, I, 11.

consolidation of power and revolution against authority. Yet, notwithstanding every precaution, the provincial officer usually robbed the government and failed to carry out the laws of the land.

The possession of all newly acquired territory was vested in the crown of Spain rather than in the government.[1] Consequently all colonial power and policy were under the king's immediate control. The sovereign being proprietor of the land, all rights must flow directly from him. The settler had no rights arising from the situation; consequently no political power developed from the people; it came instead from the king. The king treated his colonial subjects as the padres treated the natives, keeping them in perpetual political minority. The inevitable result followed; without inducement to build homes, with no hope of civil or religious liberty, with no inducement and much less opportunity to establish new laws and institutions, and hampered on every side by the laws of trade, the colonies were little beyond mere puppets in the show of government.

To facilitate the execution of the law and to enforce the adopted government, there was instituted the Council of the Indies. This council superintended all colonial affairs; and though it could not act without the sanction of the king, who met with it on stated occasions, it had a specific duty in the management of affairs, and great power in government. In the execution of the provincial laws of the government, everything and everybody was kept in subordination to the governing powers. Obedience was the great law of being, and legislation was minute and explicit to the smallest shadow of doubt. The Council of the Indies was instituted by Ferdinand in the year 1511, but was perfected by Charles in the year 1524. Its jurisdiction extended to every department, religious, civil, military, and commercial. All the laws for the government of the colonies originated here, and had to

---

[1] Bernard Moses, *Data of Mexican and U. S. History.*

receive a two-thirds vote of the members of the council and the sanction of the king before they became operative. All of the officers not appointed by the crown were named by this council; and every person filling any office of whatever nature in America was accountable to the council for the character of his administration of public affairs. This gave the Council of the Indies a control over American affairs that was destined to become entirely arbitrary. In connection with this was the Casa de Contratacion, or Board of Trade, established for the purpose of directing the course of commerce between the mother country and the colonies.[1] It was really created before the establishment of the Council of the Indies, as it dates from the year 1501. It performed a double function, as a board of trade and as a court of judicature. It regulated the course of trade, determining what goods should be imported and exported from the Indies, and the tonnage and time of the departure of the ships. It also had jurisdiction over the conduct of all persons connected with the trade between the two countries. It was subject to the control of the Council of the Indies as a court of appeal. As early as 1501, we find that the commerce of Spain must all pass through one port, that of Seville, in order that it might be better regulated. Thus the control and the direction of the colonies were placed in the hands of the central power. Nothing could be done except as it was ordered by the Council and sanctioned by the king. The local attempts at government were cut off through this arbitrary control by the mother country. There was no opportunity for the development of self-government, and hence no opportunity to develop a self-constituted national spirit. This state of affairs was precisely what the central government desired.

One of the wonderful things in the settlement of Spanish America was the union of the church and the state in the conquest of the new land. In America, as in Spain, the secular

[1] *Cf.* Chapter XIV.

and the religious powers went hand in hand; although the special aims of each seem to be more distinctly discernible here than at home. If the secular power was used to propagate the faith, religious zeal was made an excuse for plunder; if the secular arm upheld the absolutism of the church, the church in turn went forth to redeem the land in the name of the king. In both powers there was great pride of conquest; to conquer was a great principle; to save, a secondary one. By different means the two powers sought to obtain the same ends; namely, to enlarge the power and to increase the wealth of Spain. The formula for the course of action of the crown was—exploration, conquest, unity of the church, acquisition of wealth, and the increase of the territorial dominions of the king. The formula for the ecclesiastic was—spiritual conquest, increased power of the order, salvation of souls, extension of the king's domain, and, frequently, personal temporal blessings. On the other hand, soldiers and adventurers had one common thought; and that was to plunder the natives or to obtain wealth without toil. In this strange medley of conflicting motives, there seemed to be one spirit predominating the whole movement, that of conquest; in the crown it was shown in the avarice for power;. in the adventurers, by the thirst for gold; and in the ecclesiastic, by ambition to extend the territory and power of his order.

The religious party played a very important part in the colonization of Spanish America, and the institutions of the country are not to be explained without great attention to this fact. Religion performs a very important part in the making of any nation, as in all great movements; but where it is so closely connected with the government as it was in the case of Spain, what a power it must have wielded in the consummation of any plan of conquest and settlement ! The church occupied a strong position in the New World, and possessed about the same character there as in Europe. There was the same pomp and show in the organization of the hierarchy there as in the Old World. The expense of keeping up such an institution was a burden to the colonists, and the tithes imposed by law were rigorously collected. Every article of primary necessity toward which the attention of the new settlers might be turned, was taxed. The law of the Indies of the year 1501 provided for the collection of the tithes, and subsequent laws of the same body extended the list of taxable articles. Not only were the burdens of taxation grievous to be borne, but the pomp and the extravagance of the church was supported by the private donations of individuals. The influence of the religious orders was very great in every way. They not only obtained control of the religious systems but had great influence on the civil authority. The ecclesiastical system modified all forms and practices of government. The religious idea was prominent from the first in the settlement of the new continent; and its power continued to increase until the whole territory was practically under the control of the religious orders. The church system in America was a type of the system of old Spain; an expensive system, attended with the usual pomp and ceremony, and with its hierarchy, of abbots, bishops, and priests, and the usual number of religious orders. It was through the church that the tithes were collected; but by the bulls of Alexander VI., and Julius II., the revenues derived from this source were made due to the king of Spain, and were consequently at his disposal.[1] The great annual expense of the church and its fixed wealth in monasteries and churches absorbed much capital that could have been used for immediate production of wealth. It is generally conceded that the establishment of so great a number of monasteries in a new country, where it was important that the population should be rapidly increased and all of the available power utilized, was, upon the whole, a great hindrance to the development of the country, besides being a heavy drain upon the wealth of the land. Although it be admitted that the ecclesiastics did not always use the power

[1] Robertson, II, 513.

placed in their hands for the best interests of the country and the material prosperity of the colonists, yet it must be conceded that the work of the religious orders was the most sincere and faithful of that done under any part of the colonial system. Faulty as their system might be, and ignorant as were many of those who sustained it, the rule of the ecclesiastics is, after all, the only redeeming feature of the early practical results of the great theory of conquest. The missionaries, as far as possible, stood between the natives and the Europeans, and shielded the former from the oppression of unjust and rapacious men.[1] Referring to the offices of the clergy in the defense of the natives, Burke says: "This unfortunate people found their only refuge in the humanity which remained in the clergy, and the influence they had upon the Spaniards; though the clergy who went out on these expeditions were generally not the most zealous for religion; and were, as the Spanish clergy commonly were, ignorant enough, and so little principled in the spirit of the religion they professed, or in the nature of the human mind that they could boast as a glorious thing, that one of them had baptized several thousand Indians in one day without the help of any miracle for their conversion and with a degree of good life which to say the least was nothing more than common." [2]

The laws instituted by the home government for the treatment of the natives have been called the wisest of any ever recorded to regulate the treatment of an inferior race in a conquered country by the conquerors.[3] However wise the laws may have been in theory, their execution in most cases must have been a failure. And indeed the whole censure cannot fall upon the colonists and those of the new country;

---

[1] Burke, *European Settlements*, I, 164.

[2] Burke, *European Settlements;* "Learn to read, write and say your prayers, for this is as much as any American ought to know." *Viceroy, Gil de Lemos to the collegians*, I, 76.

[3] Burke, I, 164.

for those who made the laws could have understood but little of the affairs that concerned the building of strong colonies and the best means of bringing about justice. There can be, however, no excuse made, except that of bigotry and ignorance, for the manner in which the hand of avarice reached out to pluck the products of the mines and of the soil, to suppress all self-development, to drain all accumulated wealth in order to support churches and monasteries, and to fill the coffers of the sovereigns of Spain. The whole process was one of exaction from the colonists, and exaction of all their possessions. Mexico to-day feels the result of this narrow policy on the part of the church and the civil power; the priests still oppose enlightenment, still oppose the progress of the country, still oppose everything that tends in any way to better the life of human beings. They are still holding out the consolations of religion to the weak and oppressed without stimulating them to self support, self dependence, and natural growth. Since the separation of the church and state in 1857, there has been some progress made towards free education, it being compulsory in many states; but the machinations for evil by the priests still continue.[1]

Not only does the vast army of priests oppose liberty of conscience and general intelligence among the common people, but they are opposed to the introduction of industrial improvements; for they know that through these the monopoly which the church claims over the life of individuals will disappear. When Mexico is covered with a net-work of railroads, when the wooden plow is replaced by a modern patent, when the farmers use the threshing machine in place of a band of goats for threshing grain, and when universal free education has become an accomplished fact, then much of the trade of priestcraft will vanish from the land.

The system of slavery established in America partook something of the nature of feudal vassalage, although it was not

---

[1] Ballou, M. M., *Aztec Land*, 39.

everywhere the same. The feudal system had left some of its vestiges and forms in Spain as late as the conquest of America; and these elements of a transitional stage were manifest in the treatment of an inferior nation. Slavery was manifested in several different phases among the natives of the New World; it ranged all the way from a mere wardship to abject servitude. Spain held the right to conquer the Indians; for had not the Pope granted the land to the king of Spain, and should he not enter upon the possessions sanctioned by the vicar of God? And by taking the proper care of this benighted race, it would have the blessings of the gospel carried to it, and a better life pointed out to it. Such was the theory and such was the claim of the Spaniards upon the ignorant natives. If the natives did not wish to yield their land to the conquerors, then they must suffer the consequences of resistance; they must be slain or taken prisoners of war and be branded and pass as slaves. The penalty was perhaps very severe; but they might have yielded peacefully, and then there would have been no trouble. Could they not understand that the Spaniards were seeking after the highest good of the Indians, and were desirous of winning them to the kingdom of Christ as well as to the kingdom of Spain? Such was the reasoning of those who sought land by the strong arm of conquest, and so read the ancient law. Many times the following formula was repeated in various ways, setting forth the object of conquest and the warrant for invasion. " The kings, our progenitors, from the discovery of the West Indies, its islands and continents, commanded that our captains, officers and discoverers, colonizers, and all persons that are arriving at these provinces, should, by means of interpreters, cause to be made known to the Indians that they were sent to teach them good customs, to lead them from vicious habits and from the eating of human flesh, to instruct them in our holy Catholic faith, to preach to them salvation, and to attract them to our dominion." Perhaps Isabella was interested in the natives, and really did intend to give them proper treatment; but succeeding sover-

eigns were too much engrossed in the affairs of Europe to
interest themselves very deeply in the affairs of western savages, until it was too late to undo the great wrongs committed.

In the early part of the conquest, we find that there were
frequent revolts of the half subdued savages, and many skirm-
ishes between them and the Spaniards. It was in the year
1495, in the island of Hispaniola, that an insurrection was
suppressed, and some of the revolting natives were killed;
some yielded peacefully; some were taken prisoners; while
others fled to the forest, " offering themselves," says Munoz,
" to the service of the Christians, if they would allow them to
live in their own ways."[1] If this is the origin of the first
phase of Indian slavery, as Arthur Helps suggests, then slavery came as a beneficent measure, and was accepted by the
natives as the lesser of two evils, destruction and servitude.
Columbus ordered that a tribute of gold should be collected
from the natives that he might verify at the court of Spain
the fabulous reports of the wealth of the New World. As
the natives had no gold, it became necessary for them to work
out the tax on the plantations of the Spaniards. This was
the formal beginning of the *repartimiento* system, by which
lands and Indians were apportioned to the invaders. But it
was not until 1498 that letters patent were granted to Columbus, giving him power to grant *repartimientos* of land to
Spaniards, although no mention was made of the Indians.
The grantee was " to have, to hold, and to possess " the land
thus granted him. Then followed the advice of Columbus,
that the crown of Spain should grant the use of the Indians
a little while, until the colony should be in a settled state.
This was granted; and we find that Columbus apportioned
certain lands to individuals, and designated what lands should
be worked by a cacique and his people. Then followed the
edict of the sovereigns addressed to Ovando, providing that
" the natives be forced to have dealings with the Spaniards,

---

[1] Arthur Helps, *Spanish Conquest in America*, I, 147.

and that they work for wages under the guidance and oversight of caciques; the natives must hear mass, and further
were to do all of these things as free persons for so they were."
Here we find one of the early inconsistencies of Spanish
administration. The natives were to be considered as free
persons, but their land was to be taken from them, and they
were forced to till it for others; free persons, but they were
forced to hear mass; free, but forced to communicate with a
race that does not hesitate to rob, murder, and outrage them.
From this time on until the law of 1542, or perhaps until the
law of 1563 was passed, the natives were parcelled out with
each grant of land, as so many cattle, to till the soil.

The deed of these early grants ran thus: " To you, such a
one, is given an ecomienda of so many Indians with such a
cacique, and you are to teach them the things of our holy
Catholic faith."[1] The last clause was a mere fiction; as the
owners of the encomiendas cared only for the labor of the
natives. Such legislation may be very beneficent in sentiment; but it was childish, to say the least, when we consider
the circumstances and the persons to whom such grants were
made. Thus we find that at first there were repartimientos
of lands, and then repartimientos or encomiendas of Indians;
and we learn that finally the two were combined in one grant,
and with every grant of land was included a fixed number of
natives. Although the grant of the encomienda of natives
included only feudal services, or tribute from them as vassals, it permitted this tribute to be worked out; and this
system once begun, there was no distinction between it and
real slavery. The natives were permitted to live in villages, and a certain number must go on service all or a part
of the time to work out the tax or tribute. They were usually
sent to the mines and there treated as slaves. Such was the
situation of the natives before Mexico was discovered, and
these plans were still carried out in that country until a law

---

[1] Herrara, *Hist. de las Indias*, lib. V, cap. 11; Helps, I, 194.

was passed abolishing the system of encomiendas. The laws
continued to pass through many changes. At first the grant
was for one life, then for two, and again for three, then four,
and finally five, until the Indians were reduced to an hereditary feudal tenure.[1] Even after the laws were passed for the
protection of the natives, it was a long time before the Indians
were really protected.

One of the early occupations of the colonists of New Spain
was mining. The amount of gold and silver that could be
extracted from the earth was a measure of prosperity. Spain
was still laboring under the delusion that gold and silver are
the chief causes of the wealth of a nation. The precious
metals were in great demand as a means of exchange; and
Spain, along with other nations of the period, endeavored to
prohibit their exportation, and on the other hand to induce
their importation. Consequently the native cupidity of the
Spaniards for the precious metals was excited to its utmost in
the development of American mines. To perform the heavy
work of the mines Indians were necessary; and it is here that
the greatest hardships were imposed upon the natives. Upon
the whole, the laws of a country are a faithful representation
of the history of the people. Judging from the great number
of laws that have been made for the regulation of mines, and
the number that were instituted for the protection and use of
the natives, it must be inferred, that there are here represented
two important phases of Spanish colonization. In regard to
the mining laws, there was an established code regulating
from time immemorial the ancient mines of Spain; but the
regulation of the natives brought about an entirely new phase
of law. Religion, as we have seen, also introduced new conditions into Spanish law.

In the colonies the Spanish laws prevailed except where
new cases arising were provided for by special regulations
and fueros. The Siete Partidas and other bodies of laws

---

[1] Helps, IV, 325, *et seq.*

prevailed in the colonies as well as on the continent. But these laws could not meet all the exigencies of the case; consequently there sprang up a new set of laws for the government of New Spain. These laws portray vividly the attempts of the government to keep the colonies in a state of dependence and to use them for its own benefit. Evidently the colonies were regarded as fiefs of the royal domain, and the kings of Spain looked upon the colonists as their vassals or tenants. The entire code, created for the especial purpose of controlling the colonists, was made in the interests of the mother country, and particularly in behalf of the kings of Spain. But without skill in legislation in the interests of industrial pursuits or in political organization, it was a difficult task to make laws for such a vast empire as that which the kings of Spain endeavored to rule. Consequently many measures that were instituted for the general improvement of trade and the perfecting of the civil administration, turned out to be positive evils to the colonies and the mother country as well.

The laws which were enacted in Spain for the government of the colonies were issued in the " form of *cedulas, decretos, resoluciones, ordenamientos, reglamentos, autos acordados,* and *pragmaticas.*"[1] Everything done in New Spain followed the dictation of the royal government. At the slightest cause or the least friction in the governmental machinery, a cedula or reglamento was forthcoming with all the formality and dignity of the Spanish regime. The appointment of a subordinate officer must be accompanied with the dignity of an extended document, legal, explanatory, and didactic.

---

[1] Schmidt, *Civil Law of Spain and Mexico,* 93. *Cedulas* and *autos acordados* were orders of a superior tribunal issued in the name and by the authority of the sovereign. *Decretos* were similar orders in ecclesiastical matters. *Ordenamientos* and *pragmaticas* resembled *cedulas,* differing only in form and in method of promulgation. *Reglamentos,* written instructions given by competent authority without following any prescribed form. *Resoluciones* are opinions given by a superior tribunal for the instruction of an inferior.

These laws became so numerous that it was difficult for the authorities to keep informed on the subject of administration. To remedy this, a complete compilation of the laws governing the colonies was ordered ; but it was not completed until 1680, under the reign of Carlos II.   This famous code is known as the " Recopilacion de Leyes de los Reinos de las Indias," which represents a digest of the *cedulas, reglamentas,* and so on, issued at different times for the government of the American colonies.   This code was limited in its range to the regulation of the military, political, and fiscal affairs of Spanish America ; and was consequently a mere enumeration of exceptions to the civil laws of Spain.[1]   And it was expressly stated in the Recopilacion, that in cases where the laws of this code failed to provide, the laws of the Kings of Castile and of the Siete Partidas should obtain.[2]   Prior to the time of Philip IV. (1621–1665), all laws enacted in Spain applied equally in the colonies.   But at this time it was provided that no law enacted for the government of Spain should apply to America unless accompanied by a cedula so declaring it, sent out by the Council of the Indies.   It necessarily follows that many laws subsequently enacted for Spain did not apply to America ; the converse is also true, that many laws enacted specially for America did not obtain in Spain.   But after the assembly of the Cortes in Spain in 1810, following close on the French Revolution, all new laws in force in Spain were also in force in the American colonies, without special enactment.

It may be claimed with authority, that the civil laws of Old Spain were in most cases the laws of New Spain ; and that the Republic of Mexico after the revolution of 1821, adopted the Spanish laws for its government.   There is therefore but slight difference between the Mexican and Spanish laws ; for the laws of Spain passed to America where they have been subject to slight changes and new applications.   However, in recent years the promulgation of

---

[1] Schmidt, 95.   [2] Recopilacion de Indias, libro II, titulo 1, ley 1.

new laws in Mexico has radically changed in many respects the character of Mexican jurisprudence.

In concluding this part of the subject, it may be clearly affirmed that Spanish institutions were inherited by the American colonies, and the customs, the laws, and the government of Old Spain prevailed in New Spain. However, there sprang up a new set of usages in accordance with the peculiar condition of the country, even though Spain seldom legislated for the especial needs of the colonists. The system of Spanish government usually obtained, and we find that the royal audiencias of Mexico and Peru attempted to legislate and govern in a manner copied from the mother country, and also that the Spanish municipal government was transplanted to America. In dealing with the natives, a new and difficult problem continually confronted the Spanish sovereigns ; and in the zealous work of the religious orders and the church, Spain was aided in her conquests, but frequently hindered in the promotion of a healthy growth of civil administration. In her attempts to control the trade of the colonies, the home government evinced greater ignorance and less skill than even in the management of political affairs. In her general method of planting colonies, Spain differs somewhat from every other country, but most resembles Rome. In government, municipal organization, military control, laws, administration, treatment of the natives, administration of religious affairs, and in colonial life and spirit, the Spanish colonies of America had little resemblance to the colonies in America of any other nation, except, perhaps, the French.

CHAPTER V.

There is no better illustration of the philosophy of the Spanish conquest than the instructions given by Velasquez, the governor of Cuba, to Cortés before the latter set out on his exploring expedition to Mexico. Velasquez in his instructions represented the sovereign of Spain; consequently the document must have a high moral tone and a sound of piety; for nothing official could be done in Spain unless it had a religious and moral sound. In fact, nationality was clothed in a religious garb obtained by generations of warfare with the infidels. It seems impossible to suppose that Velasquez had any hope that the formal instructions would in any degree be fulfilled, nor is it certain that he cared greatly about the conduct of the soldiers. Cortés was commanded to make an exploring expedition, to search for Grijalva, and to report on the nature of the country. He was given a code of rules for his conduct and the conduct of his men. The first one required the service of God in all things and the punishment of offenders against the rule.[1] The commander of the expedition was told to observe the conduct befitting a Christian soldier; and to prohibit gambling, licentiousness, and blasphemy among his men. On no account must he molest the

---

[1] Instructions given by Velasquez, Governor of Cuba, to Cortés on his taking command of the expeditions, dated at Fernandina, October 23, 1518. Prescott, *Conquest of Mexico*, II, 514.

natives, but peaceably inform them of the Glory of God and of the Catholic King.[1] No conquest was ordered; in reality, a conquest was forbidden by the instructions. His duty, in this respect, consisted in ascertaining the secrets of the country, and in taking possession in the name of the king. But the expedition of Cortés was voluntary, and consequently the expenses were to be paid by the commander. Notwithstanding the fair showing made by both commander and governor, it was generally understood that plunder and rapine were to be the reward of the expedition. There was to be a continuation of those terrible atrocities that had been hitherto practiced by the "wolves of Spain" on the defenceless natives.

Obedient to command and the Spanish religious formula of procedure, Cortés chose for his banner a red cross on black taffeta, surrounded with the royal arms and embroidered in blue and gold. Inscribed on the border was the following motto, "Amici, sequamur crucem, et si nos fidem habemus, vere in hoc signo vicemus."[2] He also proclaimed the primary motive of the expedition to be the spiritual conquest of the country, without which temporal acquisition would be unjust. While he and his followers were absorbed by the primary motives of political and financial gain, Cortés did not forget the sacred motto under which he fought, and to which he attributed his success. Religious exercises were held regularly throughout the campaign; and the friars who accompanied the expedition found steady employment in the pursuit of their calling. The soldiers were inspired by their presence while fighting and plundering, and the outward forms of religion were practiced daily; for to neglect ceremony was rank heresy, and in those days there was no crime like heresy.

The story of the conquest of the New World by the Spaniards has often been related. The soldiers and adventurers had but

---

[1] Bancroft, *Mexico*, I, 54; Prescott, *Conquest of Mexico*, II, 515.

[2] Icazbalceta, *Documentos para la historia de Mexico*, II, 554; Bancroft, *Mexico*, I, 59; Torquemada, *Monarchia Indiana*, I, 364.

5

one common thought: plunder and gold; and this was the uppermost idea in the early explorations in New Spain. Uppermost in the medley of conflicting motives that animated the conquest, we find avarice in the crown, thirst for gold in the adventurer, and in the ecclesiastic, ambition to extend the power of his order. But the dominant motive that characterized the conquest in New Spain, was a desire for gold and a thirst for power. In considering this Burke says : " What animated these adventurers at the same time that it fixed a stain upon all their characters is that insatiable thirst for gold which appeared uppermost in all of their transactions. This disposition had been a thousand times extremely prejudicial to their affairs. It was particularly the cause of the confusion and rebellion in Hispaniola ; yet had it not been for this incentive which kindled the spirit of discovery and colonization, first in Spain and Portugal, and afterwards in all parts of Europe, America would never have been in the condition she now is ; nor would these nations ever have had the beneficial colonies which are now established in every part of the country. . . . It was necessary that there should be something of an immediate and uncommon gain fitted to strike the imagination of men forcibly, to tempt them to such hazardous designs." [1] In the attempt to excuse the conduct of the invaders, it is plain that the distinguished statesman had in mind the English theory that colonies are established and exist solely for the pecuniary benefit of the mother country. But to overcome a people for the sake of plunder, or to establish colonies that oppress the people simply to enable the home government to grow rich or carry on its barbarous wars, is far from the ideal method of propagating an enlightened civilization and aiding the development of a new country through the beneficent rule of a prosperous and happy people. Perhaps the New World was in this way more rapidly opened up to the use of the Old, but it was a terrible process.

---

[1] Burke, *European Settlements*, I, 76.

In an incredibly short time, the adventurers of Spain over-ran the country. They plunged into forests, crossed rivers, ascended mountains, and endured hardships and fatigue, led on by mad visions of sudden wealth. No matter how fertile the soil, how pleasant its climate, or how rich its vegetation, no land could tempt him to settle. The Spaniard was a swift, terrible, and cruel conqueror, who sought only plunder and gold in his merciless conquest. Let us not pause to recount the history of the conquest with its tales of cruelty and horror, nor to relate the exploits of its intrepid com-mander. However interesting the civilization of the natives, which was supplanted by the religion, government, and cus-toms of the Spaniards, and however exciting the movements of armed warriors among the helpless Indians, we must pass these by to investigate the nature of the government insti-tuted by Cortés.

The first government of New Spain was the creation of Cortés, during the period of invasion and conquest. In order to free himself from the authority of the superior officer Velasquez, the governor of Cuba, who became his enemy through jealousy, Cortés conceived the plan of forming a new government, placing himself at the head, and receiving the direct recognition of the king of Spain. His first move was to assemble the principal members of his army, whom he caused to elect a council and magistrates. He formed the new government upon the model of the Spanish corporation. The magistrates and officers took the names of similar officials in a Spanish town. Having nominated the *alcaldes*, the *regi-dores*, the *alguazil*, and other functionaries, who were properly sworn into office, Cortés tendered his resignation as Captain-General, and left the council of the Villa Rica de Vera Cruz to its own deliberations.[1] The council speedily elected Cortés, in the name of their " Catholic Highnesses," Captain-General

---

[1] Prescott, *Conquest of Mexico,* I, 276; Robertson, *History of America,* II, 24; Carta de Vera Cruz, Prescott, *Conquest,* II, 521.

and chief Justice of the colony ; and he was empowered to receive on his own account as representative of the Sovereign, one-fifth of all the precious metals to be hereafter obtained from the natives through commerce or conquest. After the foundation of the Villa, the officers and citizens dispatched a letter to their royal highnesses the sovereigns of Spain, defining their position, and explaining the nature of the new municipality.[1] The formation of the Villa of Vera Cruz represents a direct continuance of the Spanish municipality, a transference of Spanish institutions to America.

Cortés continued to form other municipalities as occasion seemed to demand ; but there was no regular system either of town government or provincial administration enforced until a later date. He was acting military governor of the conquered territory, and as such exercised supreme authority, although his election as Captain-General by the members of the army acting in the capacity of a town council, was not sanctioned by the sovereigns of Spain until three years and four months after he entered upon his active duties. Such was the slow movement of administration in those times. Having acquired the title of Captain-General, Cortés was quick to seize and hold, as best he might, the power of absolute authority. From this time forth, he acted as ruler of the conquered territory, assuming responsibility to the king alone. With the king's sanction, he continued to be the chief officer in New Spain until the creation of the supreme audiencia.

Soon after the conquest of the city of Mexico, Cortés rebuilt it and formed it into a town corporation. He granted to those who wished to settle in the town lots for building purposes (solares), and appointed the alcaldes and the regidores of the new municipality.[2] The city was rebuilt under great toil and discouragement; but the soldiers managed and the natives did

---

[1] Helps, *The Spanish Conquest in America*, II, 250.
[2] Helps, *Spanish Conquest*, III, 20.

the severe work, carrying the timbers a great distance. In all of this, Cortés managed everything with consummate skill. The aqueduct for the conveyance of water was repaired, old houses remodeled, and new ones built; and the people who had departed from the city were re-collected. Thus Mexico continued to be as it had been for many years, the chief ruling city of the provinces. It seems that other towns were created; and by this and other evidences we may discover something of the loose nature of the military government which he established; a loose government with numerous municipalities interspersed. His long marches to quell rebellious natives, and the interference of his enemies with his every attempt to establish Spanish dominion, would not permit him to establish a permanent civil government. Finally through the machinations of his enemies, he was recalled, and a *residencia* appointed through the king's justiciar Ponce de Leon.

The term *residencia* is applied to the process of sending out to relieve the incumbent of office for the time being, a royal officer, who assumes all of the functions of the officer relieved, and proceeds to sit as a judge to hear evidence against him. The origin of the word, from the Latin *residere*, meaning to reside, explains a survival of an old Roman idea in government. In the Roman Republic, officers were responsible to the people and to the courts, and could be brought to account after the close of their term of office. The Spanish officer was required to remain on the territory for a certain length of time after yielding the insignia of his office to others, that he might render an account of any misdemeanor committed during his official term. If an officer was accused of misdemeanor, this was equivalent to a process of trial. Helps traces this principle of law to the Theodosian Code, and infers that it was continued in the Visigothic Code, which was made in part from the Theodosian.[1] That the custom has its origin in Roman jurisprudence no one can doubt. The *residencia* of

---

[1] *Spanish Conquest*, III, 141.

Cortés lasted but seventeen days, on account of the early death of the judge of residence, although the usual term was from thirty to fifty days; and in some instances the residencia was allowed to drag its slow length for a number of years. Let it be stated that during this time the jealous enemies of Cortés could find nothing against his administration. However, the event caused a change in the method of government, which became more permanent and orderly.

The presence in New Spain of a supreme audiencia, created at this same time, gave a new aspect to the affairs of government. This body was created by Charles V. and his ministers in the year 1626, and henceforth became a permanent institution of the government in the Spanish possessions. The government of the Viceroys in New Spain, which obtained after the settled state of affairs, was in theory subject to the Supreme Audiencia in judicial matters; but not infrequently the vice-kings of the provinces overstepped the bounds of their even royal prerogative, and interfered with the administration of justice. The viceroy ruled with absolute authority; he was the type of the sovereign of Spain, and frequently outstripped him in assuming power. The Court of Mexico was patterned after the Court of Madrid; and was accompanied by all the pomp, show, and glitter of the royal administration of the sixteenth century. They were kings in Mexico as truly as the sovereigns of Spain were kings of the Old Dominion, with the slight exception that they were amenable to the Emperor for their conduct, and derived their glory from him. In the government established under the viceroys, there seem to have been a few dominant principles that were always adhered to, no matter what attempts were made to frame good laws for the protection of the natives, or for the benefit of the Spanish Colonists. Whatever the theory of this government might have been, it seems that in practice to obtain the largest possible sum for the royal treasury, to build up and strengthen home industries and the home government, and to extend the dominion of the church, represented the chief office of the government.

The government of Mexico was greatly modified at an early date by the arrival of the religious orders. The close union of Church and State made interference possible on the part of the religious orders and secular clergy. They exercised a watchfulness over the affairs of the government, and this led to great contention, many laws, and not a few changes in policy.

Cortés favored the religious orders rather than the regular clergy, as best calculated to do the proper work in a new country, and less liable to establish a hierarchy of power. For this and other reasons, we find that the members of the orders multiplied to a great extent in proportion to the secular clergy. From the very beginning of the expedition of Cortés, friars and ecclesiastics accompanied the army, to administer to the spiritual wants of the soldiers, and to preach the gospel to the natives when opportunity presented. History shows that for a long time they were busily occupied in praying for the success of the invaders, and absolving those who committed crimes and sins. Friar Melgarejo came to Mexico as early as 1522 on a special mission to grant indulgence to those who had committed blasphemy, or outrage against the defenseless natives. On his return he carried with him a large sum of money which was lost in a storm at sea. Later came Father Otondo and his followers, and the conversion of the natives began in earnest. Soon we find friars everywhere preaching to the Indians, whose conversion was rapid indeed if we credit the stories told by the missionaries themselves. Father Gaute himself writes without hesitation that, with the aid of a companion, he had baptized eight, ten, and sometimes fourteen thousand Indians in a day.[1] The ceremony could not have been very complete in each case; there must have been a general process for admission into the church. After baptism, the natives were taught to say prayers and engage

[1] Bancroft, *Mexico*, II, 175.

in other religious practices, and were instructed in the elements of learning; although the children were the only ones greatly influenced either by religion or education. It is said that they learned very rapidly, especially in those branches requiring great power of imitation. It was the delight of the fathers that the natives took great interest in music, and could be trained in vocal exercises and on the stringed instruments for the church service.

There was a constant feud between the religious and the secular clergy which led to contention among themselves. There was also a strife between the friars and the civil authorities, chiefly on account of the management of the Indian affairs. Add to these facts that the two chief orders, the Dominicans and the Franciscans, were bitter enemies; and we have a perplexing state of affairs. This was not improved by the advent of the Jesuits, who pushed their enterprises everywhere, and opposed all who in the least interfered with the progress of their order. The Franciscans came to New Spain in 1524, and were the first authorized by the king of Spain to engage in missionary work in Mexico. They were supported by alms, which, collected in large amounts, were used to build churches and convents. Their first province included the city of Mexico, where the famous college of San Fernando was established, the institution that figured so conspicuously in subsequent colonization. It became the mother of all of the Franciscan missions in California and Mexico. The order of Carmelites came to Mexico in 1585, and commenced immediate work with the Indians. Subsequently they became very wealthy, owning as they did, "estates in San Luis Potosi extending from the Capital to Tampico—120 leagues."[1] The Benedictines arrived four years later and were followed soon after by the Dominicans. The latter order was very poor; for it held its members to the strict rules of poverty, and forbade their meddling with

---

[1] Bancroft, *Mexico*, II, 712.

political affairs or in any way interfering with the officials in charge.

" The missionary army of New Spain was greatly strengthened in 1572 by the accession of the Society of Jesus. The Jesuits had already missions planted in Habana and Florida."[1] They built colleges and schools for the education of Spanish children, and showed great vigor and earnestness in the work of converting the natives. They showed the same spirit here that had characterized them from their earliest foundation. Called into being, at a time when other orders in Europe had fallen into disrepute, for the purpose of strengthening the Papal power by placing his authority supreme above every other, by fighting heresy, and by extending the dominion of the Church through missionary labor, they represented the most remarkable religious organization that ever existed, unless it be, perhaps, the Roman Church itself. Organized in 1534, by Ignatius Loyola, confirmed in 1540, by Paul III., the order soon had its members all over the world : in the catholic home, in the royal chamber, in protestant lands, and in the savage wilderness. The order had the strength of a military organization, and the silent working of a secret police. Notwithstanding their oath of absolute obedience to the Pope, their creed professed above everything else, the good of the order, " which was the way to God ; " consequently they were frequently found in conflict with the temporal authority and with the Church itself. " It was everywhere by the same means," says Greisinger, " and the same way, namely, by the establishment of educational institutions, by the seizure of the confessional stools of kings, by fighting with heresy, by the incorporation of the most powerful forces into their order, as also by their fanatical influence on the great mass of the people, that they succeeded."[2] By their severe discipline, their earnestness, and frequently by

---

[1] Bancroft, *Mexico*, II, 699.   [2] Greisinger, *The Jesuits*, I, 145.

crafty planning,—for with them the "end justified the means,"—they carried force wherever they went, and succeeded where others failed. But they became by an excessive development of the above qualities obnoxious to all orders, creeds, and nations. They were finally expelled from Spain and her colonies in 1767, and consequently were banished from Mexico soon after. They were the most energetic colonizers that Spain had in the New World, and their work had great influence in giving shape to the new policy and laws of domesticating the Indians.[1] Their zeal, patience, and perfect organization, made them useful allies of the Spanish government; although they were always coming in contact with the soldiers and local authorities. They did everything in the name of the king as well as in the name of the Church and of their order.

It is evident that these religious orders were of great use to the civil authorities in pushing explorations and making settlements on the frontier. It mattered not how barren the country, how desolate and unproductive, wherever natives dwelt there were to be found the members of some religious order attempting to convert the Indians. The missionaries were foremost in every expedition, first in the establishment of permanent settlements, always contending against encroachment upon their rights and the rights of the natives; they thus frequently came in conflict with the civil authority on questions of government and law, of the rights of property and of person; and it was through their influence that the beneficent laws were made for the treatment of the natives of New Spain. But with all of this we must record their interference many times with the best interests of the country. In attempting to make the conversion of the natives the only object of Spanish occupation, they frequently lost both civil and religious influence, and retarded the progress of civil and religious occupation. It must be urged

---

[1] See Chapter VII.

that, in seizing and holding such great amounts of property by building churches and monasteries and making collections for tithes, they abstracted large amounts of wealth that should have been applied to productive industries. The events which are about to be related of the attempts to explore and settle the northwest show clearly how useful they were, and also how they sometimes hindered progress. Their history is full of alternate success and failure.

Cortés continued his explorations in the northwest until, as late as 1535, he discovered the Peninsula of Lower California. From that time on, there were repeated attempts to settle the territory to the north. Expedition after expedition was fitted out, and attempt after attempt made to occupy the land; but all failed until another century had dawned. In the interior, explorations were also made to the far north in the effort to discover wealthy cities and thickly populated territories.

It is not necessary to repeat the story of the dangerous and generally fruitless expeditions of those who attempted to push exploration to the northwest; but it may be well to bring to our minds some of the more important adventures, on account of their historical relation to what follows. To Hernando Cortés must be given the honor of discovering and naming the Gulf and peninsula of Lower California. As early as 1522, this bold navigator had founded the city of Zacatula on the Pacific coast, and there began to build a fleet to be used in extending exploration to the Northwest coast and the Pacific Ocean. At that time it began to be evident to a few that Mexico was not a part of Asia; and Cortés planned to follow the coast and find, if possible, the mythical strait of Anian; and thus solve the great "Northern Mystery," concerning the connection of the two oceans.[1] The plans of the great conqueror were retarded on account of the time and attention that he was forced to give to the territories that he

_____

[1] See Chapter VI.

had already over-run and had not completely subdued. He sent out an expedition under Grijalva in 1534 to explore the coast northward, but it ended in a total failure. Grijalva discovered a bay extending into the peninsula of California, which he at first called La Paz, and afterward Santa Cruz; although they thought it an inland bay of a rocky coast rather than the peninsula that it proved to be. It was this expedition which discovered the presence of pearls in the northern waters. In the following year, Cortés commanded in person a new expedition into the same region, which resulted in nothing of permanent value. He departed from Chametla with over a hundred men, with whom he intended to plant a colony. Following his predecessor, he entered the bay of La Paz, which he called Santa Cruz; explored the coast of the peninsula, and left a portion of the colonists in its barren territory. The colony was a failure, and Cortés was obliged to send for the colonists to save them from starvation. It was from this expedition that the name California arose; a name to be applied to the peninsula and the country north. Other explorations followed. Ulloa reached the head of the Gulf of California in 1539, and Cabrillo sailed up the coast, touching at San Diego and the Santa Barbara Islands, and finally reached a latitude in the region of Cape Mendocino. This was in 1542. The celebrated voyage of Viscaino occurred at the beginning of the eighteenth century, during which the port of Monterey was discovered and entered. All of these expeditions tended to give some knowledge of the coast and to enshroud it in deeper mystery. Meanwhile the missionaries were establishing their stations in the interior and extending them to the far north. The famous exploit of Cabeza de Vaca, in his will-o'-the-wisp journey across the continent; the exploration of Marcos de Nizza and his wonderful stories; the long march of Coronado in the search for the Seven Cities of Cibola; and the subsequent settlement of New Mexico by Juan de Oñate, demonstrate the intense desire of the Spaniards to reach this northern country, and that of the

COLTON HALL, CALIFORNIA'S FIRST CAPITOL.

friars to carry the Gospel to the natives. As a result of these explorations a few rich mines were opened, a few plantations established, a few towns built, and many missions established. Upon the whole the explorations were unsatisfactory to those who made them; but they were the first steps toward the final settlement of the provinces in which they were made. The only results that could in any way satisfy the avarice of the adventurers accompanying these expeditions was the discovery of rich pearl fisheries in the Gulf of California. Ever since the return of Juan de Iturbide with a number of choice pearls, one of which was valued at one thousand pounds sterling,[1] the cupidity of the Spaniards had been greatly excited, and they hastened to profit by the new enterprise. The fisheries became so extensive as to yield a revenue to the crown as well as to the numerous persons engaged in them. Not less than $480,000 worth of pearls were taken in a single season.[2] This industry centered the thought of the people on the Californias, and a more determined effort was made to settle these provinces. But attempt after attempt of the government to plant successful colonies failed.

The authorities now proposed, owing to these failures and the supposed necessity of the early occupation of the provinces, that the work of settlement should be given into the hands of the Jesuits. Venegas, the priest-historian, with much enthusiasm for his order, records, "We have seen the zeal with which the conquest of California was prosecuted for the space of two centuries after the discovery and conquest of New Spain; at the same time there was little or no fruit of the repeated expeditions. In it the great conqueror Hernando Cortés employed all of his forces in repeated attempts. His example stimulated many private persons; governors, admirals, and viceroys entered into it on their own account. At last the kings of Spain took the work into their hands; yet all the result of such vast expenses, such powerful efforts,

---

[1] Venegas, *Noticias*, Part II, section 4.　　[2] Forbes, *California*, 68.

was that the reduction of California was considered impossible; and so indeed it was by the means made use of by men, but not by those means which God had chosen. Arms and power were the means on which men relied for the success of this enterprise. But it was the will of God that this triumph should be owing to the meekness and courtesy of His ministers, to the humiliation of His cross, and the power of His word. God seemed only to be waiting until human force acknowledged its weakness, to display the strength of His Almighty Arm, confounding the pride of the world by the weakest instruments. Possibly God was not pleased to countenance the first enterprises concerning California while the capital object was temporal good, and religion only a secondary motive. And on the contrary He prospered the design when His kingdom was the motive, and advantage of the monarchy considered only as a possible consequence." [1] This lengthy quotation has been given to illustrate the attitude of the faithful missionaries toward the conquest and settlement of the provinces of New Spain. It had become evident to the Spanish authorities that the barren waste called California could not be colonized by any ordinary process. There was nothing to induce settlement; and the explorations already made had been prosecuted at an immense cost to the government, and with little return. The last expedition to the province, before it passed under the Jesuit rule of Admiral Otondo accompanied by Father Kuhn, had cost the government $225,000.[2] But why should the government delay longer, while there were men willing to be used for the purpose, who would pay their own expenses and reduce the country on their own responsibility? There were no wealthy cities to plunder, no rich mines to explore, indeed but a limited amount of fertile soil to till. So the government by a stroke of policy made over the whole enterprise to the order, taking no part in it save that of granting the Fathers permission to enter the country,

---

[1] Venegas, *Noticias,* III, 1–3.   [2] Venegas, Part II, section 4.

to enlist soldiers on their own account, and to exercise sole authority over all concerned in the enterprise.[1] It was provided on the other hand that the Fathers should take possession in the name of the king of Spain, and that the expedition should in no way be burdensome to the government. It is evident that the sovereigns of Spain knew how to turn to account the religious zeal of the friars. On the part of the Jesuits there was no object in taking up such a work except the conversion of the natives, in which the Fathers manifested an untiring zeal.

It was in the year 1697, over one hundred and fifty years after the discovery of the country by Cortés, that the Jesuits, under Salvatierra, the President of the missions, entered the barren peninsula of Lower California. Their missions had already extended up the coast on the main land, and the Franciscans had developed to the northward on the east side of the mountains. The explorations of the secular authorities had led to numerous permanent settlements, and their endeavors were in so far successful; but the attempt was difficult enough. A great barrier lay between the colonies and settlements of New Spain and the rich countries of the north; and this barrier was California. It was given into the hands of the Jesuits as a last resort, and well did they accomplish their work. Whatever may be said of the machinations of the Jesuit order, the men who were engaged as leaders of this enterprise were above reproach; and the names of Salvatierra, Kuhn (Kino), Ugarte, and Piccolo will occupy a respected place in history.[2] They were earnest and conscientious in their work, and desired to accomplish much for the children of the forest as well as for the sovereigns of Spain. "It may be true," says Mr. Forbes, "that the means they adopted to effect their ends were not always the wisest, that the Christianity they planted was often more of form than substance, and the civilization in some respects an equivocal

---

[1] Forbes, *California*, 15. [2] Venegas, Part III, section 1.

good; still it can not be denied that the motives of these
excellent men were most pure, their benevolence unquestion-
able, their industry, zeal, and courage indefatigable and invincible." [1] The priest-historian discourses upon the motives of
missionaries who might have become wealthy at other pursuits or have lived a life of ease in their own order; but who
instead banished themselves to a life of disappointments and
fatigues to live among savages and in danger of death. Such
men, he affirms, could have had no other motive than the
conversion of Indians. [2]

Among this number of self-sacrificing men, Father Kino,
or Kuhn, is prominent; he had been formerly the professor
of mathematics at Ingoldstadt, and had been in good favor
with the Elector of the house of Bavaria. Salvatierra, the
president and manager of the reduction, had worked many
years at successful missionary work, and now had a chance
to exercise his unbounded zeal in the spiritual conquest of a
new territory. He was the chief authority on the Peninsula.
He superintended the founding of the missions and had the
supreme control of soldiers, priests and Indians. Salvatierra
believed in the improvement of the material condition of the
natives as well as the development of their spiritual natures. [3]
He taught the natives to till the soil, to construct houses, to
learn trades; and he practiced them in the observances of the
church. Their children were instructed in the rudiments of
learning. He looked out for their physical comfort, endeavor-
ing to make them happy and contented as he taught them the
arts of a new civilization.

Mission after mission was founded, and the government of
them all reduced to a system which was continued with little
variation throughout Jesuit rule. The chief authority was
the President, Salvatierra being the first, who had control of
both the civil and the military affairs of the province. As

---

[1] Forbes, *California*, 26.   [2] Venegas, Part III, section 5.
[3] Venegas, *Natural and Civil History of California*, Part III, section 11.

the country became settled, it was divided into three districts, each of which had its rector. The rector had to report every three years to the visitador, a superior officer elected every three years by the missionaries. The visitador was required to visit all of the missions within his jurisdiction at least once during his term of office, and report their condition to the Visitador-General. " Thus the Jesuit mission hierarchy consisted of missionary, rector, visitador, visitador-general, provincial, and general." [1] The provincial and the general were those who also had control of other parts of New Spain ; the general being at the head of the order.

The plan of forming a mission was to send out a padre to instruct a new tribe for a while, to prepare the natives for the reception of the Gospel, and to secure their consent to the erection of a mission in their midst. In the selection of the mission site, care was taken not to extend the system beyond easy communication with those already established. At first, a few rough buildings were constructed as a base of operation, which later gave way to better ones, as converts were collected to be instructed and domesticated. Soon the missionary in charge began to extend his work by making itineraries to the surrounding rancheries. These he later organized into pueblos, each having its Indian alcalde, who acted as governor. Thus was established a community of Christian villages, of which the mission was the capital, and the missionary the superintendent and governor in charge. The civil system in the Peninsula was under the control of the mission authorities. The soldiers were, of course, subject immediately to their own officers, who exercised civil, military, and judicial control, but were in turn subject to the direction of the visitador. The military was for the protection of the missions, which represented the important work in the province. The few settlers came under the same rule, and were subject to the

---

[1] Bancroft, XV, 430.

6

Jesuit administration.   The work of reducing California was carried on with great vigor, until missions covered its entire length.   In New Spain the fertile valleys were settled by Spaniards, who carried on agriculture or engaged in rearing stock.   The mining districts were more or less occupied by *gente de razon.*   In such districts pueblos or towns were frequently formed, and grants made to settlers of town lots and cultivable lands or stock farms.   In comparison with the inducements held out to settlers, the number of bona fide colonists was very small.   In most cases these settlements were entirely under the control of the civil system, although at first the establishments were frequently managed by a provisional or military government.   But as soon as convenient, the regular town officers took charge of the affairs of the pueblo, and reported to the provincial governor, who in turn was amenable to his superior, the Viceroy of Mexico.   The missions of Baja California continued to flourish for a time ; but under the management of inferior men they declined, and the expulsion of the Jesuits from New Spain in 1767 left them in a deplorable condition.   The change from one system to another was very detrimental ; and the Dominicans, being less aggressive than the Jesuits, had fewer means to work with.   But prior to the expulsion of the order, the padres had lost control of the natives, having no influence upon any except the children and women.   Affairs continued to decline, until by 1730 the neophyte population had been reduced to one-half of its former number.[1]   According to Humboldt, the population had continually diminished without being augmented in any way by an influx of strangers.   He held that the nature of the soil and the rule of the Fathers discouraged all immigration.   He says that most of the missions were in a wretched condition, and the Indians, poor and helpless slaves in body and mind, had no knowledge and no will but that of the friars.   Humboldt estimates that the village popula-

[1] Bancroft, VIII, 31.

tion was in 1811 not more than four or five thousand ; and that the villages were reduced to sixteen.[1]

But the decline in the peninsula of California was but a type of the condition of Spanish affairs at home and abroad, prior to the advent of Carlos III. From the time of the glory of Philip II., and his father Carlos V., Spanish affairs had been in a deplorable state. The inquisition, the power of the church, unequal taxation, and a lack of industrial prosperity, were marks of a system that must decline in the race of civilization. The great undertaking of Spain had consumed her strength without giving ample return for the investment. She had attempted to do too much in rapid exploration, in the attempt to gain and control the whole western world. The glory and strength of Spain in the days of her supremacy was in a measure due to fortuitous circumstances, although we do not detract from the tenacious energy and the fiery zeal of the Spaniards in seizing the opportunity of making the nation great. The sustaining power of the Spanish nation came from other sources than the wealth gained by substantial industry or natural growth. But there is also a deeper natural cause for the decline in the fact that, while other nations were developing constitutional and industrial liberty, while they were dealing with the new forces which the age of enlightenment had revealed to the world, Spain was still clinging to feudal ideas, and attempting to build an empire on fictitious and unenduring powers. The power of systematic labor and intellectual supremacy was lost. The natural life was grounded in principles that could but decline ; and with them declined Spain. An unwholesome spirit of absolutism, both in trade and in civil government, clung to the Spanish court. The dealing with colonists was over wise. Although the civil authorities of the home government seemed to be acquainted with the maladies that were consuming national life, they were unable to remove them.

---

[1] *Ensayo Politico, sobre Nueva España*, Lib. III, cap. VIII.

In the colonies, the missionary enterprise opened new lands, but was not favorable to the prosperity of the affairs of the state. The spiritual conquest, though joined with the temporal, was in most instances antagonistic to the healthy development of colonization. The best and strongest influences in the colonies were exerted to save another race to the exclusion of the Spaniards. But there has always been a lack of colonizing material of the right sort in Spain; there has been a lack of that sterling middle class, so useful in all lands, who represent the bone and sinew of all rational development. On the contrary, wild adventurers, gold-thirsty traders, stilted grandees, and poverty-stricken wretches, were the products of the Spanish system; and the colonies revealed these classes clearly to the world. It required more beneficent laws than the court of Spain could make, and more piety than the combined efforts of the priests could summon, to overcome such fatal conditions.

But under the rule of Carlos III, Spain awoke from her lethargy, and attempted a reform. With great efforts she sought to regain her pristine vigor, and to throw off her evil systems of government. Carlos began in the right way by first stifling the inquisition, repressing the power of the Church, equalizing government, and lowering taxation.[1] A general trade sprang up, industries were revived and expanded. The navy, once the pride of Spain, was restored; and commerce improved until the colonial trade was tripled in seven years, and the revenues of the Indies increased from 5,000,000 to 12,000,000 crowns.[2] The general prosperity was felt to the farthermost possessions of the Spanish provinces; and a general quickening of enterprises was the result. It was during this period that Upper or Alta California was settled, new laws promulgated, and a revival of the old theory of the extension of territorial power put forth.

---

[1] Coxe, *Memoirs of the Kings of Spain*, III, 517.

[2] Dunham, *History of Spain and Portugal*, V, 284.

But it was only a struggle as far as the American possessions were concerned; for Spain's opportunity had passed. The revival of power made it only more certain that the home government would be unable to cope with other powers in the maintenance of its vast possessions.

There was a growing fear on the part of the Spanish sovereigns during the eighteenth century that there was danger of the utilization of California by other nations, unless the government made haste to make permanent establishments in that territory. This fear had existed from the time of its first discovery; but was increasing every day, and Carlos ordered an immediate occupation of the country. As early as 1596, Philip II. sent an order to Count de Monterey, Viceroy of Mexico, instructing him to proceed immediately to make new settlements in the favorable parts of California. The voyage of Viscaino was the result of this order. Three years later, the order was renewed by Philip III., the successor of Philip II., and it was then distinctly stated that the western coast of the South Sea should be immediately explored, and that settlements should be made in California without delay. With the voyage of Viscaino the matter ended for the time. Again in 1665 Philip IV., just before his death, ordered that the reduction of California be completed. But, notwithstanding all these mandates, the authorities were slow in fulfilling the long felt desires of the monarchs of Spain; and besides, during this period, the treasury was usually empty.

But the reasons why California should be occupied, multiplied from year to year, and with them fear increased. It was the advantageous situation that made California so desirable.[1] Little as was known of the country, there was a growing disposition to consider it the key of the continents. Subsequent history has verified these half-formed early conclusions. There was an especial reason why Spain should hold ports along the Californian coast; for at this time the

---

[1] Venegas, IV, 4.

ships that plied their trade between the Philippines needed protection alike from free-booters and from storms. The commerce on the high seas needed protection, and there were no safe harbors along the coast for the refuge of ships in time of danger. It was therefore proposed to explore the country, and to build forts and establish colonies in favorable places. Beyond, there were threatenings of foreign invasion; and there were well grounded fears that other nations would settle the coast and occupy the harbors. At that time the Russians had explored the coast south to Lat. 55°, 36', and there was reason to believe that they would come farther. Later they became contestants for the prize. The aggressive colonial policy of England was well calculated to inspire fear in the heart of the Spaniard. "What would be the consequences if any European power should settle colonies and build forts on the coast of California?" is the significant question of Venegas; and the answer is that those who knew, felt that such establishments would prove of incalculable benefit to the nation that first made them.[1] Especially did the Spaniards recognize that the unguarded coast of Mexico would be in imminent danger should any other nation than Spain settle the northern coast.

In the first flush of victory, while the kingdom of Spain was powerful, the discoveries had been great, the explorations extended, and settlements comparatively few. Had the home country continued in power, perhaps this great extent of country might have been easily protected; but as the home government began to contract and grow weak, the colonial possessions were left in a direful condition. This constant shrinkage of power continued, notwithstanding the vigorous attempt of Carlos to prevent it, and to regain the lost prestige of Spain. But the glory of Spain continued to diminish in America, and the priest-historian does not fail to enumerate,

---

[1] Venegas, Part IV. Introduction to Appendices.

among other causes for the settlement of California, the repeated formula expressing the objects of colonization; namely,
"the growth of faith, and the extension of the king's dominion." [1] With all the reasons and all the causes for such
a settlement, it took a long time to accomplish the fact. But
it was finally brought about by the extraordinary zeal of
Galvaez, aided by the Franciscan fathers.

[1] Venegas, IV.   Introduction to Appendices.

CHAPTER VI.

THE FIRST SETTLEMENTS IN ALTA CALIFORNIA.

"Born in the purple; nestled in the past
  By a few faithful friars, grave and bold;
Under the altar-eaves thy die was cast.
  How little recked they in the days of old,
  Thy veins of silver and thy heart of gold—
When slowly plodding o'er the winding trail.
  Return, beloved band, and now behold
The harvest of thy planting! note the pale
Flush o' the almond i' the orange-scented gale!"[1]

For more than one hundred and sixty years after the expedition of Viscaino, not a European boat cut the surf of the northwest coast; not a foreigner trod the shore of Alta California. The white-winged galleon, plying its trade between Acapulco and the Phillipines, occasionally passed near enough so that those on board might catch glimpses of the dark timber line of the mountains of the coast, or of the curling smoke of the forest fires; but the land was unknown to them, and the natives pursued their wandering life unmolested, uncertain of food and shelter. It seems scarcely credible that no permanent settlement should have yet been made, after so much time and treasure had been wasted in the attempt to plant colonies in this land, concerning which so many wild stories had been circulated. The voyages of Cabrillo and Viscaino, and especially the map of the latter, had served to acquaint the inhabitants of Spain and Mexico with the nature

---

[1] Chas. Warren Stoddard.

of the country, and to excite a desire for conquest and settlement. But thirst for gold, the desire to extend the territory
of the king, and missionary zeal, all combined, were insufficient to overcome the serious obstacles to the accomplishment
of the long debated project. Although no new knowledge
of a specific character was obtained of Alta California during
the long period from 1604 to 1769, still the idea of conquest
continued to grow in the minds and the imaginations of the
people. Rumors of great stores of wealth, of populous cities
to be conquered, and of daring exploits to be performed,
served to excite further the cupidity of the Spanish mind, to
weave in it strange fancies about this mysterious country, and
to confuse real knowledge with tales of wild extravagance.

Accompanying the dreams of heaps of undiscovered gold,
was the desire to solve the great " Northern Mystery ; " the
location of the strait of Anian, which would lead the mariner
from the Atlantic to the South Sea, and by a short route
to India.[1] All explorers who desired to add glory to their
names, searched for the mysterious passage ; and many returning
adventurers on the high seas professed either to have seen the
strait, or else to have sailed through it. From the time of
Columbus the idea prevailed that there was a western passage
back to Europe by way of India. The familiar fact that
Columbus first supposed, on sighting land in the Bahamas,
that he had reached the outlying islands of Asia, caused a
search to the northward and the southward for a passage to
India. When it was ascertained that the land extended both
to the north and south in a main body, and that there was no
apparent strait, the conclusion was reached that a part of the
main land of India, or at least of Asia, was reached. Even
after the discovery of the Pacific or South Sea by Balboa,
the same opinion was entertained. It was finally believed
that the strait was not at the south but to the northward of
Mexico ; and the explorations of Cortés in the Pacific served

---

[1] Bancroft, XXVII, 5 ; Humboldt, *Nouvelle Espagne*, I, 330.

to remove the supposed location of the strait to the indefinite north.

Torquemada relates how Philip III., of Spain, found among other papers a narrative delivered by some foreigners to his father, giving an account of many remarkable particulars, which they saw in that country when driven thither by stress of weather from the coast of Newfoundland; adding that they passed from the North Sea to the South by the strait of Anian, which lies beyond Cape Mendocino; and that they had arrived at a populous and opulent city, walled and well fortified, the inhabitants living under a regular polity, and being a sensible and courteous people; with many other particulars well worth a further inquiry.[1] The Spaniards had a deeper motive than that of idle curiosity in their attempts to discover the strait; believing that the strait actually existed, they desired to discover it before other nations did, that they might control it and thus prevent foreign vessels from passing through and interfering with their possessions in the South Sea.[2] In spite of all of their efforts, the phantom channel continued to recede; while vague stories continued to direct the attention of the explorer to the northwest. It was not until the strait had receded to the Arctic zone that its existence was verified in 1728 by Behring, who sailed through from the Pacific, not into the Atlantic Ocean, but into the Polar Sea. This and subsequent voyages (1738, 1741) removed the last trace of a vague assumption that the Northwest coast belonged to Asia.[3]

Another desire worked upon the minds and the imaginations of the Spaniards, increasing their zeal for exploration, and directing their attention to the northwest; and that was the desire of gold. From the time that the supposed island of the Pacific was named California, there were floating rumors of vast fields of gold in this famous country. Even the name

---

[1] Venegas, II, Appendix, 2; Torquemada, Bk. V.
[2] Venegas, II, 230.   [3] Winsor, II, 468.

of California carries with it a vision of gold. After much conjecture concerning the origin of the name " California," it has been finally conceded by all scholars that the name was taken from a Spanish romance and applied by Cortés or his followers, or by later explorers, to the peninsula of California.[1] In the romance called *Las Sergas de Esplandian,* California is represented as an island rich in gold, diamonds, and pearls. Part of the extravagant picture is as follows : " Know that on the right hand of the Indies, there is an island called California, very close to the side of the Terrestrial Paradise ; and it was peopled by black women, without any man among them, for they lived in the fashion of Amazons. They were of strong and hardy bodies, of ardent courage and great force. Their island was the strongest in all the world, with its steep cliffs and rocky shores. Their arms were all of gold, and so was the harness of the wild beasts which they tamed to ride ; for in the whole island there was no metal but gold. They lived in caves wrought out of the rock with much labor. They had many ships with which they sailed out to other countries to obtain booty." [2] In the romance, the first edition of which was published in 1510, Esplandian, the Emperor of the Greeks, imaginary son of Amadis of Gaul, defends Constantinople against the infidels of the East. Califia, the queen of the Amazons, leads forth an army of Amazons from her dominion called " California," who fight in support of the infidels.

Mr. Edward Everett Hale holds that this name, as an omen of wealth, was applied to the newly discovered land of the northwest. He says that " as a western pioneer now gives the name of ' Eden ' to his new home, so Cortés called his new discovery, ' California.' " There can be no doubt that the name of California was derived from this romance ; but at what time, and by whom it was given, is not fully

[1] Winsor, II, 443 ; Bancroft, *Cal.,* I, 65.
[2] *Atlantic Monthly,* XIII, 263 ; Winsor, II, 443.

determined. It is supposed by some that Bernal Diaz del Castillo, an officer who served under Cortés, and who wrote, in 1539, an account of the expedition to California in 1535, applied the name to a bay on the coast of the supposed island. This is probably an error. Francisco de Ulloa, under the direction of Cortés, sailed up the gulf nearly to its head ; and not finding a channel through to the main ocean, considered that the supposed island was a peninsula.[1] Returning to the south of the gulf, he doubled the cape, and sailed north on the outside of the peninsula to the latitude of twenty-eight degrees, with the same results. The earliest use of the name known to us was in the narrative of Ulloa's voyage, written by Priciado. It was then applied to the bay or its vicinity formerly known as La Paz. Three years later, Ferrelo of Cabrillo's expedition reached the latitude of about forty-one degrees, without discovering any separation from the mainland except in the case of small islands. From this time on there was a confusion of beliefs relating to the geographical nature and extent of California ; some believing it to be an island and others considering it a peninsula. The maps of the time were as varied in their representation of the country as were the opinions of the people; and California was an island or a peninsula according to the fancy or the conception of the map-maker. Thus we find that Hennepin, in his map of 1683, made California a peninsula; but in the same plate issued in 1698, the map was so changed as to make it an island.[2] The voyage and map of Viscaino did not dispel the illusion that it was an island, so firmly was the idea fixed in the minds of the people. In fact, a lingering suspicion that the California Gulf had a northerly connection with the ocean was not entirely effaced as late as the year 1750. At that time Baja California, which had been discovered as an island by Cortés, then had existed so long as a peninsula, and again

---

[1] Bancroft, *Cal.*, I, 65.   [2] Winsor, II, 466.

San Diego Mission. Founded 1769.

was supposed for a hundred years or more to be an island, at last assumed upon the map its proper geographical form.[1]

Consequent upon the confusion of ideas relating to this half-discovered country was a great variety of names of the territory. Sir Francis Drake, landing at Point Reyes in 1577, took possession of the island in the name of the English sovereign, and called it New Albion; and with this name it again entered the realm of letters. Again, nearly one hundred years later, the whole territory was called *Las Islas Californias*, in honor of his majesty, Carlos II., king of Spain, on the occasion of his attempt to colonize the country. After the year of the settlement of California proper, in 1769, the northern country was known as the New Establishments, the Northern Missions, or *Los Establecimientos de San Diego y Monterey*. Soon, however, the upper country began to be known as California Septentrional, California del Norte, or California Superior.[2] But these inconstant names were finally replaced by the one in common usage, Alta California; although in 1804, Nueva California became the legal name and remained such until 1824, when it gave place to the other. In later times it was quite common to apply the term Las Californias to the two provinces, Alta and Baja California.

There were other considerations besides the solution of the Northern Mystery that induced the immediate conquest of California. The desire for personal glory and the cupidity for gold were uppermost in the minds of many Spanish explorers. Expeditions were fitted out either at public or private expense to search for the precious metals. These excursions led to the exploration and settlement of the country.

In another place is discussed the decline of Spain through the long period from Philip II. to Carlos III. It was not until the return of prosperity during the reign of the latter king that it was possible for the Spanish sovereign to push

---

[1] Winsor, II, 468.   [2] Bancroft, XVIII, 68.

the work of colonization with any degree of vigor. The fear
of the territory's being occupied by the Russians and other
foreigners caused Carlos, in 1767, to send orders to the
Viceroy of Mexico to proceed at once in forming settlements
at San Diego and Monterey.[1] At this time Marquis de Croix
was Viceroy of Mexico, and Jose Galvaez was Visitador-
General of New Spain. The latter arrived in Mexico in
1765, delegated with full power to investigate and reform all
parts of the government, especially the financial system. To
Galvaez the whole enterprise of the occupation of California
was intrusted; and it may be said that no better choice could
have been made for the director of an expedition of a similar
nature. Being a straight-forward business man, he avoided
the usual entanglements and delays, and prosecuted the work
according to the king's orders, with vigor. The object of the
expedition is set forth briefly and clearly in that part of the
proclamation of Galvaez which affirms that the aim is " To
establish the Catholic religion among numerous heathen people submerged in obscure darkness of paganism, to extend the
dominion of the King, our Lord, and to protect the peninsula
from the ambitious views of foreign nations."[2] In this he
but echoed the sentiments and designs of his majesty, the king.
Having made rapid preparations, Galvaez sailed from San Blas
in May, 1767; but did not reach Loreto on the peninsula
until the following July. Here he set forth his plan for the
expedition into the upper country. Viewed from the standpoint of the present, the plan seems simple in the extreme,
and the undertaking easy to accomplish. Yet there were
many obstacles to be overcome. The art of navigation was
not perfected then as now, and the vessels at the command
of Galvaez were at best clumsy affairs. The presidios were
guarded by small garrisons of poorly equipped soldiers, whose
chief duty was to draw their regular pay. The officers of the

---

[1] *Documentary History of Mexico*, II, 156.
[2] *Cf.* Bancroft, *California*, I, 120.

garrisons were appointed out of the great body of supernumeraries, and had become a helpless set and a needless expense to the government. Again, the old martial spirit of the Spaniards that characterized the days of Cortés, had departed ; and even the religious enthusiasm of the ecclesiastics had, in a measure, become subdued.

At this time the Jesuits, by far the most efficient religious order in colonization, were expelled from New Spain by the order of the king ; and the missions of Lower California were turned over to the Franciscans, of whom Junipero Serra was president. The change caused much confusion for the time being in the affairs of the peninsula ; although, the temporal affairs were administered by Captain Portolá, who exercised perfunctory jurisdiction as military and civil governor. Captain Rivera commanded the chief military force, consisting of about forty men stationed at Loreto.[1] These were the men who were to aid Galvaez in the new conquest ; for the plan involved spiritual as well as temporal aid, and the friars as well as the military had to be enlisted in the enterprise. The country was to be first conquered and then converted. Galvaez was a strong religious character and a zealous Christian, blessed with a large stock of common sense. He not only believed in the conversion of the natives, but he also believed that friars were made for use. It was not a difficult matter to find among the Franciscans, those who were ready to assist in the new enterprise. Indeed, the father president himself offered to go and command the spiritual conquest of the country.

Galvaez finally established his headquarters at Santa Ana, where he developed his plans for four expeditions to enter the territory ; two by sea and two by land. The former were to be conducted by Vicenta Vila and Juan Perez respectively, and the latter by Portolá and Rivera. Of the two sea expeditions, Juan Perez was to command the San Antonio, and Vicente Vila, the San Carlos. It was also planned that

---

[1] Bancroft, *California*, I, 115.

three priests should go by land and three by sea; Junipero Serra, the father president, accompanying one of the land expeditions. It was a theory of the Jesuits that all new missions should be furnished and equipped from the old and well established ones; and this plan was substantially adopted by the Franciscans in the preparations for the new establishments. The church furniture, ornaments, and vestments were taken from the churches already founded, and the needed supplies, such as grain, live stock, and implements, were borrowed from the missions of the south. It is not advisable to follow the details of the long preparations for the northern expedition, and the necessary delays always attendant upon such preparation, but to state that, in an incredibly short time for those days, the four expeditions set forth with orders to occupy and garrison Monterey and San Diego, and to establish missions at intermediate points. For the prompt execution of the king's orders Galvaez deserves more credit than any one else; while the final success of the expedition and the subsequent prosperity of the early missions are largely due to the courage and energy of Junipero Serra. Indeed, so closely is the life of the early missions connected with the life of this man, that even a short sketch of their history is incomplete without the careful mention of this wonderful individual.

The character of Serra has been somewhat overdrawn by his biographers and his fellow missionaries, who almost worshipped him; but in full consideration of all this, it must be said that he was the most considerable character of all of the pioneers of Alta California.[1] He was born of humble parentage in the island of Majorica, and while a child he sang in the Convent of San Bernardino. At the age of sixteen, he joined the order of monks founded by St. Francis of Assisi in 1208. Being of a religious nature, and having a strong missionary zeal, he must have found it a

---

[1] For life of Serra, see Palou, *Vida del Junipero Serra;* Adam, *Padre Junipero Serra;* Bancroft, *California,* I, 409 *et seq.*

pleasure to subscribe to the full requirements of self-renunci-
ation and devotion to the service of others, demanded by the
order of St. Francis. His subsequent life seems to indicate
that he fully realized the conception of the pious founder of
the order; and this may not be said of all of the members
of the order of St. Francis, although it may be assumed that
the Franciscan fathers have, as a rule, kept their good works
comparatively free from worldly ambition. After joining the
Order of Franciscans in 1730, Serra gave his attention to the
study of theology and philosophy; and received, on account of
his demonstrated ability as a scholar and preacher, the degree
of Doctor of Divinity. But this success was not satisfactory
to him; he had always a longing to preach to the Indians of
America. For fifteen years he worked zealously in Spain,
anxiously waiting for an opportunity to carry out his cherished plan. When the opportunity came to go to New Spain
and teach the natives, Serra was overjoyed at the prospect of
fulfilling a long cherished desire; hence he readily accepted
the offer, and he and his three companions, Palou, Crespi, and
Verger, set sail at Cadiz for Vera Cruz. After a long and
adventurous journey, they arrived at the end of their sea
voyage in October, 1749, and reached the city of Mexico, by
an overland march, in the following November. Serra went
out to his work as one who courts danger in the advancement
of a great cause; consequently the storms and hardships of
the journey were met by him with an eager courage; he
counted everything suffered and endured as so much done
in the service of his Divine Master.

At the time of his arrival, the Franciscan missions in New
Spain were under the control of the College of San Fernando,
which was, indeed, the mother of the missions of this order in
Mexico. For nineteen years after his arrival, Serra was at
service under the direction of the College, preaching the gospel
and founding missions. In the latter he was very zealous
and successful. With his enthusiasm for the spiritual welfare
of the natives, he never forgot their temporal improvement;

7

while he attempted to teach them the rites and ceremonies of
the church, and the principles and practices of faith, he also
taught them the elements of material civilization, without
which conversion is of little worth. He provided the Indians
with cattle and sheep to stock the land that they were permitted to call their own, and procured for them seed for sowing and implements with which to till the soil. All of the
alms received at masses, and all of his salary of three hundred
dollars, was spent in the purchase of seed, implements, and
supplies. As soon as the returns of the harvest were more
than sufficient to meet the needs of the Indians, the pious
monk taught them to sell the surplus and purchase for themselves with the proceeds blankets, clothes, animals, tools, and
household utensils. Even the women and children were
taught useful employments; as a rule they were more teach-
able than the men, and it was not infrequent to find these
latter classes outnumbering by far the men of the tribe who
were receiving instruction at the missions. After the natives
were thoroughly established in the way of industry, a piece of
ground was parcelled out to each, and with it were given a
yoke of oxen and a few farming utensils; the holder was
then permitted to become a separate owner and to till his
own soil, always, however, under the direction of the missionary or his agent. Thus provided for, under the fiction of
being a freeholder, the domesticated Indian began an independent life. This plan of dealing with the Indians by Serra
was substantially the method followed subsequently in Upper
California under the direction of the president of the missions;
and, in fact, it was the universal plan adopted by the Spanish
Government for the rapid civilization of the Indians. It was
intended to place them in separate ownership of the land as
soon as they were capable of management under the direction
of leaders.

With Serra's aid Galvaez was enabled to complete his
arrangements for the reduction of California. Sufficient
supplies had been collected, the necessary funds for the expe-

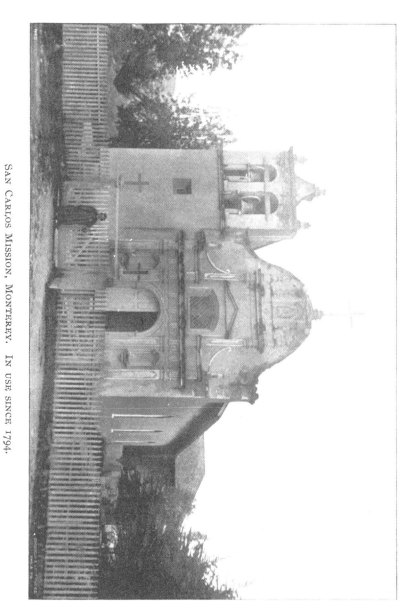

San Carlos Mission, Monterey. In use since 1794.

dition furnished, and all of the men chosen for the invasion. Everything being in readiness, Galvaez was enabled to dispatch the San Carlos, the first ship of the line, from La Paz on January 9, 1769. This vessel had arrived from San Blas in December, partly laden with stores; but being in a leaky condition, was laid up for repairs for some weeks. It is interesting to note the personnel of this small missionary group. First, there was the commander Vila, with his mate and a crew of twenty-three sailors and two boys. In addition to the sailors, the ship's company consisted of twenty-five Catalan volunteers under the command of Captain Fages: and there were also on board one Franciscan friar, Hernando Parron by name; Pedro Prat, the surgeon; four cooks; and two blacksmiths—sixty-two persons in all.[1] Before sailing, the whole band of pioneers confessed, heard mass, and partook of the communion; this was followed by a parting address by Galvaez, who set forth the object of the conquests and charged the colonists in the name of God, of the king, and the viceroy, to respect the priest and maintain peace among themselves. The second ship, commanded by Juan Perez, did not arrive at Cape San Lucas until January 25; and after being repaired, it departed for San Diego, February 15, 1769.

Meanwhile the preparations for the land expedition were rapidly forwarded in the north. The first one being in readiness, began its march under command of Captain Rivera, on the twenty-fourth day of March. The second land expedition, being delayed in its preparation, did not leave Santa Maria until May 11; and arriving at Velicata three days afterwards, paused there to found a mission,—the only one founded by the Franciscans in Lower California. From this new mission called San Fernando, the second land expedition, under the command of Captain Portolá, and accompanied by the father president, started on its journey northward on the fifteenth of May, 1769. In addition to those already mentioned, there

---

[1] Bancroft, XVIII, 128.

were in the second expedition Sergeant Ortega, ten soldiers, four muleteers, two servants, and forty-four domesticated natives of the peninsula. Having dispatched the four expeditions, Galvaez turned his attention to the affairs of Mexico, to accomplish the reforms much-needed there.

After the expulsion of the Jesuits from the province of New Spain, in 1767, the affairs of the missions of the peninsula were under the control of the Franciscans, of whom Junipero Serra was president. On his departure for the north he appointed Francisco Palou president of the missions of Lower California; although he still retained a general supervision of the work for some time after. Near together were the two friends, working in the same cause and for the same end. The famous life of Junipero Serra, written by Palou, is indicative not only of the harmony of the work, but especially of the faithful and untiring labors of the venerable Serra. It would seem, under casual observation, that when the four expeditions were finally started, with so much thoroughness and under such favorable auspices, we need have little apprehension of the result. Yet when we consider the discouragements attendant upon the establishment of a new settlement at that time, and the character of those who made up the rank and file of pioneers, it is scarcely to be wondered at that a settlement was made only by an accident, as the facts in the case go to prove. The San Antonio, commanded by Perez, containing the company which was the last to put to sea, was the first to arrive at San Diego, after a successful voyage of fifty-four days. The commander had gone too far north by nearly two degrees, and having sailed past the port which he desired to reach, he made a landing at Santa Cruz, one of the Santa Barbara islands. Perez was a skilful navigator, but was led into error by the report of Viscaino. At the islands they discovered natives who were friendly and were willing to exchange fish for beads and trinkets. When the commander ascertained that he was too far north, he took on board a fresh supply of water and sailed southward, dis-

SAN ANTONIO OF PADUA.

covering the bay of San Diego, which they entered without difficulty. Here he effected a second landing, and, as before, they were treated kindly by the Indians.

The San Carlos, which had sailed before the San Antonio, was nowhere in sight. But Perez had orders to remain for twenty days at San Diego, and then proceed to Monterey. Eighteen days of weary watching and waiting for the appearance of the flag-ship, had passed; and the commander of the San Antonio had determined to obey his orders, believing that the other ship was lost or had returned. But when he was preparing to depart, the long looked for sail made its appearance in the bay. The San Carlos moved slowly up and dropped anchor, but not a boat was lowered nor a signal given from the ship; all were sick on board; the voyage had been unpropitious; the water casks were leaky, and the crew had suffered much from want of water and from that dread disease, the scurvy. The commander, like Perez, sailing by the Viscaino chart, had gone too far to the north. After reaching the latitude of thirty-four degrees, suffering with cold and sickness, having scarcely a sufficient number of able-bodied men ·on board to man the ship, he turned southward, and as if by miracle, entered San Diego bay where he found rest and care for the sick, after one hundred and ten days of trials by sea. For two weeks the well were busy caring for the sick and burying the dead. On the fourteenth of May, the first division of the land expeditions arrived, under the command of Rivera. The men had been fifty-one days on the march from Velicata, having followed the barren and unattractive coast for a distance of one hundred and twenty-one leagues. Although the march was toilsome, no serious difficulty attended it, excepting the sickness, death, or desertion of some of the natives. At times the party were much inconvenienced by being forced to carry water for a great distance, and were hindered in their progress by heavy rains. Sometimes, also, members of the expedition, being sick, were carried many days on litters.

There was great rejoicing at the port on the arrival of the land party, and the Spaniards began preparations for permanent settlements. Under the direction of Fages, a town-site was selected to the north of their present camp, at what is now known as North or Old San Diego, and where the remains of the old presidio are still to be seen.[1] A new camp was formed, a few huts erected, and a corral for the stock; but nothing was done toward permanent foundation until the arrival of the second land expedition. To the new camp the sick were removed; and for over six weeks but little was accomplished besides caring for them. Toward the close of June, the last party with Governor Portolá and Father Serra arrived in camp. The four divisions of the invading pioneers were now united at the common port; but there were ninety-three missing from the two hundred and nineteen souls that had started on the journey. The next day was the Sabbath; and the remaining one hundred and twenty-six, the pioneers of California, celebrated the occasion with a solemn mass and the roar of guns.[2]

But this was but a temporary pause, and the journey to Monterey must soon be taken. After a conference, Rivera and Portolá decided that it would be best to send the San Carlos back to San Blas for supplies and a crew sufficient to man both vessels. Meanwhile the San Antonio should remain at San Diego, and a land expedition be sent to Monterey, the latter to be aided by the San José when it arrived with supplies. These plans were acted upon, nothing failing except the San José, which was lost at sea.

Until the arrival of Father Serra, no attempt had been made to convert the natives, who came to the camp in considerable numbers. And, indeed, it was not until Sunday, July sixteenth, that Serra raised and blessed the cross, preached the first sermon to the natives, and then dedicated the newly-founded mission to San Diego de Acalá. One of

---

[1] Bancroft, *Cal.*, I, 134.   [2] Bancroft, *California*, I, 136.

the new huts was dedicated as the church. The Indians, on the first arrival of the strangers and for a long time afterwards, were very friendly. They came around the camp more to receive the voluntary gifts bestowed upon them by the missionaries than for any other purpose. Finally, as the gifts failed to satisfy their cupidity, they resorted to begging and at last to stealing. They came in such large numbers as to give great annoyance to the missionaries, as they were not yet sufficiently well established to care for so many. And after the departure of the expedition to Monterey, the Indians, who had not yet put themselves under the tutelage of the padres, became a great nuisance and threatened the camp. At first they were entreated to keep away from the camp, then threatened, and finally as a last resort, frightened by the noise of gunpowder; but all of this was to no purpose. As a result of the attempt of the guard to repel the savages, a raid was made upon the camp. One day after Parron had gone to the ship to say mass under the guard of two soldiers, the natives made a sudden raid upon the camp and began to strip the clothing from the sick. The attempt of the guard to drive them away, was answered by a volley of arrows from the invaders, which wounded three and killed one of the Europeans. But a return fire of the guard killed three of the Indians and wounded several others, and frightened the remainder so that they beat a hasty retreat. With signs of peace, they soon returned for medical aid, and showed more respect for the strangers thereafter, although the prospects for conversions were indeed meager. There is no record of a single conversion at San Diego for over a year after the first arrival of the Spaniards.

But a settlement, apparently permanent, had been formed; and the expedition under Portolá was on its way to found a new mission at Monterey. The expedition had departed from San Diego on the fourteenth of July, with the purpose of traversing the coast line northwards until Monterey was reached; and by the aid of the San José, which was to follow them with supplies, to found a mission and build a presidio at that port. But as before stated the San José was lost at sea, and never heard of after leaving San Blas. Its loss seriously interfered with the proposed settlements. The journey up the coast was not devoid of interest, but upon the whole, very laborious. The record of the exploration, kept daily by Father Crespi, is important as being the description of the first land exploration in Alta California. The party passed through the fertile region of the San Bernardino mission, they encountered earthquake shocks in the Los Angeles country, they passed through the populous towns of the Santa Barbara Indians, and thence advanced to San Louis Obispo. Leaving these fertile and beautiful coast valleys, they tried to proceed northward by following the coast line; but found it necessary to return and pass over the mountains to the headwaters of the Salinas river and follow it to its outlet. They had passed through the richest and most desirable part of the country; and the information thus obtained was afterwards of great assistance to Serra in locating the other establishments. Upon this line of march were built a line of missions, and later there was developed a great civilization. As they approached the mouth of the Salinas, they beheld at a distance Point Pinos, one of the landmarks of the port of Monterey; but they did not recognize it as such. The extravagant description of this port given by Viscaino, whose chart they were following, and the fact that Viscaino entered it from the water highway and, consequently, that his descriptions were given from that point of view, led them into error. The present party were viewing the bay from the interior and from the northeast, instead of from the ocean and the southwest, as the other explorers had done. But even this difference could scarcely account for their apparent stupidity in the search for the location of the port of Monterey. Thus they turned from looking over the bay and continued northward, wondering where Monterey was. They had not yet reached the latitude given by Viscaino, which is known to have been incorrect by nearly two degrees. Another thing which led to their confusion was the supposition that the river Salinas was the river Carmelo; the latter having been described by the chronicler of Viscaino as a large river at full bank, while at the time of the latter expedition it was almost dry, being viewed at a different time of the year. That is, they discovered Point Pinos, Carmelo River with the adjoining ensenada, and Monterey Bay; but could not reconcile the facts with previous descriptions, and consequently they passed on, renewing their search for Monterey.[1]

After holding a conference, they decided to continue the search northward, although many of the party were sick and provisions were low.[2] They passed through the Pajaro Valley and crossed near what is now the city of Watsonville, to Soquel, the present fashionable summer resort, and thence to the San Lorenzo river at the present site of Santa Cruz. They found the mountains well wooded with the common redwood, which they called *palo colorado* (Sequoia sempervirens); this being the first mention of this famous tree in the history of discovery. Passing up the coast they came to Point Pedro, where, ascending the adjacent mountain, they obtained a view of the Farallones, Point Reyes, and the old San Francisco Bay, which they at once recognized from previous description. The Spaniards had visited this bay twice, and Sir Francis Drake had anchored in its waters. It was as well known as any point on the coast, previous to the explorations of the present party. But the great San Francisco Bay of modern fame was yet unknown to the world; it remained, however, for a few hunters of this same party, who had climbed the hills northeast of the camp, first to view the broad expanse of this great inland sea. Before this greatest discovery of the expedition was made, Captain Ortega, with a small party, had set out for Point Reyes; he reached the Golden Gate, but

---

[1] Palou, *Noticias,* I, 399.

[2] Bancroft, XVIII, 140 *et seq.;* Palou, *Noticias,* 285 *et seq.* (Crespi's diary); Palou, *Vida,* 80, 88.

having no boats with which to cross the bay, he returned to camp. On the fourth of November, they broke camp and passed over the San Bruno mountains and entered the bay region, camping on San Mateo Creek. While on the bay of San Francisco, Otego was informed by the Indians that there was a vessel anchored in the bay ; and the chief reason for the change of base was to ascertain if the lost San José was really there. After a fruitless search for the boat, the party returned to the vicinity of Point Pinos and renewed their exploration for Monterey. Not finding the object of their search, it was finally decided to wait and watch for the coming of the San José.[1] After the lapse of twelve days, they again broke camp and returned by an uneventful journey to San Diego, where they were welcomed by their friends. Before leaving the camp at Monterey, the Spaniards set up two crosses ; one on the Rio Carmelo, and one on the shore of Monterey Bay. As far as the founding of the Monterey Mission and Presidio was concerned, the expedition was a decided failure ; but the discovery of the Golden Gate and of San Francisco Bay may be recorded as one of the greatest events connected with the early history of California.

After the return from the Monterey expedition, Governor Portolá was much discouraged with the results of the trip, and resolved to abandon the whole enterprise and return to Mexico. Consequently he saved provisions sufficient for the return trip, and resolved to march as soon as the remainder was consumed, which he calculated would be about March twentieth. To this plan the zealous friars, Crespi and Serra, were bitterly opposed ; and were supported in their position by the remainder of the friars. Serra, who had accompanied the Monterey expedition, was convinced that the place where the cross was located was the Monterey which they had so diligently sought ; and consequently was unwilling to return to Mexico without attempting to make a settlement there.

---

[1] The explorers passed along the harbor of Monterey without recognizing it.

The friars found an ally in Vila, the commander of the San Carlos, who, it seems, had promised to take the friars on board his ship, and as soon as supplies should come, to take them to Monterey, and thus allow them to carry out their plans of founding a mission at that place.[1] On the eleventh of February, Rivera with nineteen men was sent to Velicata, for the purpose of obtaining supplies; but, before their return, affairs at San Diego had reached a precarious condition; the provisions were nearly exhausted; the commander of the company was disheartened, and was making daily preparations to return to Mexico on the twentieth of March. On the other hand, friars and priests were praying and fasting, and entreating the Spaniards to remain. A nine days public prayer and fasting closed on the nineteenth of March; on the morrow camp was to be broken, and the march homeward was to be begun. All day long the friars, praying, longing, and fasting, watched the horizon of the sea, as a last resort hoping that a ship might appear and bring relief. But the sun went down, and with it set the hopes of the zealous priests. But surprising as it may seem, in the clear twilight a sail appeared on the distant horizon. It bore straight for the camp and was soon anchored in the harbor. It was the San Antonio returned with abundant supplies, and the cause of settlement was safe again. The San Antonio, commanded by Juan Perez, was sailing under orders direct for Monterey. Entering the Santa Barbara channel for a supply of water, Perez was told by the natives that the Monterey expedition had returned toward San Diego; but this information was not considered sufficiently reliable to cause him to disobey orders; and had it not been for the accidental loss of an anchor, he would have continued his journey. As it was, he put in to the harbor of San Diego; and to this accident is due the success of the first colonial expedition to Alta California.

---

[1] Bancroft, *California*, I, 165.

After the return of the San Antonio with abundant supplies and with orders for Governor Portolá, nothing more was said about abandoning the new establishments and returning to Mexico. On the contrary there was immediate preparation for a return to Monterey, for the purpose of founding at that place, the required mission and presidio. The San Antonio was made ready at once, and sailed from San Diego on the sixteenth of April, having on board the commander Perez and his crew, Pedro Prat, Junipero Serra, and Miguel Costanso. There was also on board an abundance of supplies for the founding of a new establishment. On the following day a land expedition, commanded by Portolá, set out for Monterey; in this company were Captain Fages, soon to be military governor of California, and the indomitable Father Crespi, whose well kept diary has made its author famous in history. The land expedition arrived at its destination on the twenty-fourth of May, and found no difficulty in locating the Bay of Monterey. The cross set up the winter before was found adorned with sticks, arrows, feathers, meat, fish, and clams; doubtless these offerings were to the unknown god of the Europeans, and prompted by the superstition of the natives.

A week later the San Antonio arrived; fires were lighted on the rocks at different points along the coast to make safe the entrance to the harbor. The entrance was easily made, and the ship was soon riding at anchor in the bay. Before the arrival of the San Antonio, the camp, which was at first located at Monterey, had been moved to Carmelo in order to be near good water; but on the arrival of the second party, it was ordered back to Monterey, and preparation began for the planting of the new mission. In the little ravine, now crossed by the lighthouse road, under the branches of a noble oak— both made famous by the visitation of Viscaino—the company of pioneers pitched their tents.[1] After due preparation had

---

[1] In commemoration of the landing of Junipero Serra and his companions, Mrs. Leland Stanford has erected a beautiful monument at this place.

been made, the whole company assembled on the beach under an arbor to dedicate the new establishment and to consecrate their work. Bells were hung, and their long and loud peals introduced the solemn festival. On bended knees, sailors, soldiers, and priests chanted the *venite creator spiritus ;* the friar blessed the water and sprinkled the place, and then planted the cross and blessed it.[1] After the image of the holy virgin was placed on the altar, Father Serra said mass, " amidst the thunder of cannon and the crack of musketry, followed by a *salve* to the image and a *te deum laudamus.*"

It is worthy of notice that at the close of the religious services, Governor Portolá took formal possession of the land in the name of the Spanish king, Carlos III ; unfurling and planting the Spanish flag with proper ceremonies. Thus were founded presidio and mission ; and the cross of Christ and royal flag of Spain were planted side by side. The spot chosen for the site of the mission and the presidio was back from the beach near the place where now stands the San Carlos church. A few huts were built, and one of them dedicated as a church. Here as elsewhere in California, the beginnings of these new establishments were rude indeed. As at San Diego, the buildings were enclosed by a palisade, and everything was at first in common between priest and soldier.

The great importance of this permanent occupation of California was recognized in Mexico, and later realized in Spain. All those who were interested in the spiritual welfare of the natives rejoiced in the prospect of the immediate civilization of the children of the forest ; while those interested in the political welfare of their country received the news with bursts of enthusiasm. At last, after two hundred years of combined waiting and fruitless attempts, the king's dominion was extended to the northwest. In Mexico, says Bancroft, " The news was received with great manifestations of joy ; the cathedral bells rang out their glad peals, those of the

---

[1] Bancroft, XVIII, 170.

churches responding. A solemn thanksgiving mass was said, at which all government dignitaries were present; and there followed a grand reception, at which Galvaez and Croix received congratulations in the royal name for this last extension of the Spanish domain." [1] Under this favorable state of affairs it was ordered to found five new missions, and the needed funds for their expenses were promised. The names of these missions as ordered were, San Gabriel, San Louis Obispo, San Antonio, Santa Clara, and San Francisco. In addition to these, San Buenaventura was ordered to be established in connection with the mission of San Diego.

The important points of Monterey and San Diego once secured with permanent settlements, the extension of colonization was insured.

From this time on, the progress of settlement, though slow, was constant; and soon the entire coast from San Diego to San Francisco was lined with missions and colonies. For many years the founding of missions was the chief occupation of the early colonists. Under the direction of the father President, Junipero Serra, the establishment of missions was pushed zealously forward. Zealous in plans, incessant in toil, and devout in life, Junipero Serra founded and superintended eleven missions, prior to his death in 1784. [2] Afterwards, ten missions were added, making the total number twenty-one. The most important of the missions were founded in the eighteenth century, and their greatest prosperity occurred in the first quarter of the present century. [3] While their specific

---

[1] Bancroft, XVIII, 173.

[2] These eleven are, San Diego, 1769; San Carlos, 1770; San Gabriel, 1771; San Fernando, 1771; San Antonio, 1771; San Louis Obispo, 1772; San Juan Capistrano, 1776; San Francisco de Assisi, 1776; Santa Clara, 1777; San Buenaventura, 1782; Santa Barbara, 1786.

[3] The remaining missions, with the order of their founding, are as follows: La Purissima, 1787; Santa Cruz and Solidad, 1791; San Juan Bautista, San José, San Miguel, 1797; San Louis Rey, 1798; Santa Ynez, 1802; San Rafael, 1817; San Francisco Solano, 1823.

SAN BUENAVENTURA.

purpose was the education of the Indians, and the teaching to them of civilization, the missions performed a great service to the nation in occupying and holding the territory against foreign invasion. Occupying, as they did, the entire coast line, situated within easy reach of one another, and furnishing supplies to the government from the products of the soil and of the herds of cattle, horses, and sheep, their importance, aside from the immediate work of civilizing the Indians, cannot be over-estimated.

CHAPTER VII.

THE MISSION SYSTEM.

The occupation and settlement of Alta California was accomplished by a three-fold plan, involving the civil, religious, and military forces of the government. First, to guard the "mark," there were established the presidios, or frontier fortresses, which finally combined the civil with the military function, and developed into military towns; second, the purely civic community, or pueblo, composed of colonists settled on the land; and finally the mission, which was ecclesiastical in its nature, but to be eventually resolved into a civil pueblo. In the colonization of California, the mission must ever hold the front rank, more on account of the zeal and enterprise of those connected with its management, and on account of the amount of the work accomplished, than because of the nature of the settlement. Whereas the State regarded the missions as temporary institutions, the priests, to whom their welfare was entrusted, regarded them as the most important of all the institutions encouraged by the government; and consequently they threw their whole life into the work of civilizing the natives.[1] Whatever the intentions of the government might have been on the subject, it was firmly held by the padres that their work was to be permanent. As has been stated, the military and the religious forces were used by the State in the consummation of its plans. Although it was often affirmed that the object of

---

[1] Venegas, *History of California*, Part III, Section 1.

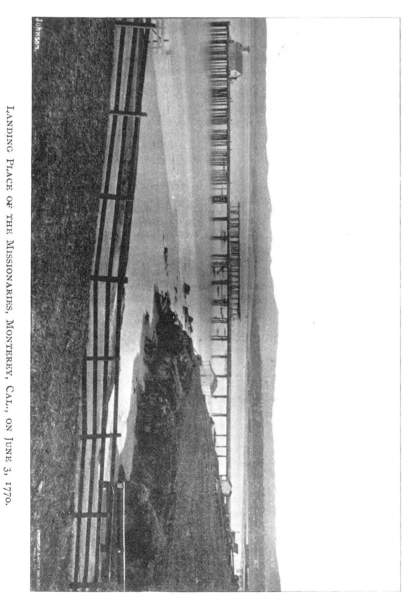

LANDING PLACE OF THE MISSIONARIES, MONTEREY, CAL., ON JUNE 3, 1770.

Spanish expeditions was to convert the natives, and doubtless it was so intended by at least some of the sovereigns of Spain, yet it was never the prime object of the State.[1] Galvaez was a zealous Christian, and believed heartily in the conversion and civilization of the Indians; but he was also in the service of the king of Spain, and believed that friars were to be made politically useful; and consequently he hastened to secure their services in the conquest of California. On the other hand, the relation of the military to the mission was that of protection against hostile invasion. Viewed from the standpoint of the ecclesiastic, the soldiers were sent to guard the missionaries and to build forts to protect them against sudden attack; and soldiers were therefore subordinate to the priests in the process of settlement.[2] This was in part true; for wherever missionaries went a guard was sent to protect them; but this guard was sent by the king or his representative, and consequently was not subordinate to the priests except by special provision. Beyond the design of protection to the missions there was the greater object of guarding the frontier against foreign invasion. The friars, like the soldiers, were to be dismissed from the service of the State when their assistance was no longer needed; and the results of their efforts in the cause of civilization were to be turned over to the civil authorities.

Prior to the conquest of California, the civil power had relied very largely upon the ecclesiastical in the management of the Indians; although the ecclesiastic was always under the direction of the civil law.[3] In the conquest and settlement of Mexico and South America, the religious orders were found very useful in domesticating the natives, and in controlling the Spanish colonists and soldiery. For this, as well as for other reasons, the extension of the faith was always encouraged by the crown of Spain. The pious sovereigns no doubt de-

---

[1] Bancroft, *Mexico*, III, 401.   [2] Venegas, Part III, Section 21.

[3] *Proclamation of Ferdinand VI.*, Venegas, III, 21.

sired to improve the condition of the natives and to save their souls; but there was involved in the process an ever-present idea of advantage to the State. During the early explorations in the New World, the natives received very little consideration, although friars accompanied each expedition to administer to the spiritual needs of the Spaniards, and to preach to the natives when opportunity offered. We referred to the fact that, in the year 1522, Friar Melgarejo came from Spain to grant indulgences to Spaniards, on account of their outrageous conduct toward the natives; and on his return he carried a large sum of gold which was lost in the sea.[1] It was not long after this that Father Otando and other friars began in real earnest the work of domesticating and baptizing the Indians; but it was many years before the work was well systematized.

In the early history of the conquest, the Indians were made slaves and disposed of at the will of the conqueror; subsequently a general law of the Indies laid a capitation tax on all of the natives, which could be paid by their working eighteen months in the mines or on a rancho.[2] In the oldest grants made to proprietors in Hispaniola, the Indians were treated as stock on the farm; and the deed of transfer of property declared the number which the proprietor was entitled to treat in this way.[3] After this, the natives were treated by what is known as the *repartimiento* system, under which they lived in villages, but were compelled to labor in places assigned them for a given period. The proprietor had a right to their labor, but could claim no ownership of their persons.[4] The next legislation in regard to the disposal of the Indians engrafted upon the *repartimiento* the *encomiendas* system.[5]

---

[1] Bancroft, *Mexico*, II, 159.

[2] *Recopilacion de leyes de los Reynos de las Indias*, libro VI, titulo 3.

[3] Merivale, *Colonies and Colonization*, 279.

[4] Arthur Helps, *Spanish Conquest of America*, Book XIV, Ch. I and II.

[5] See Chapter IV.

This required that within certain districts the Indians should pay a tribute to the proprietors of that district, which of necessity must be paid in labor ; and the lords of the soil were required to give the natives protection. It was a revival of the feudal theory in part; but the relative positions of the contracting parties rendered the tribute sure and the protection doubtful. But with all this apparently wise legislation, the condition of the Indian grew worse ; he was still at the mercy of the conqueror.

To improve the condition of the Indians the decrees of the king of Spain instructed the priests to gather the natives into villages and compel them to live in communities.[1] For lands occupied, they paid a rent to the proprietor, and a personal tax or tribute to the crown. Here they were under the immediate control of the ecclesiastics, but were granted the privilege of electing alcaldes (judges) and regidores (councilmen) of their own race for the control of municipal affairs.[2] But this was a mere show of freedom ; for the priests in charge had the power to control this election by-play as they chose.[3] Under this system, and forever afterwards, the natives were treated as legal minors under a trusteeship. The royal decrees so recognized them ; and the missionaries, in all their dealings, treated them accordingly. It was a common thing for the padres to call the neophytes their children. This was the outcome of the legal fiction held by the king that the natives had the primary right to the soil ; the Indian race was to be retained and to share the soil with the Spanish people, but to be in every way subordinate to them. However well recognized this policy might have been, the children of the conquered land usually submitted to the convenience of the conquerors. The race problem of placing a superior and an inferior race upon the same soil and attempting to give them equal rights was then, as now, difficult to solve.

---

[1] *Recopilacion*, VI, 3, 1–29. [2] *Ibid.*
[3] Humboldt, *Essay on New Spain*, I, 421.

On the other hand, the priests and the secular clergy were diligent in the salvation of souls. Thousands were baptized by the friars and taught the rites of the new religion. It is said that in a single year (1537) above 500,000 were baptized,[1] and that the Franciscans baptized, during the first eight years of their active work, not less than 1,000,000.[2] But the process of the civilization was too severe, and the treatment received at the hands of the dominant race too oppressive, to make rapid progress in the arts of civilized life possible; and the number of the natives decreased rapidly under the treatment of the conquerors.

The most perfect example of this method of civilizing the natives is that furnished by the Jesuits in Paraguay, where, in the latter half of the sixteenth century, they held absolute sway over a large part of the territory.[3] In this tract of land, granted them by the king, untrammeled by government, custom, law, and the common nuisance of settlers and adventurers, the Jesuits began their state. The Indians were gathered into towns or communal villages called "bourgaden," or reductions, where they were taught the common arts, agriculture, and the practice of rearing cattle.[4] In each town were appointed two spiritual guides, who baptized the natives, taught them the rites of the Christian faith, and taught them of religious and moral life in general.

At first all property was held in common, the labor of each person being allotted according to his strength and skill. While the villagers gave over to the community the products of their toil, they were in turn fed, clothed, and instructed. The chief occupations of the natives were agriculture and the raising of cattle; but they soon had a sufficient number of skilled artisans to manufacture all of the necessary commodities for the use of the young state, and were consequently

---

[1] Bancroft, *Mex.*, II, 408.   [2] Torquemada, *Monarchia Indiana*, III, 156.

[3] *Documentos para la historia de Mexico*, II, 204.

[4] Arthur Helps, *Spanish Conquest*, IV, 377 *et seq.*

economically and commercially independent. For many years these colonies flourished ; and there were large stores of surplus grain in the villages, while the plains were covered with herds of cattle.

At the time the territory was ceded to Portugal, there were 300,000 families gathered into forty-seven villages or districts.[1] As soon as the families had adopted the elements of modern civilization, and had shown a capability of independent life, they were permitted to hold land in severalty, to call it their own, and to have the right to the product of their own labor. There was an attempt to teach them the elements of self-government by allowing the natives to elect from their number, by ballot, magistrates to represent each district ; these, when chosen, were to be subject to the approval of the Jesuits in charge. In the formation of towns, great care was taken to locate them in fertile valleys and to lay out the town properly, allowing each Indian a house-lot with a garden attached.[2] A church was built in the centre of the town, and a convent and the caciques' houses were located near it. To those Indians who were capable of self-control, lands besides the house-lots were granted for cultivation. In all villages, whether strictly communal or partially so, public lands were reserved principally for religious purposes. These lands were worked by the Indian youth ; the products of the soil being gathered into granaries for the purpose of supplying the sick and the needy, or of providing against want. Much attention was given to the education of the children, which was considered a public affair, and the children were looked upon as belonging to the state. The Jesuits' discipline, beginning with birth and ending with death, demanded implicit obedience. But the Indians were free from care, had no taxes to pay, and received property in proportion to capability and needs. And it may be said that there was no ambition and no desire for money.

---

[1] Burke, *European Settlements in America*, I, 328 *et seq.*
[2] Helps, *Spanish Conquest*, IV, 378.

Here, away from the contaminating influences of modern civilization, was an ideal state, equal to any dreamed of by St. Simon, Fourier, or Bellamy. It was successful enough; and the natives were very happy until they came in contact with the natural selfishness and avarice of the European; for it must be understood that, while under Spanish authority, no stranger was allowed to enter this land unattended by an official of the Jesuits. But here, as elsewhere, the direct contact of the sturdy Europeans with the natives has been productive of disaster to the weaker race, and no legislation has been able to protect it. It is worthy of attention that in this, as in all other successful communistic societies, the great mass of the people must be as children before the central authority, and must subscribe to a law of absolute obedience to this central power. This same method was adopted in Mexico; but an attempt to gather the natives into villages failed, and the severe treatment that they received at the hands of the conquerors wasted them away; while the constant contact with the Spaniards prevented the adoption of systematic methods of civilization. Yet we find that certain individuals pursued the same plan elsewhere. Salvatierra carried out the same methods in Lower California;[1] and Serra, the Franciscan, adopted this plan in Mexico prior to his entrance into Upper California, where he continued to follow the same system with some modifications. It cannot be said that it was the system of the Jesuits, but rather the system founded by the laws of the Indies, and first successfully applied by the Jesuits.

As has been stated, the first colony in Alta California was planted at San Diego, in 1769, as a result of the four expeditions dispatched from Mexico by Visitador Galvaez. The first public exercises after the arrival of the colonists were to say mass and erect a cross, and this was done with the usual ceremonies. At Monterey we find the same order of exercises. Mass was accompanied with the roar of cannon and the rattle

---

[1] Venegas, Part III, Sec. 11.

of musketry, and after the ceremony Captain Portolá unfurled
the Spanish flag and took formal possession of the land in the
name of the king.[1]   At San Diego and at Monterey, a few rude
huts were thrown up at first, one of which was used as a church;
and the more permanent buildings of the presidios were erected
afterwards. As soon as practicable the friars began their missionary labor; and from that time on it was the most important
work accomplished in the occupation and settlement of California under Spanish rule. After the occupation of Monterey,
news was dispatched to Mexico informing the authorities there
of the progress of the expeditions.   The accomplishment of a
plan that had been in the minds of kings and rulers for over
two centuries caused great rejoicing in the capital city.   The
unity of the civil and religious powers in the temporal and
spiritual conquest of California is shown in the nature of the
celebration that took place in Mexico on the arrival of the
news of the grand achievement.   The cathedral and church
bells rang; a solemn thanksgiving was held in which all of
the government dignitaries participated; and a grand reception was given, at which Minister Galvaez and Viceroy Croix
received, in the name of the king, the congratulations of the
people on account of the conquest.   In the midst of this
enthusiasm, an order was issued for the completion of the plan
of conquest, and for the founding of five new missions.[2]

The usual method of founding a mission in a territory was
as follows.   After the construction of a few rude huts, the
missionaries, by a display of banners and pictures, attracted
the attention of the natives, and further gained their confidence
by gifts of food, trinkets, and bits of cloth.   A banner with
a picture of the Virgin was among the most powerful attrac-
tions held out to the natives; it appealed to their superstitious
nature, and when explained to them had a wonderful influence
in their control.   Little by little the friars induced familiarity
and confidence in the natives, who returned each day, bringing

---

[1] Bancroft, *California*, I, 170.   [2] Bancroft, XVIII, 173.

companions with them. Finally they were led to listen to the teachings of religion, and consented to engage in work about the mission buildings, as long as they were remunerated as above stated. As soon as possible, they were induced to live in huts in or near the mission, and to take up the forms of religion and civilization. The rude mission buildings soon gave place to more habitable structures, and the products of arts and industries began to accumulate.[1] Prior to the occupation of California by the Europeans, the Indians dwelt, more or less in temporary villages, later called " rancherias," where they had an imperfect government, controlled by chiefs, councils, and priests.[2]

It was the custom of the friars to go out frequently from the established mission to these adjacent villages and instruct the Indians; and this resulted in making the surrounding rancherias dependent upon the central mission. From these villages the neophytes of the mission were re-enforced. In later times, after the wild Indians became scarce, predatory excursions were made, and the natives were secured by force and brought to the mission for civilization.

It was the policy of Charles V. that the Indians should be " induced and compelled " to live in villages ; this being considered the only way to civilize them. Minute instructions were also given by this monarch for their government in the village.[3] They were to have a priest to administer religious affairs, and native alcaldes and regidores for the management of municipal affairs. It was further provided that no Indian should change his residence from one village to another, and that no Spaniard, negro, mestizo, or mulatto should live in an Indian village over one day after his arrival, and that no person should compel an Indian to serve against his will in the

---

[1] Forbes, *History of California*, 43, 56, 199 *et seq.*

[2] Powers, Stephen J., *Aborigines of California; U. S. Geological Survey*, J. W. Powell, 1888.   Dwinelle, *History of San Francisco*, 13.

[3] *Recopilacion*, Libro VI, for laws governing *los Indios*.

mines or elsewhere.[1] In all of these and similar provisions, the laws of Spain for the treatment of the natives were, upon the whole, wise and humane. Carlos III. granted special privileges to the natives, and annulled the laws providing for the repartimiento and the encomienda systems, although it was still the policy of the government to keep them in a condition of perpetual minority. It was upon these and similar laws of the Indies that the practice of treating the natives of California was based, although the method varied in its details.

As soon as a new convert was baptized, he was made to feel that he had taken personal vows of service to God, whom the priest represented, and to think that the priest had immediate connection with God. From this time on he was a neophyte, and belonged to the mission as a part of its property. As the padre in charge had full control of all of the affairs as well as the property of the mission, the relation of the missionary to the neophyte was *in loco parentis.* As far as the individual workings of the missions were concerned, there was established a complete form of patriarchal government. If a neophyte escaped from the mission, he was summoned back ; and if he took no heed of the summons, the missionary appealed to the governor, who dispatched soldiers to capture him from his tribe and return him to the mission. After his return, he was severely flogged. For small offences the neophytes were usually whipped, put in prison or the stocks, or else loaded with chains ; for capital crimes they were turned over to the soldiery, acting under the command of the governor, to undergo more severe punishment.

In the general government of the missions, the Viceroy of Mexico was the final arbiter of all disputed points ; but the immediate authority and supervision was given to a padre president, who had advisory control of all the missions. As

---

[1] " *Ninguna persona se pueda servir de los indios por via de naboria, ne tapia ni otro modo aluguno, contra su voluntad.*"—*Documentos para la Historia de Mexico, II, 212.*

there was a military governor of the entire province in which the mission was located, frequent disputes occurred between the military and ecclesiastics. In each mission were two ecclesiastics; the senior having control of the internal affairs of the mission, and his subordinate superintending the construction of buildings, the sowing and harvesting of grain, and the management of the flocks and herds.

It will be seen that by this system the neophyte was politically and economically a slave; the missionary had control of his labor-power, and had a legal right to the products of his toil. The law called for Indian magistrates; but the part played by the neophyte in this novel state was exceedingly small. The fathers utilized the leaders of the tribes, "capitans" as they were called, in the control of the natives; and frequently went through the formality of an election in appointing them as mayordomas or overseers, alcaldes or councilmen: but it was indeed a matter of form; for the power all lay with the priest.

The life of the natives at the missions varied with the nature of the friar in charge; but as a rule the tasks were not too heavy. Upon the whole, the life was quite easy enough to those who liked it; although the neophyte found the requirements of steady round of duties at the mission far different from those which the wild and reckless habits of his former life had made necessary. Under the discipline of the mission, he must undergo a ceaseless round of religious, social, and industrial duties, which must have been severe indeed to one that had been accustomed to freedom and had never toiled except by accident. Much attention was given to religious affairs; and frequently, if we may credit the report of the explorers, the temporal needs of the natives, who lived in a condition little removed from their original one, were sacrificed for the sake of religious and ceremonial practices.

As the products of the labor of the neophytes were under the control of the friars, and as a large amount of the products were spent in embellishing the churches or were hoarded in the missions, it is evident that much more might have been done to relieve the temporal condition of the natives, and, consequently, to improve their spiritual condition.[1]

At sunrise the angelus summoned all to mass; and from the several departments, directed by the overseers and led by the priest, the neophytes filed into the church to engage for one hour in public worship. At the close of the public service breakfast was served; and afterward the natives repaired, as directed by the overseers, to the fields or to the workshops, to pursue their various occupations. Seven hours of each day were devoted to labor, two to specific prayer, and the remainder of the time to rest and divine worship. The neglect of religious service was considered a misdemeanor and was visited by corporal punishment. The industries of the mission were varied. Apart from the missions were the great ranches where the sheep, cattle, and other stock, were herded or allowed to roam with the least possible care. These ranches needed attention, and were cared for by the natives under the direction of the overseers of Indian blood. Somewhat nearer the mission were the fields for sowing and the vegetable gardens and the orchards; all of these needing care and hard work. Then the creek or the river must be dammed, and the long irrigation ditch built, and all kept in repair. In seed time and in harvest, as well as while the crops were growing, there was no lack of toil for the domesticated Indian.

There were other industries carried on. Artisans were sent from Mexico to teach the natives to make saddles and shoes, to work at the forge, to spin and weave, and in fact to teach them all of the common industrial arts. The construction of the churches, the storehouses, and the dwellings, required much labor; for stones must be quarried, brick made and dried in the sun, and timber hewn and frequently carried a great distance. For all of this the native received food, clothing, and instruction. The food of the natives consisted of roasted

[1] De Mofras, II, 316.

barley (atole) for the morning meal, which was prepared while
mass was progressing, by persons appointed, one from each
cabin, as cooks for the time being.   The barley was roasted in
quantities and further prepared by boiling; and was apportioned to the neophytes daily, according to their supposed
needs.   At noon a more substantial meal was served, composed of vegetables in addition to the barley preparation.[1]
Doubtless the natives were more regularly and better fed than
when they subsisted upon the products of the chase, or on
roots, herbs, and acorns; but it may be doubted that they
were better physically under this new regime.

The clothing of the natives was always meagre; a coarse
cloth was made into blankets and shirts, which, with shoes or
sandals, made their chief covering; although sometimes a more
complete civilian dress was given.   When a ship arrived from
Spain or Mexico, small quantities of fancy goods were distributed among the neophytes.

As for shelter, the first houses of the natives in their domesticated state were made of sticks driven in the ground and
covered with straw.   They were not far removed in appearance
from the rude huts in which the natives dwelt prior to their
connection with the missions.   The sun and air had free play
in the loose structures, and the inmates suffered much from the
effect of the storms of winter; but it was maintained by the
fathers that the natives could not be induced to live in better
ones, and that these structures were more conducive to their
health than closely constructed buildings.   It was also necessary
to burn these houses occasionally in order to free them from
vermin, and it cost but little labor to replace hovels.   It is to be
noticed, however, that as soon as convenient the natives were
given more substantial houses, although the public buildings
of necessity had to be remodeled first, and especially the
church.   In the larger buildings of the mission, better apart-

---

[1] Forbes, 219.

ments were prepared for the females, who were regularly locked up for the night that they might be properly protected.

Not all of the time of the natives at the mission was occupied in religious ceremonies and the daily routine of toil. The life at the missions was relieved by social hours, in which the neophytes could engage in games, or enjoy idleness, as suited their taste. They were very fond of games and music, and the padres took advantage of these inclinations to teach them many things in a social way.[1] Besides some innocent games of chance, gambling was learned from the Spaniards and carried to criminal excess.[2] Dancing was a favorite pastime in some of the missions. In their games the Indians resembled grown children in simplicity. We must except gambling, in which, like drinking, they imitated to perfection a class of white men who were anything but childlike. The padres took great pains to teach the domesticated natives music, the use of the violin and other instruments; and as the neophytes were fond of this pastime, it helped to spend the evenings more pleasantly, and was especially useful at divine worship.

Much of interest could be added pertaining to the life at the missions; but the subject will be closed with a quotation from De Mofras describing the mission of San Louis Rey: "The building is a quadrilateral. The church occupies one of its wings; the façade is ornamented with a gallery. The building raised about ten feet above the soil is two stories in height. The interior is formed by a court. Upon the gallery, which runs round it, are the dormitories of the monks, of the majordomas, and of travellers, small workshops, schoolrooms, and storehouses. The hospitals are situated in the most quiet part of the mission, where the schools are kept. The young Indian girls dwell in the halls called the monastery, and they themselves are called nuns. They are obliged to be secluded to be secure from outrage by the Indians.

---

[1] La Perouse, II, 224.   [2] Forbes, 223.

Placed under the care of Indian matrons, who are worthy of confidence, they learn to make clothes of wool, cotton and flax and do not leave the monastery until they are old enough to be married. The Indian children mingle in the schools with those of the white colonists. A certain number, chosen among the pupils who display the most intelligence, learn music, chanting, the violin, the flute, the violincello and other instruments. Those who distinguish themselves in the carpenters' shop, at the forge or in agricultural labors are appointed alcaldes or chiefs (overseers), and charged with the direction of a squad of workmen. Before the civil power was substituted for the paternal government of the missionaries, the administrative body of each mission consisted of two monks, of whom the elder had charge of the interior and of the religious instructions and the younger of the agricultural works. In order to maintain morals and good order in the missions, they employed only so many of the whites as were absolutely necessary; for they knew that their influence was wholly evil, and that an association with them only developed those habits of gambling and drunkenness to which they are unfortunately too much inclined." [1]

The missions were all built upon the same general plan, although they differed very much in regard to convenience, quality, and magnitude of structure. At first the buildings were of the rudest nature conceivable; but these gave way to more substantial structures of stone or brick. The plan of building about a quadrilateral with the buildings opening on an interior court planted with gardens where the trades could be plied in the open air on pleasant days, was universal. The church was the principal building, upon it was lavished the greater part of the wealth of the primitive community, and upon it was bestowed the most elaborate work of the padres and their carpenters. The walls of the buildings were thick and substantial. Though the architecture was

[1] De Mofras, I, 261.

San Luis Rey Mission, 1882. Founded 1798.

somewhat clumsy, it is to-day a monument of the skill and industry of the padres.

There are traces of the Moorish architecture as modified in Spain after the first expulsion of Moors in the eighth century. The Arab-Moors introduced certain types of architecture which they derived from eastern countries; and these types became prominent features of the national architecture of Spain.[1] The Roman type was united with them in their development. This primitive architecture was transplanted to America unmodified by the introduction of the pointed arch called Gothic; indeed, there are remnants of this Moorish style in the modern architecture of Spain, the Gothic never having completely dominated it.[2] But the old architecture remains in its purest form in the Spanish provinces, thus following a universal law of development.

It has become the habit of certain writers to speak indiscriminately of the Mooresque style of the California mission buildings; but it is not easy to determine to what extent the Christians, who despised the Arab-Moors, copied the architecture of the latter people. For the architecture of Spain is as diverse in origin as the inhabitants; consequently its elements are not easily traced. In the southern part of Spain, the Arab-Moors have left distinct monuments of their architecture, to which the mission architecture of California bears a slight resemblance; but there are other distinct styles traceable in the latter, besides a certain originality of design which is attributable to the designers' seeking convenience and adaptability. Although it may be stated that the mission architecture has nothing to resemble it elsewhere in America, it may be also stated that there is nothing exactly corresponding to it in Spain. However, there is such a general resemblance to Spanish architecture that its origin could be easily traced, even though it were unknown that the missionaries brought it from Spain.

[1] Freeman.
[2] *Del Arte Arabe en España,* por D. Rafael Contreras, 101.

During the long dominion of the Western Empire in Spain, and even for a considerable time after the withdrawal of the Roman government, the Roman style of architecture prevailed. After the introduction of the Gothic, it was blended with the Roman, forming what is known as the Romano-Gothic, which became prominent in the north of Spain as late as the eighth century.[1] With the rise of the Christian kingdoms of the north, there was introduced a new combination of architecture from the Eastern Empire known as the Roman-Byzantine, frequently called Romanesque. The predominence of this style ceased with the beginning of the thirteenth century, to give place to the first native school in Spain, the Hispano-Catholic. This did not copy much from the Moors, on account of the hostility which existed between the two nations. This hostility was, in fact, the cause of the origin of the new style, brought about along with the development of the modern Spanish nation. It obtained until the sixteenth century, when it was replaced, to a certain extent, by the Plateresque or Graeco-Roman, which was the most popular until the eighteenth century. While these more or less imperfect styles of architecture succeeded one another in Spain, the Arab-Moors had introduced other styles which they had borrowed from oriental countries and modified by their own designs. This Mooresque architecture had its first origin in Persia, but was influenced by the Romanesque, the Egyptian, and that of the Moors and Berbers of Africa through whose country the Arabs passed on their way to Spain. Side by side with the various forms of Christian architecture arose the palaces and the mosques of the Arab-Moors. Of this Mooresque architecture Coppée points out three schools.[2] The first extending from the eighth to the eleventh century, is strongly marked by the Byzantine style, owing, it is supposed, to the influence of the Christian architects employed by the Arab-Moors. The next school embraces the period from the

---

[1] Coppée, *Conquest of Spain*, II, 407.   [2] *Ibid*, 408.

eleventh to the thirteenth century, and is characterized by a style more purely Arabian. The third and last school represents the purely Arabian architecture. It arose at a time when the life of the Moors and the Spaniards was almost entirely separated. It was a period which culminated with the conquest of Grenada and the final conquest of the Arab-Moors in Spain. Which of all of these styles was imported by the Spaniards to the New World, and which did the padres imitate more closely in the mission buildings? It is evident that no single style exclusively prevailed; for they were all more or less blended in Spain. Nevertheless there are many distinctive marks of several styles which the *padres* attempted to imitate, adapting them to the conditions under which they labored. Thus they attempted to imitate the Mooresque in respect to the large open courts, with fountains and gardens. The court and fountain at Santa Barbara are good illustrations of this. Another characteristic of the Mooresque architecture is observed in the square columns which support the roofs of the corridors. The corridors themselves facing the court are more Arabian than Roman; and of these there are many examples, but none better than that of San Fernando and San Miguel missions. In the cupola of the mission church at Los Angeles is a true Moorish roof covering the belfry; and one may see here and there slight traces of the horse-shoe arch, which was the purest characteristic of the Arabian architecture, and is so prominent in the Alhambra and the mosque at Cordova. So, too, the plain, unpretentious exterior is illustrative of the Mooresque; for their adornments were all bestowed upon the interior of the building. But, though all of these prominent characteristics are distinctively Mooresque, the main features of the buildings were of the Romanesque type. The predominance of the round arch, the massive walls, and the ground-plan are distinctively Roman, modified by the Christian idea. But the tile roofs, the belfry towers, and the general characteristics of the buildings, are now to be seen in the villages of old Spain.

9

The traveller views with astonishment these interesting structures that have endured the storms of a century of seasons, monuments of the wisdom and perseverance of the founders who sought not to transplant, but to build a new civilization out of crude materials. To perpetuate a historic idea, the Hon. Leland Stanford has modeled the buildings of his magnificent university at Palo Alto after the mission architecture. The open court, the long colonnades, the round arches, the corridors, and the tile roofs, present a style unique and picturesque, as well as commodious and convenient for the purposes designed.

But, though the remains of the old buildings are full of historic interest, the historian looks beyond the buildings to the ruins of the institutions there represented, and reflects upon the course of events that wrought a civilization enduring less than a century; upon the nature of the government that existed, failed, and passed suddenly away. The buildings are fast crumbling into decay; the natives are scattered, the most of them dead, and soon there will not be a vestige left of the civilization that cost hoards of treasure and many lives, and was an expression of holy zeal and long continued self-denial.

The plan of reducing the country by means of missionaries involved in the intention of the government, the changing as soon as possible of the missions into pueblos, and the replacing of the missionaries by regular ecclesiastics.[1] This plan had been adopted in Mexico and in other provinces of New Spain, and it was clearly the intention of the government to carry it out in California as soon as practicable. The patriarchal community was to be changed into a civil community, the missionary field was to become a diocese, and the president of the missions to be replaced by a bishop.[2] The mission churches were to become curacies, and the communicants of the neighborhood

---

[1] Wm. Cary Jones, *Report on Land Titles in California*, 13.
[2] Dwinelle, 20.

were to become parish worshippers. The monks, who had entire charge of the missions, having taken vows of poverty and obedience, were civilly dead; and consequently had no right to property. The missions had no right or title to the land, either by general law or grant; but held an easement or usufruct of the occupied territory. It was supposed that within a period of ten years the Indians would be sufficiently instructed in Christianity and the arts of civilized life to become citizens; and that the missions would become pueblos, all passing under civil jurisdiction.[1]

The plan of secularization of the missions was well understood by the government and the church; and there could be no doubt on any question except that of the time when the natives must be educated in the forms of industry and civil government, and prepared for an independent life. The priests were zealous in the teaching of industries, and had given to the leading Indians more or less of independence; but the entire mass of the natives was tending away from independence and self-government toward a species of slavery. They went through the daily round of toil under fear of punishment, and allowed the missionaries to think and act for them in all other matters. In fact they were becoming less and less prepared to maintain an independence in contact with a superior race.[2] The plan of secularization also involved the grant of lands to the Indians in severalty; but the church had no power to make such grants.

In choosing the lands for the establishment of the missions, the padres had wisely chosen the most fertile and otherwise most favorably located valleys; and soon a line of twenty-one missions extended from San Diego to Point Reyes, occupying all of the most fertile land of the coast. For the mission property included the missions and grounds, the tillable lands, as well as the great pasture fields where the herds of

---

[1] *Opinion of Judge Felch*, Dwinelle, 20: Moses, 9.

[2] Cf. Humboldt, *New Spain*, I, 421.

the mission were kept.[1]   Thus the claims of one mission touched the claims of another; and as no civil town could be legally founded within five miles of a mission,[2] the entire land was exempt from settlement by Spaniards.

Having lived a long time on the lands which they were accustomed to treat as their own, having accumulated property, and having governed with almost absolute sway, the friars, though they owned not a foot of soil, were never ready to give over the property to secular authority without a struggle; consequently they invariably fell back upon the fact that the neophytes were not yet fit to become citizens.   The secular clergy and the friars had been at strife on this question for centuries,[3] and many complaints had been entered against the friars by *gentes de razon* on account of the arbitrary manner in which they strove to control the lands.   Finally, to settle the matter, the Spanish Cortes passed a decree on the thirteenth of September, 1813, to the effect that missions which had been founded ten years should be given over to the bishop, without excuse or pretext, in accordance with the laws.   The friars might be appointed temporary curates, and a certain number might be retained permanently where needed, but the majority must move on to new fields.[4]

By this, the first law respecting secularization in California, the missions were to be transformed into pueblos, the mission lands to be reduced to private ownership, and the neophytes governed by town councils and by civil authorities.[5]   The last section of the decree reads as follows : " The religious missionaries shall immediately cease from the government and the administration of the property (haciendas) of said Indians, it being left to the care and election of these (Indians) to appoint among themselves, by means of their ayuntamientos, and with the intervention of the governor, persons to their

---

[1] Bryant, *History of California*, 281.   [2] *Recopilacion*, IV, V, 6.
[3] Bancroft, *California*, II, 399.   [4] Bancroft, *California*, II, 399.
[5] Tuthill, *California*, 126.

satisfaction, capable of administering it, distributing the lands and reducing them to private property, agreeably to the decree of the 4th of January, 1813, respecting the reduction of vacant and other lands to private dominions."[1] This decree took effect in portions of Spanish America; but was not officially published in California until January 20th, 1820, and was probably unknown there until its publication. At this time the Viceroy of Mexico published a proclamation, which he forwarded to Prefect Payeras and Guardian Lopez with instructions to comply with the terms of the decree at once, or as soon as demanded by the bishop. This led to a controversy, and with this the matter was dropped for the time.

After the revolution in Mexico, the subject was again agitated; and the friars continued to resist all encroachments upon the mission lands, although they were coveted by many. While it was admitted that the missions had proved the granaries of the country, and that the friars had always rendered assistance to the presidios and the pueblos, there was still a feeling that the mission system was antagonistic to the best interests of the country and the government. But the main plea for secularization was that the Indians were in a state of servitude; and, indeed, in the decrees of secularization, the term " emancipation " was used in reference to the neophytes.

Again, in 1833, the Mexican law declared that the government should proceed to secularize the missions of Upper and Lower California according to principles already laid down.[2] In each of the missions, a parish was to be established under the charge of a parish priest of the secular clergy, with a fixed salary of twenty to twenty-five dollars per annum.[3] But the priest was forbidden to collect other fees with the exception of "fees of pomp," which were to be determined by "the tariff to be formed for this object." The sum of five hundred dollars

[1] *Halleck's Report,* 125; *Hall's History of San José,* 430; Dwinelle, 39.

[2] *Halleck's Report,* 148; Rockwell, *Spanish and Mexican Law,* 455.

[3] *Mexican Law of* 1833, art. 2; Rockwell, 455.

was set apart for the support of religious worship and for servants in each mission. It was further enacted that the mission churches, with the furniture, should be handed over to supply the newly formed parishes. All of the remaining buildings were severally appropriated for the curate's house, court-house, preparatory schools, and public establishments. Ample provision was made to carry out these laws by a corps of officers of which the vicar-general was chief. Apparently apprehending the difficulties that might ensue from such a radical change, the government provided that the sea passages of the new curates and their families should be paid out of the general funds, and that in addition from four to eight hundred dollars should be given each curate for the expenses of his overland journey. Also the out-going missionaries should each receive from two to three hundred dollars to pay expenses back to their convents. The most remarkable law of the entire decree was the provision that "the expenses comprehended in this law" should be paid out of the "pious fund of the missions of California."

To enforce these regulations, Jose Figueron issued, in the following year, provisional regulations for the distribution of property and lands, and for the political government of the pueblos. After declaring that the missionary priests should be relieved from farther administration of the temporalities, and should henceforth confine their ministry to spiritual administration, the regulations proceed to give minute directions for the secularization of the missions. Article fifth states explicitly that, " To every individual head of a family, and to all those above twenty-one years of age, although they have no family, a lot of land, whether irrigable or otherwise, if not exceeding 400 varas square, nor less than one hundred, shall be given out of the common lands of the missions ; and in community a sufficient quantity of land shall be allotted them for (pasturing and) watering their cattle. Common lands shall be assigned to each pueblo, and, when convenient, municipal lands also." [1]   It was further provided that one-half of all the movable property should be distributed among the Indian citizens, and the remainder should revert to the government and remain under the care of the mayor-domos, or other appointed officers, and be held subject to the disposal of the supreme federal government.[2]   The Indians receiving property under these provisions were not allowed to "sell, burden, or otherwise alienate, under any pretext, the lands which may be given them; neither may they sell their cattle." [3]   Should contracts of sale be made, they were to be void; and the government was to reclaim the land thus disposed of.

By the regulations it was ordered that ayuntamientos or town councils should be established, and elections be provided for.   To the councils was given the regulation of the economic affairs of the pueblo; but the administration of justice was delegated to the primary judges of the nearest towns, constitutionally established.   The "emancipated Indians" were required to assist in the cultivation of the vineyards and orchards, until a resolution of the supreme government decided otherwise.   In order to carry out these regulations, a board of commissioners were to be appointed by the governor; and a long list of orders is given defining explicitly each step in the procedure of secularization.   One clause in these instructions is of interest as showing to what extent the ideas of political life had been developed in the neophytes. It asserts that "Before making an inventory of the outside property, the commissioners will endeavor to explain to the Indians, with suavity and patience, that the missions are going to be converted into pueblos; that they will only remain subordinate to the priest in matters in relation to the spiritual administration; that the lands and property will be divided out among them so that each one may work, maintain and govern himself, without dependence on any one; that the

---

[1] Rockwell, 457.   [2] *Provisional Regulations*, Articles 6, 7, 8.
[3] Article 18.

house in which they live will become their own property; and that, in order to do this, they must submit to what is commanded in these regulations and orders, which must be explained to them in the best possible manner." [1]

It was further provided that "rancherias situated at a distance from the missions, and containing more than twenty-five families, may, if they choose, form a separate pueblo; and the distribution of lands and property shall then take place in the manner pointed out for the rest." [2] The rancherias not containing twenty-five families formed wards or districts, and were attached to the nearest pueblo. In addition to the above regulations, minute specifications were given for the transference of the mission property, for the abolition of the nunnery, and for officers' salaries and debts.

Following closely on these provisional regulations of Governor Figueron, the regulations of the California Deputation, held in Monterey in November, 1834, defined and enforced certain parts of the regulations. They fixed salaries, classified curacies, provided for the location of court-houses, school-houses, public establishments, and workshops, and ordered that the missionaries should occupy the curacies until the government could provide parish priests. The regulations thus far had accomplished but little more than to throw the inhabitants of the missions into a state of consternation. However legal the regulations might be, to the missionaries the process was one of expulsion and confiscation of property long under their control. The neophytes, though excited by the prospect of "emancipation," were in sympathy with the missionaries, and were greatly influenced in their conduct by them. A reckless destruction of property began; cattle were slaughtered by the thousand, and other property quickly destroyed. To arrest the downward tendency of affairs, the Mexican Congress decreed in November, 1835, that until the curates mentioned in article second of the law of August, 1833,

---

[1] Rockwell, 459.   [2] General Orders, Sec. 9.

should take possession of their curacies, the government would suspend the execution of the other articles of the law, and the missions would remain in the state they were before said law was enacted.[1] But the affairs of the missions continued to grow more deplorable. Officers failed to comply with the law, property was wasted, lands within the villages were seized and held, and moveable property sold. To remedy existing evils, Governor Alvarado, in January, 1839, issued a long list of regulations and instructions, directed chiefly to the administrators of the mission property. He instructed them to present their accounts as soon as possible to the government; to refrain from contracting debts and making sales to foreign merchants; to keep an account of all property handled; and to prevent the slaughter of animals. Many other instructions were given pertaining to official duties and police regulations. To enforce these regulations, W. E. Hartwell was appointed as a special commissioner of inspection to visit all of the missions, enquire carefully into their actual condition, and to report the result of his investigations to the government.

But the abuses continued, and the reverses and losses constantly increased. The regulations of Governor Alvarado had but little effect in rooting out the evils of the mission management. On this account, the Governor, in March, 1840, proclaimed a new set of regulations which pertained especially to the duties of agents, inspectors, and mayor-domos of the missions. The office of administrator was abolished, and mayor-domos were appointed in their stead. They were authorized to " care for everything relative to the advancement of the property under their charge, acting in concert with the reverend padres." They were empowered to superintend the moral and religious affairs of the neophytes, to provide food and clothing for those in need, and in return to compel the neophytes to assist in the labors of the community. The inspectors had various duties and obligations.

---

[1] Rockwell, 462.

They must make contracts with foreign vessels and private persons, and attend to the public finance in relation to the missions, disbursing funds and paying debts. The document closed with a few general regulations pertaining to the administration of affairs.

Although not wanting in laws and instructions, the whole process of secularization had been thus far a complete failure. Many of the neophytes, becoming unsettled, were dispersed from the missions. Property continued to be wasted, and general disorganization prevailed. Settlers were encroaching upon the land claimed by the missions, and speculators and greedy officials were rapidly squandering the accumulated wealth of the padres. A few attempts at secularization had been made; but no stable, well organized pueblos had yet been formed. In the midst of this general confusion, waste, and injustice, General Micheltorena, to save the missions from total ruin, issued a proclamation dated March 29, 1843, which provided that the majority of the missions should again be placed in charge of the padres.[1] They were to manage them as formerly; to clothe, instruct, and supervise the neophytes, and to have charge of the mission property as prior to the law of 1833. They were instructed to collect the scattered natives, except those who had already been "legally emancipated by the superior departmental government," and those in the service of private persons. However, Indians of either of the above classes might return to the missions if they wished, and be entitled to protection; provided that, in respect to the latter class, the masters were willing, and that the padres were acquainted with the fact of their return. The grants of lands already made to Indians and others should not be revoked; but property loaned must be collected at once. The proclamation guarantees the protection of the missions and the

---

[1] This proviso included San Diego, San Louis Rey, San Juan Capistrano, San Gabriel, San Fernando, San Buenaventura, Santa Barbara, Santa Cruz, San Antonio, Santa Clara, La Purissima and San José.

SAN JUAN BAUTISTA.

prosperity of the Holy Catholic faith ; but gently asserts that one-eighth of all of the products of the missions shall be paid into the public treasury for the support of the army.

It seems that the neophytes had abandoned the missions of San Rafael, Dolores, Solidad, San Miguel, and La Purissima, and had fled to the rancherias of the surrounding country. Consequently a decree of the Department Assembly, of May 28, 1845, declared that if they did not return within one month and a day, the government could dispose of the mission property, " as may best suit the general good of the department." The decree also provided that " the Carmelos, San Juan Bautista, San Juan Capistrano and San Francisco Solano shall be considered as pueblos, which is the character they at present have."

After preserving sufficient land for the public buildings of the pueblos, the remainder was to be sold at public auction in order to pay the respective debts of the establishment ; should there be any surplus it was to be devoted to the support of religion. With the exception of the principal edifice at Santa Barbara, the remaining missions might be rented out at the option of the government, and the proceeds devoted equally to the service of the church, the Indians, and the government. The salary of the padre minister, the expenses of worship, the clothing and food of the natives, public education, and public benefices in general, were to be paid out of the surplus rents after the payment of all out-standing obligations. As to the neophytes, the decree asserted that they should " remain in absolute liberty to occupy themselves as they may see fit, either in the employment of the renter himself or in the cultivation of their own lands which the government must necessarily designate for them." [1]

In accordance with the above decree, Governor Pio Pico issued a proclamation October 28, 1845, for the rental and sale of the missions. It declared that the missions, San Rafael,

---

[1] *Decree of the Departmental Assembly,* Sec. 3.

Dolores, Soledad, San Miguel, and La Purissima, having been abandoned by the neophytes, should be sold to the highest bidder. Also all of the surplus property of the pueblos, San Louis Obispo, Carmelo, San Juan Bautista, and San Juan Capistrano, which formally belonged to the missions must be sold in the same way. It was further provided that the surplus property of missions other than those enumerated above should be sold at auction. The missions, San Fernando, San Buenaventura, Santa Barbara, and Santa Inez, were to be rented to the highest bidder, for the term of nine years. Specific regulations were made as to the method of renting, and the rights and obligations of the renters.

Again, the Indians are declared "free from the neophytism," and at liberty to establish themselves wherever they choose. The small portions of land already occupied by them were exempted from sale or rent; but those natives who occupied homes and gardens, had to apply to the government for a title for the same. It was understood that this title would not permit the Indians to alienate their lands, but asserted that they should be hereditary among their relatives according to law. It was further ordered that the Indians remaining in the missions should appoint from their number each year, four overseers to maintain public order, subject to the authority of the justice of the peace. The chief duty of the overseers was to appoint, every month, from the number of Indians "a sacristan, a cook, a tortilla maker, a vaquero, and two washer-women, for the service of the padre minister," and it mildly proclaimed that "no one shall be hindered from remaining in this service as long as he choose." Thus after all of the decrees and proclamations of Cortes, Congress, deputation, assembly, and governor, relative to the secularization of the missions and the civil rights of the Indians, the whole affair was to end in the sale or rent of the missions; and the mere shadow of a government was to be granted to the helpless wretches who had made their homes within the missions. One more decree of the Departmental

CARMEL MISSION. FOUNDED JUNE 3, 1770.

Assembly, passed on the 3rd of April, 1846, ordered the sale of the missions to prevent their total ruin. This had the effect usually produced by prior decrees, namely of complicating matters, and hastening the downfall of the missions. As some of the missions were now owing large sums, article second of the decree provided that, "attention should be had to what the laws determine respecting bankruptcies, and steps should be taken accordingly." It was a simple matter to make decrees, but the lack of timely and faithful execution rendered them useless.

The Departmental Assembly adjourned in 1846, for the want of a quorum; and Governor Pico fled the country. Soon afterwards, José Maria Flores, a captain of cavalry in the Mexican army, who assumed the governorship ad interim, organized a kind of provisional legislature which sought to save the missions from complete ruin. This Assembly passed a decree annulling the laws of Governor Pico, which provided for the sale of the missions. The Assembly authorized Flores to mortgage the missions in order to raise funds to carry on the war against the United States. But as these regulations were passed several months after the United States had taken possession of the territory, they were illegal, even could it have been established that the assembly was regularly constituted.

Thus ended the attempts of the Mexican government to secularize the missions. For thirteen years it continued to legislate, while the missions rapidly declined. When the American flag was raised at Monterey on the 7th of July, 1846, some of the property had been sold, some rented, and much squandered. A small number of the natives were still living at the missions; but the majority had returned to their rancherias in the mountains and districts remote from the settlements. Many of the lands were already in dispute as to ownership, and many preferred claims upon mission property.

At this juncture, General Kearney issued a decree on March 22, 1847, which declared that the missions and their property should remain under the charge of the Catholic priests as they were when the American flag was raised, and that the priests should hold them and preserve the property until the titles to the lands could be decided by proper legal authority.   The priests would be held responsible for the protection and pre-servation of property, and might invoke the aid of the alcalde to remove all parties intruding or trespassing on the mission lands.   But the proclamation came too late for the protection of the Indians; complete ruin had been wrought to the mission system long before.   The neophytes, collected during a long period of years, were soon scattered abroad to roam through the valleys and in the mountains in the search for food.   For this pursuit, they were in a worse condition than they were prior to their entrance to the missions; for they had been deprived of the native vigor which their wild life brought, and had received nothing of permanent value from the new civilization.   According to De Mofras,[1] there were connected with the missions in 1834, 30,650 Indians.   In 1842, not more than 4,450 remained.   The property of the missions had declined far more rapidly.   Of the 424,000 horned cattle belonging to the missions in 1834, there remained only 28,220 twelve years later.   These twenty-one missions, ex-tending in an irregular line for over six hundred miles along the coast, linking together the most fertile valleys of Cali-fornia, produced in 1834, 70,000 bushels of wheat, and 30,000 bushels of smaller grains.   One hundred thousand cattle were slaughtered every year, yielding a product of ten dollars per head.   The total annual productions of the mis-sions was valued at $2,000,000 ; and aside from the valuable property in buildings, orchards, and vineyards, the movable stock was valued at $3,000,000.[2]   In addition, the annual income of the so-called pious fund amounted to $50,000.

Aside from the general plan of secularization instituted by the Cortes of Spain and carried out .by the Mexican authori-

---

[1] De Mofras, *Exploration de l' Orégon, des Calafornies, etc.*, I, 321.

[2] De Mofras, 1, 321 *et seq.*

ties, there were several minor reasons for the immediate change from religious to secular administration. The government was in need of funds, and many officials thought the mission property would do good service in supplying the deficiency. Others opposed the mission system as detrimental to the best interests of the country, and therefore desired a change. The system was well enough for the subjugation of a country; but it had now become a hindrance, and therefore needed to be abolished. In addition to this, the avarice of individuals who saw an opportunity to increase their own wealth and advance their own interests, continually urged the subject before the government. The immense claims of the missions to property extending far beyond their legitimate boundaries, led to constant strife with those desiring to settle on the land. In this the padres were frequently inconsistent, and lost much prestige thereby. However, it is evident that the government had lost its zeal for the conversion and civilization of the natives, and the only question remaining was as to the proper disposal of the property.

In speaking of secularization, Mr. Dwinelle says : " These laws, whose ostensible purpose was to convert the missionary establishments into Indian pueblos, their churches into parish churches, and elevate the Christianized Indians to the rank of citizens, were after all executed in such a manner that the so-called secularization of the missions resulted in their plunder and complete ruin, and in the demoralization and dispersion of the Christianized Indians." [1] He considers that there was a perfect understanding between the government of Mexico and the leading men in California, that the government should absorb the "Pious Fund" as a quasi-escheat, while the co-actors in California should appropriate the local wealth of the missions by the rapid and sure process of administering the temporalities.[2] Whether so planned or not, the ruin of the missions and of their civilization built up through

---

[1] Dwinelle, *Colonial History of San Francisco*, 54.   [2] *Ibid.*

a period of more than sixty years, was wrought in an incredibly short time.

The " Pious Fund " mentioned above, was created by gifts and donations of wealthy persons to the religious orders for the purpose of carrying on missionary work among the natives. After the failure of the Spanish Government to conquer and settle California, the work was undertaken by the Jesuits in 1697; consequently Fathers Salvatierra and Kino were empowered to make the temporal and spiritual conquest of the country.[1]   One of the conditions of this contract was that the missionaries should not " waste anything belonging to the crown, or draw on the treasury without an express order from the king.[2]   The two zealous friars had already commenced to collect a fund to advance missionary work.   This fund was constantly increased, and placed in the hands of the missionaries, in trust, to forward the specific ends of the extension of religious conquest.   Donations to the amount of nineteen thousand dollars were soon made, and the treasurer of Acapulco granted the use of a galleon to transport the missionaries to their place of work.[3]   It was then determined to create by subscription a permanent fund for a perpetual endowment of the missionary work in California.   Ten thousand dollars was considered a sufficient sum for each mission, as it would yield an income of five hundred dollars per annum.   It now became quite fashionable for wealthy Catholics to endow a mission.   Not less than thirteen missions were thus endowed in lower California.   From this time the fund accumulated until it reached the sum of about two million dollars.   The pious fund was managed by Jesuits until their expulsion from Mexico in 1768.   By order of the Viceroy, the missions were then placed in the hands of the Franciscans.   Subse-

---

[1] Cf. Chapter V.   [2] Venegas, Part III, Section 1.
[3] The "Pious Fund" of California, John T. Doyle, *Overland Monthly*, Sept., 1890.   Also see a full discussion of the subject by the same author in *Cal. Hist. Assoc. Pub.*, Vol. 1.

quently, by a royal cedula dated April, 1770, the missions were divided equally between the Franciscans and the Dominicans; and by an agreement between the two societies, two years thereafter, the missions of Lower California were to be managed by the Dominicans, and those of Upper California by the Franciscans. Consequently the income of the Pious Fund was divided equally between the two orders. After the expulsion of the Jesuits, the crown seized all of their temporalities, and therefore became the administrator of the Pious Fund, holding it in trust for the missions. Officers were appointed to control it. After the revolution, the government of Mexico succeeded the crown of Spain in the administration of the trust. In 1836, a law of the Mexican Congress granted, for the support of the proposed Bishopric in California, an endowment of six thousand dollars per annum; and " conceded to the incumbent, when selected, and to his successors, the administration and disposal of the Pious Fund." [1] In February, 1842, Santa Ana, then President of the Republic, abrogated that part of the Mexican law relative to the disposal of the Pious Fund, and it again reverted in trust to the Mexican government. In the following October, the greater part of the property was sold for the sum of about $2,000,000. The reason for sale as given, was that there had been waste and mismanagement by public officials. The proceeds of the sale were paid into the public treasury, and were finally absorbed by the government. Through the management of John T. Doyle, Esq., interest to the amount of over nine hundred thousand dollars was reclaimed, in 1870, by the award of the mixed American and Mexican Congress which met at Washington. Doubtless the existence of the Pious Fund had something to do with the reckless legislation relative to the missions.

After the United States government obtained the territory of California, it was decided by Congress that there were two classes of mission property: one consisting of the mission

---

[1] Doyle, *Overland*, XVI, 93, 238.

10

itself and its immediate surroundings; the other comprising the large farms with pasture fields attached, and situated either near by the mission buildings or at a remote distance from them. Therefore it was legally declared that the missions, with a suitable amount of ground and all movable property connected therewith, should be considered as belonging to the church; and all other property should revert to the government. The titles of the Indians had never been formally recognized, and consequently they were not tenable. There were many general decrees concerning the location of the Indians, and they were placed upon land which they were permitted to call their own. As colonists and settlers came in, these lands were taken up under the law, regardless of their occupants who could show no legal title. That much injustice was done and great wrongs committed no one can deny; but the case shows little variation from the continuous treatment of the Indians for three hundred years by colonies and governments. Once removed from the protection of the friars, the semi-civilization of the natives collapsed before foreign aggression and immigration. The common theory that the neophytes should settle in self-organized and self-governed communities, and occupy lands to which they held a clear and indisputable title, in severalty, was never realized in practice. The process of secularization, and the subsequent American invasion, destroyed the semi-civil communities; and with few exceptions left the natives with no title to the land.

The result of an attempt to organize an Indian pueblo under that portion of the secularization act of 1834, relating to the formation of pueblos and rancherias at a distance from the mission,[1] is well illustrated by the history of the San Pasqual village. This village was formed by about one hundred neophytes attached to the San Louis Rey mission. The Indians were granted the lands, and although they could not show a modern title, had a clear and just right to them.

---

[1] Section 9, General Orders.

They tilled the soil to a certain extent, and possessed large herds of horses, sheep, and cattle. They lived a quiet, peaceful life, not even disturbed by advancing civilization. The whole valley was finally reserved by executive authority for their temporary residence; but the order was revoked and the valley thrown open to settlement. Then the process of displacing the Indians began; and in a short time there were no Indians in the village, but in their place a small white settlement. The neophytes had scattered to the foot hills, where they maintained a life similar to that of their fathers prior to the Spanish invasion. Sometimes they worked for wages on the neighboring ranches, and sometimes the priest made them a visit, collecting them for worship; but the brush shed that sheltered them, their mode of life, and their meagre subsistence and clothing, disclosed anything but a state of civilization.

Many criticisms have been offered from time to time on the methods adopted by the priest colonists in their management of the Indians. It may be well said that there are many objections to the methods adopted; but that everything was done in good faith by those hardy pioneers. The Indian problem has always been and is yet a difficult one. But comparing the methods used by the Jesuits and the Franciscan friars, and those adopted by other missionaries in different parts of the world, it is doubtful whether a more successful plan has obtained anywhere than that of the California missionaries. The preparation for citizenship was indeed slow; and the means employed did not always tend toward independent citizenship. But the same difficulty is experienced everywhere in the attempt to civilize barbarous tribes. Our own civilization rests upon thousands of years of progress and self-evolution; and an attempt to force it suddenly upon a race not yet entered upon the pastoral stage of development must end in a failure. In dealing with uncivilized tribes, civilized nations have not given sufficient attention to their relative stage of progress, and consequently, have attempted to force the process of domestication too rapidly. The result has been that an artificial system has been superimposed on a barbaric nation, which seeks at every opportunity to throw off the burden.

The slow development of a race on a natural basis, through the pastoral and agricultural and the industrial stages, is the only process of civilization that will lead to permanent results. The native should be taught to practice the industrial arts, and should be inspired with a desire to become self-sustaining in competition with civilized races, before there is any hope of real culture. In this respect, we find the padres teaching the natives the care of flocks, the process of agriculture, and the common industrial arts. All the while they allowed them to live in semi-civilized condition, and treated them as children. It was a slow process; and could they have had time enough—a few more generations at least—possibly the results would have been satisfactory. But the movement of modern institutions is too swift; modern progress cannot wait for the slow evolution of utopias. Steam and electricity are great disturbers as well as great civilizers, and they frequently destroy instead of building.

We find that our national Indian schools, Haskell Institute and Carlisle, are adopting the same means of education as those practiced by these early pioneers on the Pacific slope. Industrial education is made the foundation, and intellectual culture and citizenship the superstructure, of civilization. But the difficulty of the transition from school life to that of practical citizenship obtains now as well as then. The government now falls short of its duty, if it does not follow the Indian boys and girls into the actual business world, and see to it that they are able to make the connection of individual culture with social life. It should place them in a life work, make them self-sustaining, and protect them in this new life so that all opportunity and all desire to return to the blanket and the gun may be cut off.

The friars certainly had poor material on which to work. It was true that the natives were docile and easy to subdue;

but they were also dull and of an inferior race. It was necessary to keep them subordinate to the severest discipline in order to accomplish anything. La Perouse, the most just of all of the visitors to the Pacific coast, thought that "The neophyte was too much a child, too much a slave, too little a man."[1] He censures the padres for neglecting their temporal welfare and their instruction in the common individual arts for the "heavenly interests" of the natives.[2] This is the worst feature of the whole system, that their zeal for the prayers and rites of the church far outran their interest in the temporal welfare of the natives. It has been fully demonstrated by experience that the surest development of Christianity rests upon economic advancement; and that Christian teaching, which is not backed by permanent social and industrial improvements, will prove evanescent.

The neophytes were quite readily controlled through the religion taught them; for they believed that the missionaries had a direct communion with God, and that they daily prevailed upon him to descend upon the altar.[3] Thus by appealing to superstition, the priests took the place of the native caciques in the control of the Indians. But there was frequent insubordination; rebellion had to be put down, and consequently punishment had to be inflicted. At Monterey, in 1786, "men and women were seen loaded with irons, others were fixed in a frame resembling stocks, and the noise of the strikes of the whip assailed the ears of all present, a proof that this punishment is permitted here, although it is said not to be exercised with severity."[4] Other writers have spoken of the neophytes' being treated as a race of slaves. In some instances this was true, in others not. Subordination and docility are the first requisites to effective civilizing. La Perouse held that to the principles of Christianity there might

---

[1] Bancroft, *California*, I, 436.
[2] La Perouse, *Voyages and Travels*, II, 26, (Pelham).
[3] La Perouse, II, 27.   [4] La Perouse, II, 25.

have been gradually added the practice of legislation ; so that little by little, the neophytes might have been transformed into citizens. Mr. Forbes and Mr. Beechy both criticise the methods employed by the missionaries, but Mr. Dwinelle shows a desire to give full credit to their work. He says, " It was something, surely, that over thirty thousand wild, barbarous, and naked Indians had been brought in from their savage haunts, persuaded to wear clothes, accustomed to a regular life, inured to such light labor as they could endure, taught to read and write, instructed in music, accustomed to the service of the church, partaking of its sacraments and indoctrinated in the Christian religion, and this system had become self-sustaining under the mildest and gentlest of tutelage ; for the Franciscan monks who superintended these establishments were from Spain, and many of whom were highly cultivated men, soldiers, engineers, artists, lawyers, and physicians, before they became Franciscans, always treated the neophyte Indians with the most paternal kind-ness, and did not scorn to labor with them in the field, in the brick-yard, the forge, and the mill." [1] Again, he says, " When we view the vast constructions of the mission buildings, includ-ing the churches, the refectories, the dormitories, the work-shops, the granaries, and the rancherias, sometimes brought many miles on the shoulders of the Indians, and look at the beautiful ribbed stone arches of the church of the Carmelo, we cannot deny that the Franciscan missionary monks had the wisdom, sagacity, and patience to bring their neophyte pupils far forward on the road from barbarism to civilization, and that these Indians were not destitute of capacity." [2]

It may be said, however, that suitable as this system was for the docile California natives, it failed when applied to the treacherous Apaches and the warlike Moqui. It was a system especially adapted to pueblo Indians and non-warlike races. But with sufficient discipline and sufficient time, the youth of

---

[1] Dwinelle, *Colonial History of San Francisco*, 84.   [2] Dwinelle, 84.

FRANCISCAN MONKS, SANTA BARBARA.

every tribe to-day in America could be made self-sustaining. They could be taught the arts of industry, and given sufficient intelligence to make them good citizens. They could be taught to hold their land in severalty, and to till the soil. And all this and more of the same nature is essential to the solution of the Indian race problem.

Another method which was tried by the missionaries on the river Colorado ended in complete failure. It was designed to combine at once the three-fold plan of civil, military, and mission pueblos. The proposed colony combined the attributes of missions, pueblos proper, and presidios.[1] "The soldiers, under a sub-lieutenant, were to protect the settlers, who were to be granted house-lots and fields; while the friars were to act as pastors," attending to the spiritual interests of the colonists, and at the same time acting as missionaries to the Indians. In this plan the priests were to have nothing to do with temporal affairs. As soon as the Indians were domesticated, they could obtain lands and live in the pueblos with the Spaniards. After a while they were to come under civil and military control. Each mission was to have ten soldiers, ten settlers, and six laborers, all *gente de razon*, to form the principal organization of each pueblo. But the removal of the friars from the duty of managing land and secular property in general, the inequalities of the separate races, and other difficulties, led to a revolution among the Indians; and a massacre resulted, bringing to a speedy close all efforts for civilization on the Colorado.

No other system came so near accomplishing the reduction of the barbarous races to a state of civilization as that of the padres of California. Their work was done in a very short time; for fifty years is but a span in the course of civilization. Certainly one thing was accomplished: under the supervision of missionaries the pioneer work of a great state was begun. The natives did the greater part of the work. Indian labor

---

[1] Bancroft, *California*, I, 357.

constructed all buildings, sowed the grain, harvested the crops, planted the vineyards and orchards, and herded the cattle and sheep. Indeed every variety of industry was cultivated among the neophytes, and labor and worship were their discipline. Considering that there were but a handful of monks to organize and superintend the work, that they worked under so many disadvantages, and that they received but little substantial aid from the civil or military authorities, the result of their occupation of California for the period of sixty years, is indeed marvelous. The old mission buildings are the most conspicuous remnants of this early Spanish and Mexican domination. But they with other relics of this evanescent civilization will soon be obliterated. Some missions have crumbled to dust, others have been transformed in attempts to preserve them, and all will soon be forgotten in the new civilization of the Anglo-Saxon; the civilization of steam, and electricity; of free institutions and universal intelligence, the civilization wrought by wheat, fruit, and gold.

CHAPTER VIII.

SPANISH COLONIAL MUNICIPALITIES.

The purely civic colonies of California were called pueblos to distinguish them from missions or presidios. The term pueblo, in its most extended meaning, may embrace towns of every description, from a hamlet to a city;[1] and consequently might apply equally well to the missions, with their adjacent Indian villages, to the small villages springing up around the presidios, or to the regularly settled colony. However, in its special significance, a pueblo means a corporate town, with certain rights of jurisdiction and administration. In Spain the term *lugar* was usually applied to towns of this nature; but the Spanish Americans have preferred and persistently used the term pueblo. But the word may be used in several distinct ways, each of which may be entirely correct. In the first place it had a political significance when it was applied to the jurisdiction of all the legal voters within a certain territory; second, it applied to the judicial jurisdiction represented by an alcalde of the pueblo, which did not always coincide with the political jurisdiction; and third, the pueblo had a proprietary existence defined by the rights to certain lands given by the grant; and when complete it had a town council (*ayuntamiento*), composed of councilmen (*regidores*), judges (*alcaldes*), and a mayor.[2] This view gives to the term

---

[1] *Ciudad*, is the term usually applied to a city; it also admits of flexibility of use.

[2] Instructions of the Governor of California in a letter to the Ayuntamiento of Monterey, Jan. 25th, 1836; cf. Dwinelle, 51.

a wider signification than its most common one, that of a collection of houses (*aldea*).

The use of these terms remind us that the origin of this institution, like that of many others in Spanish America, belongs to an early period of Old Spain. It is quite remarkable that, in our so-called Anglo-Saxon nation, there should have existed, as late as the present century, so many of the customs and usages of a Romance people; and that there still remain in some of our States vestiges of the laws and judicial procedure of Old Spain. Spain has ever been a conservative nation, in spite of frequent revolutions; and her customs and laws have been preserved throughout the centuries. This is made apparent by a comparison of the numerous codes of Spain; for an old code was seldom repealed on the introduction of a new one, consequently the former was appealed to in all cases not covered by the latter. After the transmission of laws and customs to the colonies, there was a tendency to preserve old forms; so that the provinces record institutions, customs, and laws, that the progressive centers of civilization have out-grown. While colonies are young and feeble, and before they have developed an independent life and growth, it is universally true that they have a tendency to retain ancient forms.

Not only was Spain the first territory to be fully colonized by Rome, but the first to develop the municipal system, the first to allow the communes representation in the general assembly, and the first, in fact, to formulate a code of modern laws. It is difficult to point out the exact origin of the Spanish municipality, although it is easy to assert in general terms that it is Roman in its source. It is claimed by some that the Roman municipality was never entirely obliterated, and consequently retained its identity throughout the invasions of the Moor and the Goth, and under the feudal regime. Considering the general effects of the Northern invasions upon the Roman law and the Roman government, especially in reference to the municipality, this is very plausible. It is evident that the forms of government and their own time-honored rights still remained in the minds of the people. At the risk of repetition, the writer will again refer to the continuity of the Roman municipal polity.[1]

Although the early period of Spanish history is upon the whole obscure, it is not wanting in definite knowledge on specified subjects. That Spain was covered with Roman municipalities and colonies, there is abundance evidence; but as to the nature of these colonies and municipalities, as to their laws and government, it could only be affirmed that they were Roman. This would give them a general characterization, and beyond this, little could be said of their nature, were it not for the discovery of bronze tablets in a brick-pit near Malaga and Salpensa, two towns in the province of Baetica in Spain. These tablets not only show the nature of the municipal laws of the period, but they demonstrate the continuity of the municipality during the early empire. The laws were compiled in the time of Vespasian, and were doubtless in force a long time thereafter. Although they were only partially recovered, they reveal sufficient truth to supplement knowledge from other sources, and to establish beyond a doubt the character of the municipal organizations in the provinces. In the Roman province there were several classes of towns; there were free federated towns, free non-federate, and the *civitas stipendiariae* possessing no privileges; all of which were non-Roman. But the group that especially concerns us includes the Roman towns. Of these there were three main classes; municipia, coloniae, and praefecturae. These all had either Roman or Latin rights. They represented a part of the Roman system of citizenship. It was the custom of Rome to govern the provinces largely through the towns. The municipia and the colonies differed but little in privileges; their chief differences lay in their historical development. As respects internal arrangement and constitution the

---

[1] Cf. Chapter II.

chief difference lay in the fact that the colony had *duoviri*, while the municipium had *quattuoviri*, although a town might have both sets of officers.[1]   The municipium was received into the Roman system from without; while the colony was founded by sending out citizens from within.   The colony or municipium might be with or without suffrage, as they were admitted either to the full Roman or the Latin rights.

Thus their constitutions would vary with their privileges granted; and in this respect the Roman towns may be classed together.   Every Roman municipal town had a senate of a hundred members in which sat the magistrates.   The superior magistracy consisted of two aediles, two questors, and two duumvirs; and the two duumvirs were changed each year.   These officers represented the administration of justice, and the management of the revenue of the municipium.[2]   The senate (*decuriones*) represented the chief executive body of the town, and formed a town council of more power and less responsibility than modern town councils.[3]   The members of the council were usually elected by the whole body of citizens; but with the election, the power of the people ceased; the town council became a strong oligarchy.   It was the chief executive of the municipal organization, and in many instances the other officers were held responsible to it.   In the election of magistrates, the whole number of candidates was made out and posted before election; and from the whole list the designated number of officers was elected.[4]

These early Roman municipalities established in Spain laid the foundation for the later Spanish municipalities.   Rejecting the problem of identity, the historical continuity is shown by the repetition of forms and methods of government.   So marked is the similarity between the early Roman and the later Spanish municipality, that there can be no question as to

---

[1] Allus Gellius, XVI, 13.   [2] Lex Malicitana, section 67.
[3] Arnold, *Roman Provincial Administration*, 224.
[4] Lex Malicitana, section 51.

their relation. The towns passed through many changes and through a period of obscurity; but they reappear in the eleventh century with the old forms and a new spirit. In the place of decuriones we have the town council (ayuntamiento), composed of councilmen (regidores) elected by the people. And as in the case of the Roman municipality, the magistrates of the town have seats in the council. The alguazil, or town treasurer, takes the place of the Roman quaestor; and the alcaldes or judges supersede the Roman duoviri. In the Roman municipium, the duumvir acted not only as judge, but he conducted the case throughout. He procured the witnesses and appointed arbiters or jurymen to decide the case. In the early Spanish municipalities, the alcaldes performed a variety of duties, and probably combined the functions of constable, city attorney, and judge. In the more fully developed town, there was a special officer (procurador syndico), or city attorney, who shared part of the duties which formerly fell to the lot of the Roman duumvir. Thus in the principal officers and in their respective powers, the Spanish pueblo bears a close resemblance to the Roman provincial town. This resemblance is especially marked in the grouping of the functions of officials; there was no clear classification of the judicial, legislative, and administrative powers, as in modern government.

Although the Roman municipality was not obliterated by the conquest of the Goths nor by the dominion of the Arab-Moors, it was greatly modified by feudal society, until its modern phase possesses some characteristics entirely different from the original. Federalism, though not as complete in Spain as in other nations, had its peculiar effect on the status of towns. The manorial system prevailed to a considerable extent; and at a very early period we find the lords giving charters containing privileges to the burgesses of the towns. These privileges were, at first, of a simple nature; referring chiefly to the inheritance of property, and to the right to their own judges, either chosen by the people or appointed by a

higher power.[1] The town was composed of lords and com-
moners, who were accorded the privileges of the town; but
there were connected with the municipal government the
counts or *companeros* of the king, who were charged with the
defense of the country and the re-population of the frontier.
The modern Spanish commune had its origin in the attempt
to repeople the frontier wastes made desolate by the wars
against the Arab-Moors.[2] Inducements were held out by the
government to settlers to form towns, and certain chartered
rights and privileges were granted to the colonists (pobladores).
The earliest record of a charter of this nature is that granted
to the city of Leon in 1020. This grant is remarkable, as it
recognizes the municipal council as a time-honored institution.[3]

The progress of municipal freedom was necessarily slow, on
account of the power of the feudal lords and the centralization of authority in the crown. That some progress in self-
government was made is assured from the fact that the towns
were granted representation in the general assembly, about the
middle of the twelfth century.[4] There are references that seem
to indicate a much earlier representation; but it is certain that
the towns were represented in the Cortes of Leon in 1188.[5]
But there were many difficulties with which the new municipalities had to contend. In the first place, the precedent of
the Roman municipality which represented the officers as
proprietors of legislative action to the exclusion of all representative privileges, was opposed to the development of an
urban democracy. The proprietorship of the feudal nobility
strengthened this tendency to aristocracy, and further repressed the rising power of the people. Again, the rights

---

[1] Alberto Lista, Del Regimen municipal en España, Knapp, *Spanish
Readings*, 173.

[2] Dunham, *History of Spain and Portugal*, IV, 99.

[3] Hallam, *Middle Ages*, Part II, chapter II.

[4] Popular representation occurred about a century later in France, England,
Italy, and Germany. Hallam, Part II, chapter 2.

[5] Dunham, IV, 154.

accorded those who formed themselves into organized communities, with town councils and local and other officers, were largely nominal, on account of the forces that opposed them. The election of magistrates, the enjoyment of revenues of the forests, and the right to the succession of property, were greatly interfered with by the oppressive feudatories. The elections were seldom governed by the free and independent choice of the people. Take, for example, the town Saragossa, (an old Roman colony), in which the mode of choosing the municipal officers was partly guided by the choice of the people and partly left to fortune. The names of persons thought fit for office were written on slips of parchment which were inserted in wooden balls. The balls were placed in a bag. Then a child, possibly not more than ten years of age, selecting a ball from the bag, elected the person whose name was found within.[1] By this method and by others, a few leading spirits had the opportunity of controlling the rights of the people. Although there was more of form than of real liberty in the Spanish municipalities, they grew to have power in the government, and gave rise to a distinct portion of Spanish law.

The establishment of towns with municipal charters, and with rights of representation in the Cortes, developed that branch of the law known as fueros, consisting of chartered rights, privileges, and decrees. These laws formed a component part of the famous Siete Partidas, which was formulated by Alfonso X. in 1258, and which later became the basis of the common law of Spain.[2] This body of ancient law and customary usage formed the basis of the royal decrees, made for the settlement and the government of the colonies. The kings of Spain, especially Charles V., Philip II., Philip III., and Philip IV., made laws and gave decrees based on this code for the settlement and government of Spanish America.

---

[1] Ordinaciones de la Ciudad de Zaragoza, 4 (1693), cited by Arthur Helps, *Spanish Conquest*, IV, 404.

[2] Dunham, IV, 121.

The municipalities in the colonies were formed after the manner of those in Spain ; and as far as government was concerned, they were exact copies of those in the mother country. Not only was the newly colonized territory considered a part of the national domain, but the laws and ordinances for its government were promulgated from the central government. In this, as well as in the idea of peopling and guarding the frontier, the Roman method was closely followed. All details had to be reduced to law and pass through a process of administration before any action was taken ; nothing was left to be decided by the needs of the colony arising from peculiarity of situation, or from subsequent development.

Nevertheless the Spanish sovereigns endeavored to work out in detail those laws best suited to the supposed condition of the settlers ; and in later times they endeavored to consider the exact condition of the colonists before making laws for their control. But it was not until the time of Carlos III. that there was any show of liberality on the part of the sovereign in regard to self-government. The reform of Carlos III. was directed equally against the practices of the church, the inquisition, and the civil government. The nation had already been aroused from lethargy during the reign of Ferdinand VI. ; but Carlos stifled the inquisition, repressed the power of the church, lowered taxation, and equalized government.[1] During his rule a general trade sprang up, the navy, once the pride of Spain, was restored, and prosperity began on every side. The trade with the colonies increased from 5,000,000 crowns to 12,000,000 crowns.[2] At this time the old spirit of conquest and colonization was aroused, and Alta California was settled. There was an attempt to give colonists better opportunities for self government. There was at this time, after two hundred and fifty years of occupancy of the land, evidence of original development, of the modification of the old laws, and of provincial independence. But it was

---

[1] Coxe, III, 517 *et seq.*　　　　[2] Dunham, V, 284.

very slight, as we find the laws of two and a half centuries being enforced with little modification. The colonies were servile; and as far as administration was concerned, they developed but little vital liberty.

There was, however, one distinct feature of the Spanish American town which separated it from others of its class in he old world—and that was uniformity. Made after the same pattern, the towns and colonies were quite similar. Not so in Europe; for there it was common to find a single province containing towns of every variety, one holding its lands in full proprietary right, another by mere usurpation, another in common with a neighboring lord, and yet another in partnership with a bishop, a church, a convent, or a monastery. All liberty in the towns of old Spain was either purchased, forced from the power of feudal nobility, or received directly through chartered rights granted by the sovereign.

There was at least symmetry in the foundation of the rights of the towns of Spain; and this led to the formation of all the towns in the colonies upon the same general type, or at least after special types.[1] This had a tendency to guarantee the rights of the town, and to free it from irregularities and exactions. As has been already stated, the general laws and regulations governing the province and the provincial town proceeded from the crown. Nevertheless the provincial governors were recognized as having special privileges, and their recommendations were frequently followed, especially during the latter part of Spanish rule; and under Mexican domination, the provincial governors were recognized as having still more independence in administration.

Although laws for the settlement of the new territories were made by Charles V., the first general system of laws regulating colonization were enacted by Philip II.[2] There were two principal methods set forth in the royal decrees. The first

---

[1] Dwinelle, 34.

[2] *Recopilacion de leyes de los reynos de las Indias,* II, 19.

11

vested the land by proprietary right in the individual, provided that he founded a colony after prescribed rules. The second plan granted the land to a company of individuals, and reserved to them certain rights as citizens and colonists. The first method allowed the proprietor to settle a town by contract, with Spanish colonists, and to provide it with a town council (ayuntamiento) composed of alcaldes and regidores; and required the proprietor, as a guarantee of the grant, to establish within a given time stated in the contract, thirty settlers, each provided with a house, ten breeding cows, four oxen, and additional small stock.[1] The proprietor had to procure a priest for the administration of the sacrament and to provide a well furnished church for divine worship. The priest was at first temporarily appointed by the proprietor; but the king reserved the right to make all subsequent appointments. Should the proprietor fail to comply with all the requirements of the law as manifest in his bond, the improvements already made were to revert to the king, and the proprietor was to be subjected to an additional fine of one thousand *pesos* of gold; on the other hand, should he succeed in founding the colony according to agreement, he was then entitled to four square leagues of land.

By the second method it was provided that ten, or more, married citizens might form a settlement, with the customary pueblo grant of four leagues of land. They were accorded the common municipal rights, and granted the privilege of electing annually alcaldes of the ordinary jurisdiction, and a common council.[2] This guaranteed to the settlers certain democratic rights, and represents in this respect the type of the true Spanish pueblo. More laws were added to these from time to time, the Spanish sovereigns always giving explicit instructions concerning the minutest details of procedure.

[1] *Recopilacion*, libro IV, titulo V, ley. 6.
[2] *Recopilacion*, libro IV, titulo V, ley. 10.

Even so small a matter as sending irons for branding cattle had to receive the royal sanction.

The laws for the colonization of California, though based on the laws above referred to, were set forth in regulations proclaimed by Philip de Neve, governor of provincial California in 1779; but did not receive the royal approval until 1781. The first settlement in Alta California had been made ten years prior to this proclamation, and several missions and presidios had been founded in the intervening time. These regulations mark the beginning of a new enterprise, that of an attempt to settle the province with Spanish people (*gente de razon*). They represent but little that is new in the law; but are rather a development and explanation of the laws of the Indies. The regulations relate to all departments of the government of the province, but title fourteen treats especially of political government and colonization. The instructions are set forth clearly and in detail, embracing the methods to be employed in founding colonies, and the rules to govern the colonists.[1] In the introduction, the governor stated that it was desirable to found colonies in California in order " to fulfil the pious intentions of the king," and to secure to his majesty " the dominion of the extensive country which occupies a space of more than two hundred leagues, comprehending the new establishments, the presidios, and the respective ports of San Diego, Monterey, and San Francisco." Another reason of prime importance was urged; that towns should be established in the interest of the state in order that the people might encourage agriculture, cattle breeding, and other branches of industry, to such an extent that in a few years the produce of the colonies would be sufficient to supply the garrisons of the presidios. San José had already been founded with this

---

[1] Halleck's *Report*, Ex. Doc. 17; 31st Con., 1st Sess., 134–9; Hall's *History of San José*, 450 *et seq;* Dwinelle's *Colonial History of San Francisco;* Bancroft, *Cal.*, I, 333; *Archives of Cal.*, 732, 762, 746.

idea in view, and another pueblo was contemplated, to be peopled with settlers (*pobladores*) from Sinaloa and Sonora.

In this way it was hoped to obviate the great risks and losses which the royal government might suffer in the transportation of supplies so great a distance. Still another consideration must not be overlooked ; namely, the new colonies would supply recruits for the presidio garrisons, and at the same time prove a means of defence to the entire country. The law provided that each *poblador*, to whom house lots or lands were granted, should be obliged to hold himself " equipped with two horses and a complete saddle, musket, and other arms " for the defence of his particular district, subject to the call of the government.[1] It would not be difficult to trace, in this grant of land on consideration that the receiver hold himself in readiness to defend the king's territory, something analogous to the old feudal régime.

Prior to the regulations of Neve, each settler was entitled to receive annually one hundred and twenty dollars, with food for the first two years after enlisting as a colonist, and provisions alone for the three following years. At the end of five years he might be put in full possession of the land, provided that all of the conditions had been fulfilled. By the new regulations this law was changed so as to give to each settler one hundred and sixteen dollars and seventeen and a half cents for each of the first two years, and sixty dollars per annum for each of the remaining three years. The colonists were to enter upon their possessions at once, their salaries, stipends, and rations beginning with the enlistment.[2] But these provisions were simply a part of the inducements offered to settlers by the Spanish government. Each settler was entitled to receive a house-lot, a tract of land for cultivation, another for pasture, and a loan of sufficient stock and implements to make a comfortable beginning. In addition to these, he received two mares, two cows and one calf, two sheep, and two goats

---

[1] *Regulations of de Neve*, XIV, 16.   [2] Neve, XIV, 3.

(all breeding animals); two horses, one cargo mule, and one yoke of oxen or steers; one plow point, one spade (of wood with steel point), one axe, one sickle, one wooden knife, one musket, and one leather shield. In addition to these, there were given, for breeding purposes, the males of the different kinds of animals and females of certain kinds were distributed to the settlers. These were granted to the community at large, and were therefore town property. The town also had one forge, one anvil, six crow-bars, six iron spades, the tools necessary for carpenter and cast work, and other necessary tools and utensils.

The implements and stock granted to the settlers were to be repaid within five years, in horses and mules, " fit to be given and received." But the surplus produce of the colonists was to be purchased by the government for the use of the presidios ; and a certain part of this return was to be set aside each year for the payment of the loans.[1] All of the above regulations were approved by his majesty the king, according to the laws of the Indies.

In the process of founding the town and laying out the land, the instructions were not less explicit. By an ancient law, a pueblo grant was four square leagues of land, laid out in the form of a square or an oblong, according to the conditions of the country.[2] The first point to be chosen was the plaza, which in an inland town had to be laid out in a rectangular form at the centre of the town, or in case the town was on a river or bay, it was to be located on the water front.[3] Having located the plaza, the surveyors proceeded to lay out the town, dividing it into blocks and lots.[4] At the center of the plaza was located the pueblo courthouse (juzgado), sometimes with a jail attached ; and facing the plaza were the public buildings, the council house, the church, the store rooms, and others ; while the remaining frontage was occu-

---

[1] Neve, XIV, 15.   [2] *Recopilacion*, II, 19.
[3] *Recopilacion*, V, IV, 6.   [4] Bancroft, *Central America*, I, 496.

pied by dwelling-houses.[1] There are traces of these old plazas
yet remaining in some of the towns of California, although
the majority have been used for public parks or for the location of public buildings. After the location of public buildings, the land composing the remainder of the proposed towns
was divided into building lots, and granted to the founders
(*pobladores*). The Spanish law provided that each settler
should receive a building lot thirty *varas* square, separated
by streets of ten *varas* in width between each block of two
lots.[2] However, there were variations in the size of the house
lots. The lots of Los Angeles were twenty by forty *varas*;
and by the Mexican ordinance of 1828 for the colonization of
the territories of the Republic, each lot was to be one hundred
varas square.[3]

Thus the town proper was laid out for the erection of
dwellings, and for religious and political purposes. But in
considering the Spanish pueblo, it must be remembered that it
included a large area, ten thousand varas square, of which the
collection of houses represents but a small part. In this
respect it resembled a New England town; as it included not
only village lots, but small farms of tillable soil, the commons,
common pasture, and common woodland.[4] Consequently there
were, in addition to the town lots, five classes of land to be
considered in the formation of a town, as follows: First,
there was a certain strip of land, called *ejidos*, lying on one
side of the town, or else surrounding it entirely, which must
be reserved for the convenience and common benefit of the
colonists, and where they might pasture a few milch cows or
tether a horse.[5] In its use it bore a close resemblance to the
commons of the New England town. The *ejidos* belonged to

---

[1] See Figure 1, B.

[2] A *vara* is a Spanish yard of 33⅓ inches, and is still used as a measure in
selling city lots in California towns.

[3] Halleck, Sec. 15, 142.   [4] See Fig. 1, A.

[5] *Recopilacion*, IV, VII, 7, 13, 14.

CHURCH OF THE ANGELS, LOS ANGELES.

Fig. 1.—An Ideal Pueblo after the Laws of the Indies.

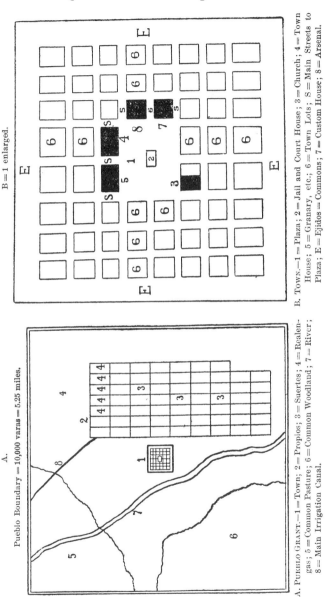

A.

Pueblo Boundary = 10,000 varas = 5.25 miles.

B = 1 enlarged.

10,000 varas = 3 leagues = 5.25 miles.

A. Pueblo Grant.—1 = Town; 2 = Propios; 3 = Suertes; 4 = Realengas; 5 = Common Pasture; 6 = Common Woodland; 7 = River; 8 = Main Irrigation Canal.

B. Town.—1 = Plaza; 2 = Jail and Court House; 3 = Church; 4 = Town House; 5 = Granary, etc.; 6 = Town Lots; S = Main Streets to Plaza; E = Ejidos = Commons; 7 = Custom House; 8 = Arsenal.

the town, and could not be alienated from it except by royal order permitting its occupation by new settlers.[1] It seems that this was one method employed to allow the town to expand after all of the lots of the original survey had been taken. Although the laws are explicit in guaranteeing to each pueblo *ejidos* assigned out of the public domain, there seem to have been differences of opinion and of usage at different periods concerning their disposal.[2]

It was held by Gutierrez that the *ejidos* must be maintained as vacant suburbs for pasturage of cows and horses, and for ventilation, walks and alleys; but that they could be sold, if necessary, by the town for building lots.[3] Dwinelle and Hall each assert that the Spanish law resembles that of the ancient Hebrews in regard to the " field of the suburbs," which says : " But the field of the suburbs (or pasture lands) of their cities may not be sold for it is their perpetual possession."[4] The situations of the Hebrew commonwealth and the Spanish monarchy were so widely different that little is to be gained by the comparison, although there is a striking resemblance in the law and the usage in both countries. The king of Spain being absolute proprietor of the land, in theory and in practice, all grants of public lands to towns gave to those towns the full right and title to the lands, which the king could not revoke, although he might usurp these rights. Nevertheless, the grant to a town was not equivalent to a grant in fee simple ; but was rather a guarantee of perpetual use. The grants to settlers were of similar nature; and consequently, when the king granted the occupation of the lands to settlers, it was a transfer of use only ; and the king could maintain a right to allow the occupation of these towns by his own decree, although the

[1] Ibid., 13.

[2] Dwinelle holds that the term "*ejidos*," used in a general sense, meant all of the common lands attached to a town, but that it also had a particular meaning of "commons," as described above. Gutierrez gives the same explanation. Dwinelle, 32, 337.

[3] Dwinelle, 52.   [4] Dwinelle, 11 ; Hall, 52 ; *Leviticus,* XXV, 34.

town could not.   Under Mexican rule, Gutierrez assigns the
right of transferring land, formerly held by the king, to the
town council.

Within the pueblo, and some distance from the village,
were located the arable lands or *suertes*, which were granted to
the settler for the purposes of agriculture.   These grants were
provided for in the laws of the Indies to which the regulations
of Neve apply more specifically.   After the reservations of
the land for town lots and for the suburbs were made, all of
the remaining land was divided into two classes; the irrigable
and the non-irrigable.   One-fourth of the lands having been
reserved for new settlers, and another portion for the town, the
remainder was divided among the first founders.   If there
were sufficient lands to allow it, each poblador received two
suertes of irrigable land and two of non-irrigable; the latter
suitable for pasture or crops without irrigation.   As each
suerte consisted of a lot two hundred *varas* square, every
settler received, under favorable circumstances, about twenty-
eight acres of tillable land besides his own lot.   All citizens
were treated alike in the distribution of lands.   In this respect
the Spanish colony differed from the Roman, in which land
was allotted according to the rank of officers and civilians.

The conditions attached to the grants indicate the strong
hold the king retained on the lands.   By the laws of the
Indies, colonists were forbidden to sell or otherwise alienate
their lands until after the fourth year of their occupation.[1]
But this law must have been changed; for we find the regulations of 1791 forbidding, under any conditions, the disposal of
land by sale.   The houses and lands were to remain forever as a
perpetual inheritance to the sons and daughters of the colonists,
with the exception that the daughters should receive no land
unless married to useful colonists who had received no grant.
Although the lands were to be kept " indivisible and inalien-
able forever," the owner of the *suerte* might, if he chose, will

---

[1] *Recopilacion*, IV, XII, 1.

it to one son, provided he were a layman. Another precautionary measure asserted that the colonists and their successors could not impose upon the house or parcel of land allotted them, "either tax, entail, reversion, mortgage (*centa, vincula, fianza, hipotica*) or any other burden, although it be for pious purposes." The penalty for failing to comply with this law was the entire forfeiture of the property in question. This law, in part, survived the revolution; for we find, in the decree of 1824, that lands shall not be transferred in mortmain.[1]

Among other conditions of grants worthy of notice is that within five years after his first occupation each settler was to possess two yoke of oxen, two plows, two points, two hoes, and other instruments for tilling the soil; and by the end of three years he must have a house entirely finished, and "supplied with six hens and a cock."

The colonists were forbidden to kill any cattle granted them, or their increase, within the first five years; but sheep and goats might be disposed of at the age of four years. The penalty for the breach of this law was the forfeiture of the amount of a year's rations.[2] The colonists were exempt from the payment of all tithes and every other tax on the products of the lands and cattle given them, provided that, within one year from the date of settlement, they built a house to live in, constructed a dam for irrigation, and set out fruit or other trees on the boundaries of their possessions. But the community had to complete, during the third year, a store-house to keep the produce of the public sowing, and within the fourth year suitable government buildings. Also from the third to the fifth of one almud (one-twelfth of a fanega, or one peck) of corn must be given by each poblador for the sowing of the public lands; and these lands must be tilled and the grain harvested and stored by the labor of the settlers. These were forms of municipal taxation, and the harvested grain was stored as

---

[1] Halleck's *Report*, 140; Rockwell, 451; Schmidt, 341.
[2] Neve, Sec. 12.

public revenue. But after the expiration of said term of five years, the new pobladores and their descendants were to pay, in the acknowledgment of the direct and supreme dominion which belongs to the sovereign, one-half of a fanega[1] of Indian corn for each *suerte* of cultivable land.

The colonists of the civil establishments of California formed in no respect a community where goods and property were held in common; but there are to be noticed in the founding of the towns several characteristics which are marks of the old village community. Within the four square leagues of land included in the pueblo grant, there were reserved from sale and permanent occupation a common pasture land and a common woodland, which were secured to the settlers by law. The pasture land was necessarily limited; but as it was established by law that each pueblo should be located at least five leagues from every other village or settlement, there was sufficient room for the pasturage of the large herds outside of the pueblo limits.[2] These lands outside belonged to the king; but they could be used by the inhabitants of the town; in fact, the great pasture fields (*dehisas*) were guaranteed to each town.[3] Over these the large herds belonging to the inhabitants of the town usually roamed without any special limits of territory, except that of convenience. Other property, set apart for the common good of the community, was the royal lands (*realengas*); these were devoted to the raising of revenue for the support of the town government. Portions of these were set apart and assigned to the care of the town council; and were consequently called "*propios*," or the estates of a city corporation. These lands were to be leased to the highest bidder, for a term not exceeding five years; and the proceeds of the rental were used, in lieu of taxes, to defray the city expenses.[4] The "*ayuntamientos*" had full control of these lands, fixed the minimum price of rent, and conducted the rental. Not all of the expenses of the

---

[1] One bushel; a fanega being about two bushels.
[2] *Recopilacion*, VII, IV, 14.   [3] *Ibid.*   [4] Dwinelle, 8, 51.

town government were met in this way, but enough of them to relieve taxpayers.

The fact that a government, having sole right and title to the land, founded a town in a new country, and reserved a part of the public domain to defray the expenses of city government, thus lessening taxes, appeals to our sense of justice, and is a subject for the consideration of the modern political economist.[1] Since it would not be well to free a people entirely from taxation, the above method is a legitimate and rational way of lightening the enormous burdens of taxation that fall upon the people of large cities. Many cities have surrendered lands when they should have held them for future use; and were consequently obliged to purchase at great expense that which should have been reserved by right.

Another very important grant of land was termed a sitio (site); which, in its primary legal sense, meant the individual grant of a square league of land. It obtained a general signification as applied to all of those grants of land made to individuals outside of the pueblo for the purpose of rearing cattle. It was through this process of obtaining land that the extensive Spanish grants in California originated. The sitio gradually increased in size, until under Mexican rule the law fixed the maximum grant that might be made to a single person at eleven square leagues of land, or about seventy-one and one-half square miles, or nearly two legal townships. The regulation of 1834 provided that no person should be allowed to receive a grant of more than one square league of irrigable land, four superficial ones dependent upon the seasons, and six superficial ones for the purpose of rearing cattle.[2] In 1828 the maximum amount of grants to a single individual, of irrigable land, was two hundred *varas* square; of land dependent upon the seasons, eight hundred *varas* square; and

---

[1] There is a parallel to this law in the Hebrew custom of reserving certain lands for them that serve the city. *Ezekiel*, 48, 18.

[2] Halleck's *Report*, 139.

for breeding cattle, twelve hundred *varas* square.[1] The legal
titles to these Spanish grants have been the source of a great
deal of legislation in the California courts.

Having thus outlined the method of colonization as established by law, it remains to give a brief description of the few

Fig. 2.

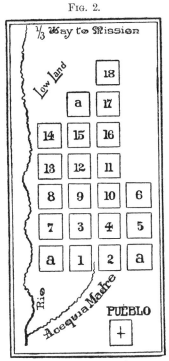

MAP OF SAN JOSÉ.
Bancroft, *California*, I, 350.
a, a, a, = Realengas.   1, 2, 3, etc. = Suertes.

examples in history of the application of these laws in California.   Like all laws, and especially like all Spanish laws of
the period, we shall find that they were far more exact in

---

[1] Hall, 142.

theory than in practice. Philip de Neve was governor of
Lower California, with a nominal supervision of Upper California prior to the year 1775, when a royal order directed him
to take up his residence at Monterey as governor of the
province, and required Rivera, then at Monterey, to return to
Loreto to act as lieutenant-governor.[1] The order was repeated
the following year, and the change was directed to be made at
once. Philip de Neve believed in making permanent settlements of Spanish people (gente de razon) in the province, as
the only means of successfully holding the territory against
the encroachments of foreign nations. He also had the courage
to undertake measures for the encouragement of agriculture,
commerce and other industries, trusting to receive royal sanction for his actions. Having resolved to form a pueblo, he
proceeded to establish San José according to law, and then
reported to the Viceroy what had been done. The matter
was communicated in form to the king and received his royal
sanction.[2] In his communication to the Viceroy in 1776,
before leaving Loreto, Neve had recommended the sowing of
certain fertile lands for the purpose of increasing government
supplies.[3] After taking a survey of Alta California, he concluded that his object could only be obtained by founding two
pueblos, one at Los Angeles and one at San José. He therefore asked the authorities for laborers and necessary supplies
for this purpose; but without waiting for a reply, he took
nine soldiers who knew something about farming, and from
the presidio of Monterey five other settlers; and with these,
proceeding to the Gaudalupe river, he made an informal
settlement of San José in 1777. Five years afterward, Don
Pedro Fages, then governor of California, ordered Don José
Moraga, lieutenant-commander of San Francisco, to go to San

---

[1] Bancroft, *California*, I, 307.

[2] The informal settlement was made in 1777, but the royal sanction of the
foundation was not received until 1781.

[3] Bancroft, *California*, I, 311.

MISSION ST. JOSEPH.

José, and in accordance with the royal regulations to give in the name of the king full possession of the lands to the nine pobladores, residents of San José.[1] It would seem from this, and the method pursued in the founding of Los Angeles, that it was customary to consider the contract with the settlers formally closed after five years of occupancy, and the settlers then went into full possession of their rights. At least, it is so provided in the laws of the Indies.

The commissioner placed each settler in formal and legal possession of the soil, and located all of the public lands according to his best judgment, always complying with the regulations of Neve.[2] The commissioner chose two witnesses and proceeding with the nine settlers to the land, in the presence of all he located each man's grant. Each title was signed by the two witnesses and the one to whom the land was granted, and then forwarded to the governor to sign.[3] A copy of the deed was held by the settler, and it was properly recorded in the register of the city council or " book of colonization." Each colonist received one house lot (*solar*), and four *suertes* for cultivation. Soon after the site for the town had been selected and the land surveyed, houses were constructed for the colonists. They were at first very rude, being constructed of palisades or posts driven in the ground, plastered with clay, and roofed with poles and earth or with tiles. The rude structures were not greatly improved for many years ; but finally they gave way to more substantial dwellings of adobe. It is difficult to realize, as one walks the streets of the magnificent modern town of San José, that its first foundation was represented by a few inferior mud-bedaubed cabins. After the construction of the houses for shelter, a dam was thrown across the river,

---

[1] Hall, 25.

[2] The settlement of a colony by a commissioner resembles the Roman method of sending out the colony in charge of the *agrimensor* or of three magistrates. Livy, XXXII, 29.

[3] Hall, 26.

and ditches were constructed for irrigation. The town was situated on an eminence by the river; and near it were laid out the *ejidos,* fifteen hundred varas long and seven hundred varas wide. On the other side of the river, a tract nineteen hundred and fifty-eight varas long was measured for *realengas* and *propios.*

The growth of San José was very slow; and for many years the town consisted of a few scattered houses of settlers, who barely obtained a meagre living with the help of the lands and supplies generously granted them by the government. The town was first located about a mile and a quarter north of the old market street plaza on which the City Hall now stands. The old town was located on the Alviso road, or First street, where it crosses the first bridge on the outskirts of the present town.[1] As the Santa Clara Mission was located at that time somewhat east from the present situation of the old mission church, which now stands within the precincts of the Santa Clara College, the pueblo and the mission were not far apart; and the latter was very nearly west of the former. The proximity of the mission to the town gave rise to much contention, and the governor concluded that the respective properties of the two settlements were too near each other. Another more potent reason for the change of site was that the town-site was located on low ground, and consequently was subject to frequent floods. In the winter of 1778–9, water stood nearly three feet deep in the houses of the Santa Clara Mission, and in the new pueblo.[2] Direct communication was cut off between the mission and the pueblo, and a circuitous path of three leagues was the only safe route between the two places. The Indians, being better acquainted with the ground than the settlers, took the opportunity to commit depredations. To be relieved from the evil effects of a life on this low, marshy ground, the colonists petitioned the governor to remove the pueblo farther south

---

[1] Hall, *History of San José,* 46.   [2] Hall, *San José,* 46.

to higher grounds.   After the manner of Spanish administration, the governor forwarded the petition to the Comandante-General of the Intendencia at Arispe, Sonora.   So grave a matter had to receive due consideration, and the Comandante-General referred the case to the king's attorney, who, it seems, gave advice for the removal.   Consequently, nearly two years after the petition was first presented, the Comandante-General transmitted to the Governor a decree authorizing the settlers to remove to the "adjacent *loma*, (little hill) selected by them, as more useful and advantageous, without changing or altering for this reason, the limits and boundaries of the territory or district assigned to said settlement, and to the neighboring Mission of Santa Clara, as there is no just cause why the latter should attempt to appropriate to herself that land."[1]   The new site was within the limits of the pueblo lands, on higher ground, and in better communication with the mission.   The change was not made, however, at that time; and we find that the subject was under discussion again in 1797, and it is supposed that the pueblo was removed to its present situation during that year.   After the removal, there sprang up between the missionaries and the colonists a great controversy, pertaining to the ownership of a tract of land, lying between the property now known as the "Cook place" on the northwest, and the Guadalupe river on the southeast.   Both parties claimed the territory, and after a long controversy and investigation, the Guadalupe was fixed as the boundary between the pueblo and the mission.

The extent of the pueblo lands of San José was greater by far than the law allowed; greatly exceeding four square leagues, as fixed by the law of the Indies, and confirmed by subsequent decrees.   It seems that the boundaries of the public lands or *ejidos* belonging to the city, as well as those known as *realengas*, were never definitely fixed; or, if definitely fixed, the land-marks were lost.   Consequently we find that the citi-

[1] Quoted by Hall, *San José*, 47, 48.

12

zens of the pueblo continued to use a wide extent of land beyond
the confines of the town, occupying or renting it for cultivation or pasturage, until the land used and claimed by the
pueblo covered not less than twenty-five square leagues.[1]
Without doubt, many lots were temporarily occupied for
cultivation, without any title to the land.   Permission was
given to use lands for pasturage, a small rent being collected;
and there were some special grants outside of the regular
pueblo limits.   In 1837, a survey of the pueblo was made by
commissioners appointed by the ayuntamiento (town council),
by the direction and consent of the governor.   The commission proceeded upon the basis of the ancient pueblo; but
acknowledged that only the northwest by west line had monuments upon it.   Consequently, it was concluded by the commission that it remained to be shown how much land should
be allowed to *sitios*, and how much set apart for *ejidos* and
proprios (reservations); in other words, that the size of the
pueblo should conform to the needs and prosperity of the
community.   It was further urged that they ought "to carefully guard against any want of accommodation or conveniences
for the raising of cattle, which had become important to trade
and the subsistence of families."[2]   The plan was to observe
the ancient boundaries as far as they could be discovered, and
to expand the town according to the needs of the people living
in the town.   It was further decided that private lands within
the boundaries of the town must pay a tax for the support of
the town.   The holders of land within the prescribed area
would continue to hold the land until the government should
decide respecting private rights.   The survey included a tract
of land, with an east and west line measuring about eleven
and one-half leagues, and with a north and south line of about

---

[1] The Mexican league was the same as the old Spanish league of 5000
varas of about 33½ inches each. This would make the area of the pueblo
lands about 171 sq. mi. in English measure.

[2] Hall, 129.

two and one-fifth leagues. The area of the pueblo was at least twenty-five square leagues.

The report of the commission was recommended by the ayuntamiento, but the government failed to act upon it. However, it became the basis of the United States survey of the San José Pueblo lands, made in 1866 by George H. Thompson. In 1847, there was a considerable immigration of Americans to San José, which made it necessary to reduce the chaotic town into some systematic order with carefully defined limits. There were no roads or streets laid out by any method, but only crooked cow-paths, wandering from one house to another of the straggling village. A survey was made of the town and all streets and village lots were located. In the following year a re-survey was made, and the St. James and the Washington squares were located. Subsequent surveys were made, and the city boundaries were enlarged from time to time. In 1851, the United States passed an act confirming to all towns in existence prior to 1846, the rights to the lands within the boundaries of the pueblo surveys. This led to other surveys and to a long litigation between the city and the land companies, the history of which will not be given here. It is sufficient to say that the city of San José, after many decisions and reversals, finally obtained the right and title to the lands in dispute.

The social development of San José was of necessity slow. For many years the inhabitants went on Sunday to the mission, about three miles distant, to worship and to say mass. Worship was well practiced by the people, although they were obliged to go a long way to attend church. In 1803, for the sake of convenience, a church was built at San José. The church was dedicated on the twelfth of July, near the present site of the Catholic Cathedral. This chapel remained until 1835. It was of very simple construction, being made of adobe and roofed with tiles. A council house (juzgado) was built in 1798. It also was of simple structure, and remained until 1850, in which year it was torn down. Schools were established as early as the year 1811, and subsequently some progress in learning was made.   There are many interesting things in connection with the early history of San José, of the Santa Clara Mission, and of the San José Mission founded at a later date; but for the present they will be passed by.   The earliest settlements in Los Angeles county were the missions of San Gabriel and San Juan Capistrano; the former founded in 1771, and the latter in 1776.   These missions soon became flourishing settlements of the native population.   Their flocks and herds soon covered nearly the entire county.   In 1797, another mission, San Fernando, was added to the list.   In 1802, the three missions had gathered within their walls 2674 converts; and in 1831, the number was over four thousand. By the labors of the Indians, superintended by the missionaries, large tracts of land were reduced to a state of cultivation. Orchards and vineyards were planted; wheat, barley, and corn were cultivated to a considerable extent.   This was the early pioneer work of the county.   The construction of buildings, the breaking of a virgin soil, the cultivation of the cereals and fruits, the rearing of large herds of domestic animals, and the domestication and instruction of barbarous Indian tribes, are the first results of the early civilization in California.

The town of Los Angeles was founded in 1781, according to the instructions of Philip de Neve.   In general, the instructions followed the principal regulations set forth in 1777, and sanctioned by the king in 1781; but in a few particulars the details of founding a pueblo are set forth more clearly than in the general law.   The town was located with regard to the facilities offered for irrigation of the sowing lands (suertes).   After the sites for the dam and the irrigation ditch had been selected, the location of the town was fixed on higher ground, about two hundred varas distant from the dam.   The plaza of the pueblo, measuring about two hundred by three hundred feet, was laid out with its corners toward the cardinal points of the compass, and three streets running perpendicu-

San Gabriel Mission, 1885. Founded 1770.

larly from each of the four sides.[1] The dimensions of the solares, or house lots were twenty by thirty varas, and these solares were to be equal in number to the available *suertes*

FIG. 3.

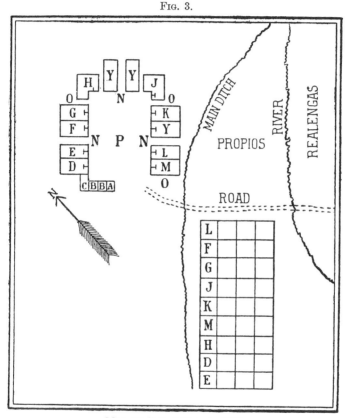

MAP OF LOS ANGELES, 1786.
Bancroft, *California*, I, 348.

A = Guard House.　　　　　C = Trozo del posito.
B = Town Houses.　　　　　D, E, F, etc. = Town Lots (solares).
L, F, G, H, etc. = Suertes.

The map of the pueblo (P) is a scale five times greater than that of the fields (L, F, G, etc.).

---

[1] Bancroft, *California*, I., 345; the dimensions of the plaza are usually given as 100 x 75 varas, cf. Bancroft, who gives 200 x 300 ft.

of irrigable ground.   The east side of the plaza was reserved
for the public buildings.   On the opposite side of the river the
realengas were laid off, extending rather indefinitely.   One of
the remarkable features of the settlement of Los Angeles is
found in the fact that the settlers were all treated alike in the
apportionment of lands, as respects the amount of land; but to
settle the position of lands, they drew lots, in accordance with
an ancient law.[1]   For many years the records of the pueblo of
Los Angeles are very meagre.   Nor is this surprising when
the character of the settlers is considered.   There were enlisted
under contract, "twelve settlers and their families, forty-six
persons in all, whose names are given, and whose blood was a
strange mixture of Indian and negro with here and there a
trace of Spanish."[2]   It is indeed surprising that there could
have been an effective settlement at all, with such diverse
elements.   However, the majority of the colonists went to
work, and soon mud-roofed houses were built, which served
as a protection while they engaged in the construction of the
dam and the irrigating ditch.   By 1784 the temporary dwellings had been replaced by substantial adobe houses, public
buildings had been completed, and the foundation of a church
laid.   Meanwhile there had been some changes in the settlers.
Two of the contracting settlers never entered upon their possessions, five were sent away on account of their idle habits,
and four new ones were admitted.

The formal distribution of lands did not occur until 1786,
five years after the first settlement.   At this time Governor
Fages appointed Alférez José Argüello commissioner, who
proceeded to confer upon the colonists the full right and title
to the lands.   He appointed two witnesses, and "summoned
each of the nine settlers in succession, and in the presence of
all granted, first the house lots, and then the four fields, and
finally the branding-iron by which his stock was to be distinguished from that of his neighbors."[3]   A separate document

[1] *Recopilacion*, IV, vii, 7, 13, 14.
[2] *California*, I, 345.   [3] Bancroft, *California*, I, 347.

was drawn for each grant (twenty-seven documents in all); and the nature of the grant and the conditions under which the pobladores received it were fully explained. Each colonist signed his name to his document by means of a cross, as not one could write his own name. The measurement of lands was not very specific, and the boundaries of the public lands were not definitely fixed. Definite boundaries were not necessary then, for land was plentiful; but carelessness in this respect led to much subsequent trouble here and elsewhere. The town was founded under circumstances very favorable, with the exception of the character of the colonists, who, even though industrious enough, might not be the best material for the settlement of an important municipality. The pueblo continued to grow slowly, until, in the year 1800 nineteen years after its foundation, its inhabitants numbered three hundred and fifteen persons. In 1836, the number of inhabitants increased to 2228, including 553 domesticated Indians. But this latter number included all of the inhabitants over whom the pueblo government had jurisdiction, or those of the entire county of Los Angeles.

Gradually there came to live in Los Angeles a better class of inhabitants, chiefly of old Castilian blood, who gave way to the later emigration of Americans from the Atlantic states. The town assumed some importance in early times on account of its connection with the trade with New Mexico. There were many large ranches in the vicinity of the town, and the whole valley was in a fair state of cultivation; orchards and vineyards abounding. These and other considerations made the pueblo a place of much wealth and of considerable importance. But its recent marvelous development far exceeds the most favorable promises of the early period of Spanish occupation.

Notwithstanding the liberality and care exercised by the Spanish government in the foundation of colonies, they were not prosperous. They continued an insignificant existence for a period of nearly twenty years after their establishment.

The explorations of the French, English, and Americans on the Pacific coast awakened renewed interest in the question of peopling California with Spanish colonists. The sudden agitation of this subject resulted in a determination to create a new settlement on an approved plan, and finally led to the founding of the villa of Branciforte on the site of the present city of Santa Cruz. It was at first decided that the new villa should be located near San Francisco; but as this spot was described as a bleak, sandy place, without wood or water, and with a creek whose bed was so low that it would not admit of irrigation, the proposed site was abandoned. After exploring the coast from San Francisco to Santa Cruz, it was finally decided to locate the villa at the latter place.[1] Palou, during his first trip to Santa Cruz had stated that " this place is not only fit for a town, but for a city, without wanting any of the things necessary." He thought that the town could be put a quarter of a league from the sea, and have all the advantages of good land, good water, pasturage, timber, and nearness to Monterey. The plan of the town of Branciforte partook somewhat of the nature of a presidial pueblo, although the cultivation of the soil and the practice of industries were associated with the defense of the country. It was to be situated on the coast, and resembled in design the old Roman military town constructed for the defense of the frontier; but, in real existence, Branciforte was but a third-rate pueblo. An attempt was made to form a town of a higher class than those already established; consequently the governor requested the Viceroy to send robust country people from temperate or cold climates to engage in farming, together with artisans, smiths, carpenters, stonecutters, masons, tailors, tanners, shoemakers, tile-makers, and sailors.[2] The inducements held out to the settlers were very favorable. Each civilian was to receive one hundred

---

[1] There was much prejudice against San Francisco at this time. It was said to be the " worst place on the coast for a town."

[2] Bancroft, *California*, I, 568.

and sixteen dollars annually for two years, and sixty-six dollars annually for the remaining three years, besides a house, live stock, and farming implements. Each soldier was to receive a house, a year's pay, and a supply of live stock and farming implements. A peculiar feature of the laws for the settlement of Branciforte was the order to grant every alternate house lot to an Indian chief, who, living among citizens, officers, and soldiers, would thus become accustomed to civilized life, and lead his tribe to adopt the laws and customs of *gente de razon.* This is evidence that the original plan of the Spaniards to unite the two races in the possession of the soil had not yet been abandoned. The greatest difficulty in the way, in this particular instance, was that there were no Indian chiefs in that locality.

The first colonists were to come from the surplus populations of San José and Los Angeles, and subsequently the artisans and soldiers were to arrive. The rules made for the government of the colonists were very fine indeed. They were enjoined to live in harmony, to refrain from drunkenness, gambling, and concubinage.[1] The penalty for neglect to attend mass on holidays was three hours in the stocks; prayer with the rosary must close the day's labor; the annual communion and confessional must be attended, and certificates must be forwarded to the governor that these requirements had been met.

Branciforte was founded in 1797, but the Franciscan fathers had preceded the colonists by six years, and had founded a thriving mission on the bank of the San Lorenzo. It was on the 25th day of September, 1791, that Fathers Salazar and Lopez pitched their tents upon the present site of Santa Cruz. They brought with them cows, oxen, and horses from Santa Clara, oxen from San Francisco, and mules from El Carmelo. These and other supplies for the missions enabled them to make a beginning of the new settlement. They began at once

---

[1] Bancroft, *California,* I, 569.

the foundations of a new mission, and before the year closed ninety-one Indians had received baptism. In 1794, they completed and dedicated a church, constructed of stone and adobe. Success attended their zeal and untiring energy in the conversion of natives. Nine years after the founding of the mission, the neophytes numbered four hundred and ninety-two; and the production of grain for the year 1800 was four thousand three hundred bushels. The missionaries contended that the new town was encroaching upon the lands of the mission; and consequently, as the new settlers were not desirable neighbors, they petitioned to have the town removed. But no action was taken respecting the petition, except that the governor expressed the thought that the town would do no harm, as there was room enough for all.

The new town was not very prosperous, and the settlers were of no great credit to the country. They came, for the most part, from the region of Guadalajara, and were considered an undesirable class. Judging from the instructions of the governor, and the regulations of the pueblo, they were not a very good class, and deserved all of the admonitions of the authorities to care for property, to avoid drunkenness and crime, to observe religious duties, and to live sober and industrious lives.[1] The first settlers, though mostly Spaniards, were of an inferior class, whose numbers were increased from time to time by invalids and discharged soldiers. But here, as elsewhere in California, the character of immigrants improved until the settlements were represented by some of the first families of Spain and Mexico.

It would seem that these liberal inducements and fair prospects should have brought an industrious and thrifty class of settlers to found a thriving town; but, with all of this, the villa was a failure; and the colonists, if not a criminal class, were at least a worthless class. The commandante Guerra, writing to Arrillaga, said that "to take a charitable view of the sub-

---

[1] Bancroft, I, 571.

ject, their absence ' for a couple of centuries, at a distance of a million leagues,' would prove most beneficial to the province, and redound to the service of God and the king." [1]

There were many causes that brought about the failure of the civil colonies in California; but none greater than the character of the majority of the colonists. The class of thrifty pioneers seeking homes, so notable in the English colonies of the Atlantic coast, was wanting. Spain had a minimum of this class, and they were needed at home. On the other hand, the policy of shipping criminals to a new country was suicidal to the interests of the colonies and to those of the parent country. The colonies on the Atlantic coast had common cause of complaint on account of the same practice; but they were more fortunate than the Spanish colonies in this respect. The majority of the colonists of New England came to build homes, to accumulate property, to engage in industries, and to establish civil and religious liberty. A great purpose dominated their entire life and controlled every adventure. Without assistance from the government, they wrought out their own destiny by the master-stroke of toil; they were true founders and builders. On the other hand, the Spanish colonists were given lands upon which to build, lands to till, live stock, tools, and rations, and then paid a salary to occupy territory and live a life of ease and laziness. The close proximity to the domesticated Indians, who could be either hired or forced to work, had a tendency to degrade all labor. Nearly all of the labor was done by the neophytes, who were given a certain percentage of the crops for tilling the soil, or were hired from the padres at the missions. There were many other difficulties in the way of success: there was no market for produce, and but little commerce. The general policy of Spain in the treatment of her colonies was detrimental to the best interests of the provinces. The colonies were for use; and though recognized as an integral part of the kingdom, there was a continual

---

[1] Bancroft, *California* II, 155.

process of subordination of the interests of the colonies to the interests of the home government. And all of this was carried on with mistaken notions of advantage. The chief officers controlling the provinces were sent out from Spain by appointment, and they carried with them an abundance of legislation, which always tended to suppress any tendency toward freedom or self-government.[1] The religious orders were first in the field, and always zealous and aggressive. They monopolized the products of Indian toil, appropriated the best lands, and opposed the civic communities. Under these circumstances of constant discouragement, it is little wonder that Spanish colonization was a disappointment and a failure.

The local administration of the provinces was represented by the pueblos, which were the units of local government. The decree of Philip II. provided that the pobladores of the colony should elect their own magistrates ; that is, alcaldes of ordinary jurisdiction, and members of a town council.[2] In accordance with this act, Philip de Neve, with the approval of Carlos III., provided that for the good government of the pueblos, the administration of justice, the direction of public works, the distribution of water privileges, and the execution of the regulations of the governor, they should be furnished with ordinary alcaldes and other municipal officers in proportion to the number of inhabitants. It was provided in this law that the governor should appoint the alcaldes for the first two years, and for each succeeding year the people should elect their own officers. But the regulations of local government in California under Spanish dominion are based upon the provisions of the Spanish Constitution of March 19, 1812, and the decrees of the Cortes in 1812 and 1813.[3] These laws became effective in the departmental and local government of the

---

[1] Merivale, II.   [2] *Recopilacion,* V, III, 12.
[3] Cf. Moses, *Establishment of Municipal Government in San Francisco,* 12 ; Hall, 102.

provinces, but had little authority in California until after the Mexican revolution. It was enacted that every pueblo should be governed by an ayuntamiento, composed of alcaldes, regidores, and syndicos (city attorneys); and that the alcalde should be president of the council, or, if there were more than one alcalde, the first one elected should be president. Every town, of at least one thousand souls, had to establish an ayuntamiento. Each year, in the month of December, the citizens of the pueblo were to meet and choose electors, who should, in the same month, elect the requisite number of officers. The duties of the ayuntamientos were clearly specified. Among other things, they were to care for the comfort and health of the people, provide for raising taxes, for charities, public highways, the encouragement of agriculture, trade, and other industries; in fact, they were to attend to all of the "politico-economic" affairs of the town.[1]

The decrees of the Cortes gave more specific directions for the municipal administration. The ayuntamiento was composed, in its simplest form, of one alcalde, who was mayor and president of the council, and a limited number of councilmen. Section four of the decree of 1812 asserts that "there shall be one alcalde, two regidores, and one *procurador-syndico* (city attorney), in all towns which do not have more than two hundred inhabitants;" in towns having more than two hundred and less than five hundred inhabitants, the number of regidores (councilmen) shall be increased to four; in towns having above five hundred and less than one thousand, there shall be six councilmen; in towns having over one and less than four thousand inhabitants, there shall be two alcaldes, eight councilmen, and one *procurador-syndico*; and in the larger towns, the number of regidores shall be increased to twelve. In the capitals of the provinces there must be at least twelve regidores; and should these towns possess over ten thousand inhabitants,

---

[1] Schubert, *Verfassungs urkunden*, II, 44 *et seq.*

the number of regidores must be sixteen.[1] The official term of an alcalde was one year, the time fixed by Philip II. The term of the city attorney was the same, and that of the councilmen was two years.[2]

The electors chosen by the people to elect the town officers were appointed as follows: Towns having less than one thousand people were entitled to nine electors; those having more than one and less than five thousand were entitled to sixteen; and those having more than five thousand were entitled to twenty-five electors. To avoid confusion which might occur in a large town or in sparsely settled districts, it was decreed, that each parish might constitute an electoral district, and choose the number of electors to which it was entitled according to the population; each parish, unless it contained less than fifty inhabitants was entitled to at least one elector.[3] Small towns, having less than one thousand inhabitants, and in need of town councils, might apply to the Deputation of the Province, which might in turn apply to the governor for permission to establish an ayuntamiento; and all other towns must attach themselves to the nearest ayuntamiento, or to the one to which they previously belonged. Thus the pueblo system formed a complete local government.

The above laws remained in force until repealed in 1850. However, changes were made in regard to the basis of population, and also, in 1837, in regard to the general provincial regulations of towns. This law of 1837 provided that, "the capital of the department, ports with a population of four thousand inhabitants, interior towns of eight thousand inhabitants, towns which had ayuntamientos previous to 1808, and those to whom the right is given by special law, shall be entitled to ayuntamientos or town councils." [4]   The number of town officers was to be

---

[1] Section 3, decree of 1812; Hall, 103.

[2] Moses, 13.   [3] Moses, 12.

[4] Sec. 5, Art, I; *Debates in the Convention of California*, Appendix V, Art. III.

determined by the departmental legislation acting in concert with the governor; but the number of alcaldes, regidores, and sindicos, could not exceed six, twelve, and two respectively.[1]

The chief results of the laws of 1837 were to strengthen the central government, and to detract from the powers of the local government. The province was managed by a governor, a department legislature, prefects, sub-prefects, ayuntamientos, alcaldes, and justices of the peace. The ayuntamientos were responsible to the sub-prefects, the sub-prefects to the prefects, and the latter to the governor; and they had charge of the police, health, comfort, ornament, order, and security of their respective jurisdictions. Their duties were carefully specified. They were to supervise the food and liquor, to insure its good quality, to care for drainage, hospitals, prisons, and the like.

The duties of the alcalde in California were multifarious, although he was of more importance in old Spain, where he was the chief officer of the local government. But in California he was arbiter of disputes, and was in duty bound to settle difficulties, and to prevent, if possible, cases coming into court.[2] His function was judicial, in that he tried cases which were subject to appeal to the royal audiencias. His duty was also administrative, as he executed the decrees of the governor. Sitting at the head of the council, he had to do with the politics and economics of the town; and in addition he combined the function of police judge with those of policeman and constable.[3]

---

[1] Section 5, Art. III.

[2] Cf. *Mining Camps*, Chas. H. Shinn, 83, 104.

[3] *Recopilacion*, V, III, 1, 2.

CHAPTER IX.

To protect settlers against the attacks of Indians, and to secure permanently the country against foreign invasion, it was the policy of Spain to extend a line of forts along the frontiers of remote provinces. These forts were called presidios after the Latin term presidium, meaning a garrisoned town or fortress. As the Latin word has changed into a Romance, so the Roman presidium has become the Spanish presidio. The design of the presidio was the same as that of the Roman presidium; and the method of establishing a line of presidios to protect the frontier was similar to that employed by the Romans in the protection of the empire, and analogous to the lines of castles (hence the name Castile) established by Spain during the conquest, for protection against the Arab-Moors. But the part which Christianity played in the settlement of the territory and in the civilization of the Indians introduces an entirely new element into the colonial system of Spain. The employment of the religious orders in a " spiritual conquest " of the country necessitated the establishment of garrisons for their protection. The conquest of the aborigines of America was complete; for the Spaniard brooked no opposition and tolerated no institutions of the native race, all of which he considered unworthy of preservation. As soon as possible the natives were to be taught the language, religion, laws, and the habits and customs of civilized life. The conquerors recognized no religion but their own, no rights and privileges of local government; but demanded an entire transformation of

192

everything that pertained to the life of the barbarians. Consequently, "spiritual conquest" meant complete subjugation or final extermination. The nations which the Romans conquered were somewhat farther advanced in civilization than the tribes of the New World; but the Roman plan of treating a newly acquired territory differed from the method adopted by the Spaniards. While, in colonization and conquest, Rome held the imperium, great respect was shown for the local institutions of the conquered, where they did not interfere with the central authority. Therefore the religion and the customs of the conquered were frequently allowed to remain until absorbed by the higher civilization which the conquerors introduced.

In respect to the growth of the town around the fortress, the conditions of Spain were analogous to those of Rome. Around the presidio were located the traders, the families of the soldiers, and numerous settlers, who combined to form a community; and this, together with the garrison, formed the military town. These garrisons, located in every province of Spain, were the germs of towns which in later times frequently developed into thriving cities. As the missions were established in the Californias, presidios were located by their sides to guard the missions and to protect the entire interests of the country. From the presidios two soldiers were sent to each mission, to protect the padres against the natives.

The early government of the province of California was of a military character. The governor was the chief executive officer, and his superior was the viceroy of Mexico. The province was divided into military districts with a presidio in each district, over which the commandant of the presidio had jurisdiction. In the management of local affairs, the commandant of the pueblo exercised great authority; even to the extent of appointing the alcaldes for the civic towns, allotting lands to settlers, and enforcing all of the general regulations of local government. But the commandant was always subject to the governor, who was at the head of the

13

military organization.   Of the three powers, the ecclesiastical, the political, and the military, the last had the highest authority in the government of the province.   In the actual development of the country, however, the political and ecclesiastical powers greatly exceeded the military.

The first presidios, like the first missions, were usually temporary structures, but were improved from time to time.   The Spanish law respecting the plans of the presidios was very precise.   It provided for a uniform method of procedure, but the slow movement of Spanish administration permitted one portion of a fortress to decay while another part was being built.[1]   The presidios, as a rule, were composed of barracks for the soldiers, necessary public buildings, and a half-finished or half-decayed castilla, where a few cannon were mounted.   In most instances, the buildings were in a poor state of repair, and the soldiers poorly clothed and poorly equipped.   Duflot de Mofras has given in his terse though graphic style a general description of the presidios.   He says, " All of the presidios were established on the same plan.   Choosing a favorable place, they surrounded it with a ditch twelve feet wide and six feet deep ; the earth of the ditch served as an out-work. The enclosure of a pueblo was formed of a quadrilateral, six hundred feet square.   The rampart, built of brick, was twelve to fifteen feet high by three in thickness ; small bastions flanked the angles.   Its armament consisted of eight bronze cannon ; eight, twelve, and sixteen pounders.

" Although incapable of resisting an attack of ships of war, these fortifications were sufficient to repel the incursions of the Indians.   Not far from the presidios, according to the topography of the land, was an open battery, pompously styled the castle ; within the enclosure of the presidio were the church, the quarters of the officers and soldiers, the houses of the colonists, store-houses, workshops, wells and cisterns.   Outside were grouped some houses, and at a little distance was the

---

[1] Vancouver, II, 318.

king's farm (El rancho del Rey), which furnished pasturage to the horses and beasts of burden of the garrison."[1]

The soldiers who formed the garrisons of New Spain were dressed in a quaint uniform, the description of which brings to mind the age of the decadence of chivalry. Besides their ordinary cloth uniform, they wore a suit of buckskin like a coat of mail, which descended to their feet and was impenetrable to the arrows of the Indians. "They wore the uniform only while in the field, and at the moment of combat, with a double visored helmet; a leathern buckler worn on the left arm served to ward off arrows and thrusts of the lance in single combat. But while they defended themselves with the sabre and the lance, they could use neither their pistols nor their muskets. Their horses, like those of the chivalrous knights of old, were covered with a leathern armor."[2]   In this Quixotic equipment, these brave knights of the cross sallied forth to pursue a few spiritless and unwarlike Indians, who had been stealing from the mission or the pueblos. All of the travelers who visited the coast of California, including Vancouver, Mofras, La Perouse, Dana, and others, speak of the weakness of the coast defences, and of the dress and equipment of the soldiers. But these travelers never fail to speak also of the courtesy and hospitality of the Spaniards. True, the soldiers were usually an idle class, but there was no necessity for severe toil. Here, as elsewhere in California, there was no need of haste, and the inhabitants took their own time for the accomplishment of a set task. What matter if a year, or even two years glided idly by in this land of sunshine and ease, where time records were scarcely kept, and where progress was so slow that change seemed impossible. The erection of buildings, the necessary attention to herds and flocks, and the cultivation of the soil frequently fell to the lot of the soldiers; but they soon learned to employ the neophytes for every ser-

---

[1] Eugene Duflot de Mofras, II, 276.   See figure 4.
[2] Duflot de Mofras, II, 276.

vice except military duty. This duty involved occasional exploring expeditions, bear hunts, the recapture and punishment of run-away neophytes, and the care of the government property. It was necessary to give some attention to the stock on the king's farm, and the soldiers occasionally spent some time in the supervision of this; provided that they could do so without dismounting from the saddle.

The king's farm, referred to above, was a tract of land situated outside of the four-league grant of the presidial pueblos. It was used chiefly for the pasturage of horses and stock belonging to the fort; but it was to be perpetually held as royal land. The *rancho del rey* of Monterey was located at some distance from the fort in the fertile valley of the Salinas, in an easterly direction from the town and presidio. A *rancho del rey* was established at San Diego about 1795, for the purpose of rearing cattle and horses, that soldiers might be relieved from the task of driving them from the north. A king's farm was established in 1777, at San Francisco, and stocked with one hundred and fifteen head of cattle. In 1791, the stock, then numbering twelve hundred, was transferred to Monterey at the request of the padres.[1] Eight years thereafter, the San Francisco rancho was re-established, being located ten or twelve miles south of the presidio. Stock was purchased from the neighboring missions and placed upon it. But this did not prevent a renewal of the old complaint against encroachment; for the friars protested vigorously against it. They claimed that all of the land was needed for the pasturage of the mission herds, and that Governor Borica had acted contrary to the king's wishes in allowing the rancho to be located there. But their protests availed nothing. The viceroy, deciding with the governor, ordered the rancho to be maintained. There is excellent evidence that the fears of the friars were groundless; for fertile grazing land was plentiful. It is a curious fact that

---

[1] Bancroft, *Cal.*, I, 707.

the friars assumed absolute control of all the lands in the province, when in reality they had no legal right to a foot of the soil. They had located the missions in the most fertile valleys of the coast, and had extended their claims as far as their flocks and herds could pasture. The land of one mission, consequently, joined that of the next, and their claims covered a large portion of the most desirable parts of the coast valleys. Having obtained possession and developed power, they were continually at strife with the civil and military authorities. The friars always assumed complete control over everything connected with colonization, and could tolerate no opposition to their opinions and methods. At first they claimed entire control of spiritual affairs, and finally, as they grew stronger, demanded the right of administering the temporalities. The missionaries opposed the free use of the lands for settlements by Spaniards, and watched with jealous care every attempt at encroachment by the civil and military powers. It is true that the Spaniards in the garrisons, in the towns, and on the private ranchos, were not in sympathy with the missionaries in their attempts to civilize the Indians. They thought the missions useful only so far as they assisted in the preparation of the country for the habitation of *gente de razon.* However indolent the Spaniards might be, they considered that they had a superior right to the soil, and so far as legal title was concerned, they were, no doubt, correct. On the other hand, the missionaries magnified their own work and assumed great power. They also zealously defended the supposed rights of the neophytes. To a certain extent this was necessary; but it must be conceded that their policy was narrow in the extreme. To assume that the fairest portion of a conquered territory could be set apart for the maintainance of an inferior race, which, prior to conquest, scarcely held claim to the land by permanent occupation, was not in accordance with the usage of conquering powers. A more liberal policy on the part of the padres would have had a tendency to invite the permanent settlement of a good class of citizens. Whereas, though it was designed that every presidio should develop into a pueblo, very little attention was given by the authorities to carrying out the law on the subject. The presidios remained mere centres of military districts down to the close of the eighteenth century. A few inhabitants had collected around the forts, living for the most part outside of the stockade of the presidios. Each presidio was entitled to four square leagues of land, but little care was taken to locate the land or to give titles to permanent settlers. The first regulations which might be construed as a partial provision for extending the settlements of the presidios were given in 1773, by Bucareli, Viceroy of Mexico, to Don Fernando Rivera y Moncada, the newly appointed commandant of Monterey and San Diego. Bucareli states that, in order to people the country more speedily, he grants " the commandant power to designate common lands, and also to distribute lands in private to such Indians as may most dedicate themselves to agriculture and the breeding of cattle ; for, having property of their own, the love of it will cause them to radicate more firmly." [1] But they must have their residences in the town or mission to which they have been attached. The same privilege was granted to colonists. The lands were to be distributed according to the merit and means of labor of the founders. Those accepting such grants were obliged to live in towns, and all grants had to be in conformity to the laws respecting the establishment of new towns. The commandant was instructed to exercise care that the new settlers should have the requisite number of arms for their own defense and for the purpose of assisting the garrisons of the presidios and missions. It seems that these instructions were somewhat general and could apply equally well to all kinds of pueblos, whether military, civic, or ecclesiastic. The last clause refers especially to mission pueblos, but it may not exclude presidios. It

---

[1] Executive Document No. 17, 1st session, 31st Congress, p. 133.

SAN MIGUEL.

asserts that " when it becomes expedient to change any mission into a pueblo, the commandant will proceed to reduce it to the civil and economical government which, according to the laws, is observed in other pueblos of the kingdom, giving it a name and declaring for its patron the saint under whose auspices and venerable protection, the mission was founded."[1] However comprehensive this regulation might have been, it had little effect on the growth of presidial towns. As no specific laws existed for colonizing and for the regulation of towns at this time, except such as were set forth in the Laws of the Indies, it is presumable that the above law was intended to be provisional for all settlers in every place.

There was another famous law relating to presidial towns, which applied specifically to the town of Pitic, in Sonora, but which is supposed to apply as well to the regulations of Branciforte, San Francisco, Santa Barbara, and San Diego. The general regulations were called " the plan of Pitic," and were ordered by the king to be observed throughout the *commandancia* in the foundation of other towns.[2] Prior to the publication of this plan for the settlement of Pitic, it appears that a mission had been founded at Guaymas for the purpose of converting the Seris Indians. But as the Indians were savage and warlike, they revolted and destroyed the mission. To protect the missions and those Indians still remaining loyal, the presidio located at San Miguel de Orcavitas was removed to Pitic. The union of the mission with the presidio formed a presidial town with civil functions.

In these regulations, it was left for the Governor to decide whether the new settlement should be city, town, or village; and the character of the government of the pueblo had to be determined in accordance with his decision. It was provided that in

---

[1] Regulations of Bucareli, article 15.

[2] For references to these regulations, see Bancroft, *California*, I., 610; Dwinelle, *Colonial History of San Francisco*, 29; *California Archives*, I., 853 *et seq.*

the absence of a town formed by contract, the *pobladores*, or colonists might form such town.   In this as in many other provisions, the laws of the Indies were merely re-written. Thus four leagues of land were guaranteed to each town, (*en quadro ē prolongo*); and it was provided that the town should be more than five leagues from every other town.[1]   There is also the re-assertion of the design of the home government respecting the amalgamation of the two races, in the requirement that the village of Seris Indians should be removed within the suburbs of the town.   They were to be subject to the same jurisdiction and to enjoy the same public and private benefits as other citizens.   The Indians retained the privilege of choosing their own alcalde and regidores.   The object of these apparently beneficent laws was to inspire the natives with a desire for self-government; since, previously, on account of their lack of intelligence and application as well as on account of their indolence, they had no rights.   Thus the Indians were to dwell together, and one race was to learn the art of civil government from the other.   On the other hand, the presidio at San Miguel was to be moved near the settlement for the protection of the same; but it was to be under civil, not military control.   Thus the presidio was transformed into a pueblo.[2]

As soon as there were thirty settlers, it was necessary to form a town-council (ayuntamiento), consisting of two ordinary alcaldes, six councilmen (regidores), and one *mayordomo de proprios*.[3]   The duties of the ayuntamiento thus formed consisted in looking after the economic regulations, the police, and the food supply of the town.   The members of the town council were at first chosen by electors named by the people, and vacancies were filled thereafter by the council itself.   The two

---

[1] *Recopilacion*, IV., 6.

[2] When the first town-council was formed in San Francisco, the pueblo, which had been formerly under military authority, became a town having a civil administration.   Moses, 18.

[3] The mayordomo cared for the public lands and attended to their rental.

SAN MIGUEL CHURCH, SANTA FE. FOUNDED 1550.

alcaldes acting conjointly with the first alcalde, or commissioner, exercised royal jurisdiction ; that is, ordinary civil and criminal jurisdiction in the first instance. The decisions of this court were subject to appeal to the royal supreme court.[1]

The law guaranteed the tract of four square leagues of land, and all the privileges of pastures, woods, water, hunting, stone-quarries, fruit-trees, and others, for the common use and benefit of the Spaniards and Indians residing therein or in its suburbs, the village " de los Seris." The natives and founders were to share equally in all of the common rights of the citizens. Provision was made for the location and distribution of the town lots and the cultivable lands among the citizens, according to their needs. The pasture land (dehisas) and the commons (ejidos) were guaranteed their respective users.[2] It was further provided that eight suertes of irrigable land should be set aside as proprios to be rented, and that the proceeds be devoted to the payment of municipal expenses in lieu of taxes. The care of the proprios, their rental, and their entire administration devolved upon the mayordomo; but the fields had to be sown the first year by the colonists. The suertes were to be two hundred varas wide by four hundred varas long, and the commissioner was to determine the number to be assigned to each settler, provided that no one should have over three suertes. The settlers were to cast lots for the choice of position of building-lots and suertes.[3]

As in the regulations of Philip de Neve, certificates were to be given to each settler, and a register was to be kept for the record of titles. Section eighteen provides that town lots should be distributed and granted in the name of his majesty, the king, to be held perpetually, for ever and for ever, and by right of inheritance for themselves, their children, and their descendants. The grants were made on the express condition

---

[1] Cf. *Recopilacion*, V., iii. laws 1 and 2.

[2] *Recopilacion*, IV., vii., 13, 14; Cf. Chapter VIII.

[3] *Recopilacion*, IV, vii, 11; Plan of Pitic, article 16.

that those receiving them should keep arms and horses, and be ready to defend the country from insults of enemies who might commence hostilities against it, and to march against the enemy whenever ordered. Lands could not be alienated nor hypothecated, nor could the holders subject them to any incumbrance during a term of four years after entering upon their possession. During this period of four years, the colonists must build houses and reside in them with their families. At the end of this period, if all of the legal requirements of the grant had been fulfilled, the land might be sold, provided that no sale be made to any ecclesiastic community, church, or monastery. A very essential law was established respecting irrigation. In every colony founded by Spain on the Pacific Coast, irrigation was almost a necessity for the proper cultivation of the soil. It was therefore essential to regulate the use of a scanty supply of water by the community. By this provision, the water was divided equally among the settlers, and an alcalde was appointed for each main ditch. If a founder failed to irrigate his land at the proper time, then the alcalde in charge might do it for him and at the owner's expense. The clearing and repairing of the main irrigating canal was a public trust, the expense of which was to be met by a tax.

The foregoing laws are derived almost entirely from the laws of the Indies, many of them having been in existence for over two centuries. They were compiled and readjusted in parts to meet the conditions of the " new establishments." They resemble the laws of Governor Neve,[1] although they are more thorough and systematic. The laws of Governor Neve forbade the sale or alienation of land ; while those of Pitic, agreeing more closely with the ancient Spanish laws, allowed sale after four years' occupation. Also, in the regulations of Neve, all settlers were treated alike ; while in the regulations of Pitic, the lands were distributed according

---

[1] See Chapter VII.

to the needs of the settlers. The rules and regulations for colonization, laid down with so much care and exactness, were not always strictly observed. The government was very punctilious in making and recording laws, but very dilatory in their execution. But this is not unlike the whole structure of the Spanish government. It was difficult to carry out the letter of the law, and not until population had greatly increased were specific land regulations needed.

The first explicit regulations, pertaining to the formation of presidial pueblos in California, were given by Pedro de Nava, Commandante-General, who then resided at Chihuahua.[1] He authorized " Captains of Presidios to grant and distribute house-lots and fields to soldiers and citizens who may solicit them to fix their residences on." These lots were to be granted within the extent of four common leagues of land belonging to the presidio. The four leagues were to be "measured from the centre of the presidio square ; viz., two leagues in every direction."[2] The grants of land under this provision could not in any way interfere with lands beyond the limits of four square leagues, nor could they be located on the lands belonging to the royal *hacienda*. "There is no clear evidence," says Bancroft, "that any such grants were made," as those authorized in the above proviso. Prior to this ordinance, General Ugarte, in 1786, had authorized the granting to private individuals tracts of lands not exceeding three square leagues in extent. These grants were to be outside of the presidio, and were not to interfere with the lands of the mission rancherias. However, it seems that no such grants had been made prior to 1793 ; although Captain Fages had issued permits to settlers to occupy temporarily certain lands. In 1794, Arrillaga gave permission to several persons to settle temporarily on the Rio de

---

[1] Dwinelle, *Colonial History of San Francisco*, 34 ; *California Messages and Documents*, 1850, 139 ; Bancroft, *Cal.*, I, 610.

[2] This is a mistake ; for, two leagues in every direction from the centre would make sixteen square leages. Under this law, Los Angeles claimed sixteen leagues, but the claim was not granted. Cf. Bancroft, *Cal.*, I, 610.

Monterey, from three to five leagues from the presidio. Governor Borica was opposed to the granting of lands to Spanish settlers; on the ground that it could not yet be determined what lands the missions would need, and would cause trouble between the owners of the land and the neighboring rancherias.[1]   He therefore recommended that settlers of good character should have permission to occupy the land provisionally.   But whether any of the above laws were strictly observed or not, we are aware that the number of soldiers and their families continued to increase around the presidios, that other settlers came to occupy the lands, and that soon a small village was formed around each presidio.   It is further evident that the foregoing laws represent the principles on which the four presidial towns, Monterey, San Francisco, San Diego, and Santa Barbara, were founded.   Upon these laws rest the title to lands, and the early forms of municipal government. Although San Diego was the first presidio to be founded, Santa Barbara, San Francisco, and Monterey early assumed more importance in civil and military affairs.   In the early period, Monterey was the most important of all the towns of this class; but in a later period, her glory was surpassed by San Francisco.

The central location of Monterey gave it great military importance.   It was long the residence of the military governor. The place was of importance on account of its tolerably good harbor, its pleasant climate, and its convenience to wood, water, and pasturage.   All of these points gave Monterey significance in the early history of California.   Until the discovery of gold, Monterey was the capital of California, and the chief place on the coast.   In 1843, Richard Henry Dana wrote : " Monterey, as far as my observation goes, is decidedly the

---

[1] When convenient, the friars of the missions allowed the natives to remain in their own villages or rancherias situated at some distance from the mission.   The friars appointed overseers for their control, and exercised the same spiritual and temporal oversight concerning them as was given to the neophytes or the missions.

OLD MISSION, SANTA BARBARA, CAL. ESTABLISHED 1786.

pleasantest and most civilized-looking place in California. In the center of it is an open square, surrounded by four lines of one-story buildings, with half a dozen cannon in the center; some mounted and others not. This is the Presidio or fort. Every town has a presidio in the centre; or rather every presidio has a town built around it; for the forts were first built by the Mexican government and then the people built near them for protection." [1] At this time the presidio at Monterey was open and unfortified. There were several officers and about eighty soldiers in the garrison. The fort was under the the immediate care of the commandant; but the governor, who was chief military commander of the province, resided at Monterey. The local officers of the town consisted of two or three alcaldes and regidores, elected by the inhabitants of the town. There were civil officers who attended to the small municipal affairs, the superior officers regulating everything pertaining to the general government, to the military, and to the foreigners. Mr. Dana wrote that " No protestant has any political rights, nor can he hold property, or, indeed, remain more than a few weeks on shore, unless he belong to a foreign vessel." [2]

Vancouver, who visited Monterey in 1792, forty-six years before Mr. Dana's visit, gives a graphic description of Monterey and environments. He praises the situation and the climate of Monterey; but does not hesitate to point out the defects in the harbor, and speaks decidedly of the dangerous coast. The presidio was very much the same as when it was first built in 1770.[3] " The buildings form a parallelogram, or a long square, comprising an area of about three hundred yards long by two hundred and fifty yards wide, making a complete enclosure. The interior wall is of the same length and is constructed of the same material." [4] Around the square are

[1] Dana, *Two Years before the Mast*, 89, 90.

[2] Dana, *Two Years before the Mast*, 90.

[3] Vancouver, *Voyage de Découvertes, a l'océan Pacifique du Nord,* Book III, chapter 2.

[4] Vancouver, III, 319.

situated the church, the officers' quarters, and the other public buildings. The whole has a forlorn appearance with the exception of the officers' apartments, which are constructed of better material and are more commodious than other dwellings. In consequence of the absence of windows in the outer walls, the whole structure has the appearance of a prison. The windows and doors open on the interior plaza. At each corner of the square is a small bastion, which projects a little beyond the wall. Before the entrance, which faces the bay, are seven cannon, four of which are nine-pounders and three, three-pounders. These guns are on the ground, without any fortifications. They are so far from the bay and are so ill protected that they serve but poorly as a means of defence. Indeed, Vancouver criticises the whole line of coast defenses, which are all about the same, with the exception of San Diego; the latter being better prepared for defence.

The only population of the presidio, at this time (1792), was military; composed of soldiers, ex-soldiers, and their families. Vancouver speaks very favorably of the hospitality and generosity of the Spanish people. "Their amiable conduct and hospitality prove daily the sincerity of their protestations." They were ever ready to render all kinds of service within their power. To this all travelers testify, and many speak of the excellent society at Monterey; for it was always noted for its excellent society during the Spanish and Mexican rule. The situation of Monterey is superb, resting on a gentle slope, with the hills covered with forests rising above. The bay lies before; and the coast line sweeps with a curve away to the northwest, toward Santa Cruz. The town is protected from the southwest winds by Point Pinos. The town grew away from the old presidio, and developed coastward, so that the ruins of the old fort are on the hill back of the town. In the suburbs of the present town, on an open plain toward the northeast, is the old mission church. About nine miles south on the Carmelo river, are the ruins of the mission, San Carlos. Vancouver rode from Monterey to the mission in 1797, and gave a graphic description of it and its surroundings. It is noted as being for a long time the home of Fathers Serra and Palou.

It was a long time before the presidio of Monterey, subject to military rule, became a town with a civil administration. In 1820, an order was issued for the formation of a town council.[1] The only evidence we have that the order was carried into effect, is that alcaldes are mentioned for the years 1820, 1823, and 1826. In 1826, fifteen citizens petitioned the Governor to appoint a judge with civil jurisdiction over the one hundred and fourteen civilians living at Monterey. This would indicate that military rule continued to this date. Following the order of the Governor, an *ayuntamiento* was elected in December. This ayuntamiento continued to be elected for four years. In 1828, it issued a series of municipal laws for the government of the town,[2] and in 1830, the territorial *deputacion*, recognizing the needs of the town, proceeded to designate the extent and position of the town lands.[3] The town from this time had a feeble civil government which was somewhat overshadowed by the military power.

The origin and growth of the presidio and town of San Francisco offers an excellent example of the manner in which a military town became transformed into a civil pueblo. The founding of the San Francisco presidio and mission marks a great event in the annals of California. It has already been related how the party in search of Monterey discovered, in 1769, the harbor of San Francisco. Three years later, Pedro Fages and his companions caught a glimpse of the Golden Gate from the foothills east of Oakland. In 1775, Bucareli, the

---

[1] Bancroft, *Cal.* II, 611.

[2] These regulations had a special reference to public and private order of citizens. Religious duties must be attended to; persons must not leave church after the sermon begins; gambling and drunkenness were forbidden; persons were not allowed to have company late at night, and might not be out late, etc. Bancroft, II, 612.

[3] Bancroft, II, 612.

viceroy of Mexico, gave directions for the founding of a presidio and a mission on the recently discovered bay. On the
12th of June of the following year, an expedition left Monterey
for the purpose of founding the new establishments. The
little company was composed of Moraga, the commander, seven
settlers, one sergeant, and sixteen soldiers; besides herdsmen,
servants, and others. They drove a pack train, and two hundred head of cattle with which to stock the presidio. The
supplies and equipment of the new settlement were shipped
by sea in the vessel San Carlos. After some controversy as to
situation, the presidio was founded in September, about thirty
days after the arrival of the San Carlos. The usual ceremonies were observed on taking possession of the presidio.
Mass was held, the Te Deum sung, and salutes of cannon and
muskets were fired. The first buildings, consisting of the chapel,
store-houses, and dwellings for the officers, men, and their
families, were rudely constructed; but they were the beginnings
of a great city. The presidio was constructed after the usual
plan. Vancouver has given us a minute description of the
establishment as it appeared in 1793. After the usual and
legal manner, a plaza was laid out and the buildings were distributed on its sides, all facing toward the interior. The
houses and public buildings were made of adobe brick; all
were rude enough, having open spaces for windows, and the
bare earth for floors.

At a somewhat later period, the *castillo* was established on the
point, and the mission further inland. Between the mission
and the presidio, and to the east of a line connecting them,
sprang up the civic town of Yerba Buena, the nucleus of the
modern city. Prior to 1834, San Francisco included the presidio, the mission, and the small town, Yerba Buena, which
had sprung up between them.[1] Until this date these establishments were under the control of military organization. The
territorial governor imposed taxes and license fees, and the

---

[1] Moses, *Municipal Government in San Francisco*, 18.

commandant acted as judge of the first instance. It was in November of the year 1834 that Governor Figueroa wrote to the military commandant at San Francisco in respect to the change from a military to a civil organization. In this letter he stated that the territorial council had ordered the partido[1] of San Francisco to elect an ayuntamiento, composed of an alcalde, two regidores, and a syndico. The ayuntamiento must hereafter exercise the political functions which had hitherto been exercised by the commandant. The alcalde must henceforth attend to all judicial duties of the pueblo; the commandant having to do only with those cases which were referred to the governor. The military and civil power was thus divided; the commandant attending to the administration of the former, and the town council to that of the latter. The jurisdiction of the town council (ayuntamiento) extended over a large territory. It embraced not only the entire peninsula, including presidio, mission, and town, but extended to the inhabitants of the opposite bay coasts; Contra Costa, Sonoma, and San Rafael. Thus we have a pueblo organization embracing the small populations of the peninsula and its surroundings.[2] The officers of the new government met sometimes at the mission, sometimes at the Presidio, sometimes at Yerba Buena. Upon investigation, it was ascertained that there were sufficient inhabitants on the peninsula to allow the organization of a pueblo under the existing laws. Consequently, in December, 1835, nine electors were chosen who proceeded to select members of a town council. From this time on, the inhabitants of the opposite shores were merely aggregated to the pueblo of San Francisco.[3] And henceforth until 1839, at which date the town gave up its ayuntamiento but retained its charter, the town exercised the powers and privileges of a fully organized pueblo.[4] How-

---

[1] Moses, *San Francisco*, 18.

[2] Dwinelle, *Colonial History of San Francisco*, 48.   [3] Dwinelle, 51.

[4] The ayuntamiento of San Francisco was suspended by a law passed in 1836, which required a greater population for the privilege of having town officers.

14

ever, it must be inferred from the records that the pueblo of
San Francisco, like the other settlements in California, was of
very slow development, and that its government was informal
and irregular. The municipal organization during the Spanish
and Mexican rule, was of a meagre character. Professor
Moses relates a curious incident respecting this deficiency in
government machinery. It seems that in 1839, more than
sixty years after the foundation of the pueblo, the authorities
had the criminal, Galindo, on their hands, without any jail in
the town. The inhabitants of San Francisco petitioned the
Governor to have the prisoner removed to San José, where
there was a prison. In urging this removal on account of the
absence of a prison, they stated further that the inhabitants of
the pueblo were so scattered, caring for their herds and flocks,
that there were not enough remaining in the town to guard
the prisoner.[1]

The petition was heard and the prisoner remanded to San
José, which was fortunate enough to have a prison. It is
not necessary to relate the few changes in the municipal government which occurred from time to time, prior to the American conquest. Under the new government, the ayuntamiento,
with a full quota of town officers, was elected under the law
of 1836. The castillo was in a dilapidated condition and
usually unfit for any effective service. When Vancouver
entered the harbor in 1793, he was saluted by a brass three-
pounder tied to a log. He saw another cannon mounted on a
decayed carriage in front of the presidio. But, from this time
on, strenuous efforts were made to build the famous Castillo
de San Joaquin on Fort Point. Although much time and
labor and a considerable sum of money were spent in the construction of the fort, it was faulty and useless as a means of
defense. It was not until commerce sprang up that San Francisco's superiority as a site for a great city was made known.

---

[1] Moses, *San Francisco*, 22.

SAN FRANCISCO MISSION.

Santa Barbara presidio was established in 1782. There was no fort at Santa Barbara; consequently the garrison was composed of cavalry. The buildings of the presidio, in 1793, were said by the governor to be the best in California. Santa Barbara was especially noted for the excellent buildings at the mission as well as at the presidio. It was noted also for its great herds of live stock, the products of the soil, and the successful instruction of the Indians in the industrial arts. Quite a number of invalids were sent to Santa Barbara to live, on account of the healthful climate, and a small voluntary population gradually accumulated about the presidio. The number of the inhabitants in the town at the close of the eighteenth century was three hundred and seventy, fifty-nine of whom were soldiers on active duty, and seventeen were pensioners. We infer from this that the town was increasing under military rule. The town has always been noted for cleanliness and healthfulness. Vancouver was well pleased with the surroundings. He says that he found here, " the appearance of a far more civilized place than any other of the Spanish establishments had exhibited. The buildings appeared to be regular and well constructed, the walls clean and white, and the roofs of the houses were covered with a bright red tile. The presidio excels all others in neatness, cleanliness, and other smaller though essential comforts ; it is placed on an elevated part of the plain, and is raised some feet from the ground by a basement story, which adds much to its pleasantness." [1]

It seems that there was no *rancho del rey* at Santa Barbara ; but a large number of stock belonging to the presidial company was pastured on the surrounding lands. There were, in 1797, four thousand horses and cattle and six hundred sheep in charge of the presidio. The yearly product of grain was 1650 fanegas.[2]

---

[1] Bancroft, *California*, I, 667 ; See Fig. 4.
[2] A fanega of grain is equal to about two bushels.

Mr. Bancroft states that "the municipal records of Santa Barbara have been for the most part lost, so that respecting

Fig. 4.

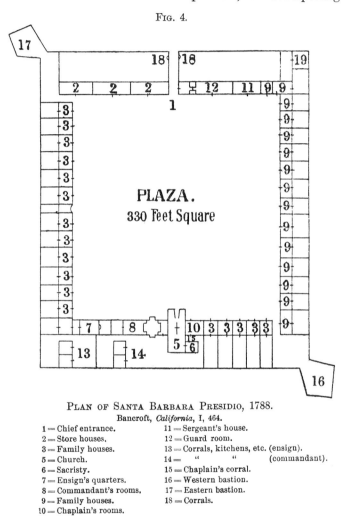

PLAN OF SANTA BARBARA PRESIDIO, 1788.
Bancroft, *California*, I, 464.

1 = Chief entrance.	11 = Sergeant's house.
2 = Store houses.	12 = Guard room.
3 = Family houses.	13 = Corrals, kitchens, etc. (ensign).
5 = Church.	14 = " " (commandant).
6 = Sacristy.	15 = Chaplain's corral.
7 = Ensign's quarters.	16 = Western bastion.
8 = Commandant's rooms.	17 = Eastern bastion.
9 = Family houses.	18 = Corrals.
10 = Chaplain's rooms.	

the pueblo government, administration of justice, criminal cases, and even list of officers, only a slight record can be formed from miscellaneous scattered documents."[1] There can be recorded for it a quiet prosperity and a simple organization. Especially prosperous were the missions in the vicinity. The natives were of greater intelligence here than in other parts of California, and reached a more advanced stage of culture under the new civilization. Wealth in herds and flocks, in buildings and furniture, and in the products of the soil increased rapidly. That the pueblo was granted an *ayuntamiento* in 1834, is evident; but the subsequent government of the town is scarcely mentioned, although an occasional reference to alcaldes and regidores would indicate that some part of the municipal government existed. Without doubt the presidio expanded into a town with civil administration; but being under the shadow of military power, in all probability the commandant continued to exercise chief authority, and the old régime predominated until the American invasion.

As far as situation is concerned, San Diego is one of the most important points in California. Its harbor is next to that of San Francisco, and it is situated nearer Mexico. It was highly important that it should be strongly fortified as a coast defence. The presidio was established in 1769, as one of the pioneer foundations in California. Notwithstanding the fact that San Diego was an important harbor, favorably situated for coast defences, and that it was the first colonial settlement in California, it was always a weak fortification and wanting in general prosperity. Vancouver, who visited San Diego in 1793, twenty-four years after the founding, says, "The presidio of San Diego seems to be the least of the Spanish establishments. It is irregularly built, on very uneven ground, which makes it liable to some inconveniences, without the obvious appearance of any object for selecting such a spot. With little difficulty it might be rendered a place of considerable strength by establishing a small fort at the entrance of the port; where at this time there are neither works, guns, houses,

---

[1] Bancroft, *Cal.*, III, 653.

nor other habitations nearer than the presidio, five miles from the port, and where they have only three small pieces of brass cannon."[1] In the same year, following the report of Governor Borica relative to the condition of the presidio at San Diego, the viceroy of Mexico ordered the presidio to be repaired. In the following year, the viceroy, in a letter to Borica, expressed a desire to have the fort at Monterey built similar to that of San Francisco, "without cost to the king." Subsequently considerable sums of money were expended in an attempt to remodel the fort, but with little effect.

But the fine harbor of San Diego could not fail to attract the outside world, after the beginning of trade and commerce. A small town, which grew in later times to considerable proportions, sprang up around the presidio. Though the presidio was of little importance as a coast defence, it was an important station in California; and San Diego obtained considerable attention as a pueblo, prior to the American invasion. There was no civil government of San Diego until sixty-eight years after its foundation. During this period the rule was strictly military. The military company gradually diminished, and with its decrease the rule of the military power declined. The presidio was abandoned in 1837, although one soldier was reported on duty in 1839. The presidio buildings were abandoned in 1835, and by 1840 were in complete ruin. "Probably much of the material was brought down to build the little town of thirty or forty houses that had sprung up at the foot of the hill."[2] The castillo, which was built farther out on the point, likewise fell into ruin.

The separation of the civil from the military government of San Diego occurred in 1835, when the first town council was installed. This town council was composed of one alcalde, two regidores, and a syndico.[3] For three years the ayunta-

---

[1] Bancroft, *Cal.*, I, 649; Cf. Vancouver, Book IV, chapter 8.
[2] Bancroft, *Cal.*, III, 610.   [3] Ibid., 615.

miento continued to serve; but in 1837 the town was placed under the control of a justice of the peace (*juez de paz*) appointed by the Governor. This change was caused by a law of 1836, which provided that towns must have a requisite population in order to have an ayuntamiento; and San Diego's population fell below the limit. This law is referred to in another place.[1] The administration of justice and the management of the affairs of the town consisted of trials for petty misdemeanors and punishments by flogging, fines, or imprisonment. The rules for municipal government were excellent for the time, though quite severe in reference to personal liberty. Gambling and drunkenness were forbidden by law and punished according to the degree of the offence. There were many fines for petty theft and fraudulent practices.[2] In 1839, San Diego formed a part of the prefecture of the partido of Los Angeles. The former could not have been very important at this time, for there was not sufficient population to make it a sub-prefect.

Thus it is seen that the four towns, Monterey, San Francisco, Santa Barbara, and San Diego, grew up around a fortress; that they were for a long time under military rule; but that finally each one had its own civil government. The transition from a military garrison, with a military rule, to a municipality or civil pueblo, with a town council and local magistrates, was necessarily slow. The causes are many. The slow increase of the population in and around the presidio was the primary one; but the inactivity of Spanish and Mexican life and the crude state of society prevented the formation of anything like a systematic organization. Nevertheless, these examples serve to illustrate the principles of government; and had not the easy-going Mexican life been overtaken by the rapidly moving, energetic American civilization, doubtless

---

[1] See Chapter XIII.

[2] Mr. Bancroft gives a long list of town records from 1830 to 1840. *California*, III, 610 *et seq.*

each one of these towns would have developed into a thriving city. As it is, the wisdom of choice in locality is fully demonstrated by the later development of the great maritime city of San Francisco, the thriving towns of Monterey and Santa Barbara, and the recent evolution of San Diego. In the selection of sites for towns and for missions, the wisdom of the early founders has been fully demonstrated. It is not the province of the present volume to follow the details of events of these cities after the institution of the American rule. The period of transition from Mexican to American institutions is interesting. That the transformation is complete, no one can doubt who looks upon the metropolis of the Pacific coast, or gazes at the ruins of the old Spanish buildings of the other towns mentioned, around which have developed modern cities.

CHAPTER X.

The Spanish Occupation of Arizona, New Mexico, and Texas.

In the early period of Spanish conquest, a mystery hung over the country of the north now included within the present boundaries of Arizona and New Mexico. The fabulous stories of the "Seven Cities of Cibola" were recited over and over, and distorted from their original fictitious forms. Reports of populous cities to be plundered and a new empire to be conquered greatly excited the cupidity of the Spanish invaders, and created visions of immediate and boundless wealth in the minds of the adventurers. Dreams of another Mexico to be taken awakened their avaricious desires to such an extent that they were ready to undertake the most hazardous expeditions in order to satiate their thirst for gold. The origin of these fabulous stories was very simple. They started with the account given by the Indian slave, Tejos, who told his master·Nuño de Guzman that he was formerly accustomed to visit this fabulous country in company with his father for the purpose of carrying on a trade in feathers. The trader went from place to place exchanging his wares for silver and gold, which were said to be plentiful in the interior. Tejos accompanied his father once or twice as far as the seven cities which were large and populous like the city of Mexico. Slight as this information appears, it contained the magic idea which moved every Spaniard to action; it told of populous cities and prospects of gold and silver. Relying upon this information, Nuño de Guzman, the head of the Royal Audience of Spain, collected four hundred Spaniards and twenty thousand Indians and plunged into the wilderness on a prospective journey of six hundred miles.[1] It was thought by some that Guzman was inspired, in part, by the current, fabulous stories relative to the Island of the Amazons, situated somewhere in the north, in which there was an abundance of gold and silver.

Without doubt this story of the Island of the Amazons originated from that of the island spoken of as California in the Spanish romance referred to elsewhere.[2] But Guzman did not find the island, and the seven cities receded. The discouragements of a pathless wilderness and the return of Cortés from the south brought the expedition to a close.[3]

Soon after this, the arrival of Cabeza de Vaca and his companions, the survivors of the Narvaez expedition to Florida, caused the renewal of the reports already current of this famous country.[4] Cabeza told of passing through the country of a civilized people with permanent habitations; dwellers in large houses situated in populous towns. The news of the arrival of Cabeza and his companions and of the fabulous stories which they told was communicated to Antonio de Mendoza, Viceroy of New Spain, who in turn dispatched it to Francisco Vasquez Coronado, the governor of New Galicia. The repetition of the accounts of those famous cities of the north again inflamed the breasts of the Spanish cavaliers with a desire for conquest. As soon as possible, Coronado dispatched Fray Marcos de Nizza with a few companions on a preliminary expedition to gain more definite information of the land. It is not necessary here to follow the adventurous journey of the company headed by Fray Marcos and guided by the negro Stephen, a former companion of Cabeza. It is sufficient to

---

[1] *The Relation of Casteñada*, Terneaux-Compans, IX, 1.
[2] See Chapter VI.
[3] Haynes, *Early explorations in New Mexico*, Winsor, II, 473.
[4] *Relation of Cabeza de Vaca*, Ternaux-Compans, V.

relate that the stories told by the friar on his return are to be classed preëminently among the marvellous. As Fray Marcos continued his journey, the cities of Cibola again receded; and, although finally discovered, he was not permitted to enter them, but was compelled to retreat with the loss of the negro Stephen. On his return, all New Spain resounded with stories of populous cities, of fabulous wealth, of prizes awaiting conquest. Even the religious orders took up the subject, and preached a crusade and spiritual conquest. With this new glow of enthusiasm, Coronado proceeded to collect the forces for a new expedition; and with him the epic of the Seven Cities is completed.

Coronado soon collected an army, composed of three hundred Spaniards, including many gentlemen of noble families, and eight hundred Indians.[1] So many persons of noble birth and rank volunteered for the expedition that the Viceroy found great difficulty in making his appointments. The old cavalier spirit was fully aroused, and the Spanish grandees were eager for the foray. Owing to the delays usual on such expeditions, the column was not ready to advance until February, 1540. Then began the famous march over mountains, across rivers, through parched and dreary deserts, to conquer and despoil the rich cities of the north and add another province to the royal domain. But the members of this brave and hardy band were doomed to suffer extreme disappointment. The fatigues and discouragements of the expedition were sufficient to cool their ardor; for the cities of Cibola receded as the adventurers pursued their way in the desert, and, when discovered, dwindled into the merest villages in comparison with the populous towns which their imagination had pictured to them. They indeed found "Cibola" and "Quivira," but in no respect the Cibola and Quivira of famous story. They discovered wonderful ancient remains and marvelous villages peopled with semi-barbarous natives; but no gold, no wealth and no plunder.

---

[1] Bancroft, XV, 83; Winsor, II, 481.

Indeed a bare subsistence and threatened starvation were the only rewards in store for the volunteers upon this most famous of all the Spanish explorations, excepting those of Cortés. They discovered a land rich in mineral resources, but others were to reap the benefits of the wealth of the mountain. They discovered a land rich in material for the archaeologist, but nothing to satisfy their thirst for glory or wealth. They returned after accomplishing only a temporary conquest, and solving the mystery of the "Seven Cities of Cibola." But the conquest was merely temporary ; for only two friars of the entire expedition remained. These two determined to remain and win this newly discovered people to the Christian faith.[1] They were soon forced to pay by death the penalty of their invasion, and "received the martyr's crown." It remained for others in a later period to colonize and permanently settle New Mexico.

Within the present bounds of Arizona, the permanent results of Spanish occupation were very meagre, although the territory is not wanting in the historic lore of this early period. The expedition of Espejo, following full forty years after that of Coronado, added but little to the knowledge of the territory. Espejo, traveling to the northwest, entered the territory of "Arizuma" and discovered rich silver ore in the mountains about forty-five leagues southwest of Moqui. Over a hundred years after this expedition, the Jesuit missionaries penetrated southern "Arizuma" and established permanent missions. The two pious fathers, Francisco Kino and Maria Salvatierra, pushed northward ; establishing missions and preaching the gospel to the various tribes with which they came in contact. They were zealous missionaries and energetic explorers. There was no country so rugged or desolate as to forbid their entrance, no tribe so fierce that they would not attempt to carry to them the blessings of the gospel; though it must be confessed that their success with the Apaches

---

[1] Castañeda, *Ternaux-Compans*, IX, 214.

was not very great. A large majority of their converts were of the Pima tribe, who are now called " Papagoes ;" and a few of them were domesticated Apaches. The first mission within the territory was established at Guevavi, near the present southern boundary of Arizona. Soon after, the Mission of San Xavier del Bac was established, about twelve miles southwest of Tucson. At first its buildings were small and inferior ; but about a hundred years later the present magnificent building was erected, which stands as a monument of the early mission architecture. The missions continued to be prosperous for many years. The natives were taught not only the tenets of the Christian religion, but to till the soil, and attend to the rearing of cattle as well. Large tracts of land in advantageous situations were cultivated, and flocks and herds soon dotted the landscape. But they were destined to receive a severe blow by the constant raids of the Apaches and the rebellion of the Pimas in 1751. However, the greatest blow to the prosperity of the missions of Arizona was the expulsion of the Jesuit fathers, and the transferral of the missions to the Franciscans.

According to Mr. Bancroft, there were only two missions and three visitas, or dependent missions, established north of the Arizona line; although there were many more recorded on the older maps of Venegas and others.[1] Although Kino made many excursions to the north, discovered and named rancherias, enumerated the inhabitants, and requested missionaries to be sent to these places, the missions were never established. Kino pushed his explorations to the banks of the Gila and across to the Colorado. The missions established during Jesuit rule were mostly south of the present boundary of Arizona. Kino laid the foundation of a church at Bac in 1700, but it was not completed at the time ; for it was not until twenty years afterwards that a permanent mission was established there. Notwithstanding the many con-

[1] Bancroft, *Arizona and New Mexico*, Chaps. XV and XVI.

flicting statements, it appears that no missions were established in modern Arizona until 1720, and Mr. Bancroft seems to prefer the date 1732 for the first foundations.[1] After the expulsion of the Jesuits in 1767, the missions were put in charge of the Franciscan friars, who found affairs in a bad condition; owing, in part, to the change of authority. The neophytes refused obedience to authority thereafter, and held that they should do only that which they chose. The missions were maintained with more or less prosperity for many years. The buildings were constructed of adobe, and roofed with grass, timber, and earth. The structure now standing at Bac bears the date of 1797, which was the probable time of its completion. Bac was known as a rancheria until 1720, from which time it became a mission. The missions were quite well filled with neophytes, and the success of the missionaries was satisfactory in many respects. The Jesuits were the best colonizers in the employ of Spain, especially for rough and wild countries. The Spanish settlements were very meagre; they were limited to a few hundred haciendas or estates, where land was tilled and cattle reared to a considerable extent. In addition to these, a large company of Spaniards settled around the presidios of Tubac and Tucson. It appears that the presidio of Tubac was established for the protection of the missions in 1752, soon after the revolt. In 1764–7 it had a population of about five hundred persons. The presidio of Tucson was established somewhat later, at first by moving the one at Tubac. But at least as early as 1826, garrisons were maintained at both places.[1]

Among other industries mining was carried on to some extent. Many mines were opened and some of them worked; but not to the extent indicated by the numerous exaggerated reports. From 1790 to 1822, the region enjoyed a period of peace and prosperity. Almost all that was accomplished under Spanish rule may be referred to this period. But the establishments

---

[1] Bancroft, *Arizona and New Mexico*, 374.

were destined to end in disaster. The constant raids of the Apaches, the neglect of the garrison, and the failure of the Spanish government to make proper provisions for the protection of the establishments, as well as the revolution in Mexico, helped to hasten the downfall of the missions. Soon the haciendas were deserted, the missions abandoned, and the working of mines was stopped. Nothing is related of the missions since 1826–8, and in all probability this is the end of their active existence. The present church of San Xavier at Bac is under the care of the tribe which the missionaries converted, the Papagoe Indians, who care for the property.[1] Exploration, invasion, the establishment of a few institutions, the foundation of a few towns, afterwards to be destroyed, and the opening of a few mines to be abandoned, is the history of the struggling pioneers of Arizona.

If we turn our attention to New Mexico, we shall find that a more permanent foothold was obtained here, and consequently with more lasting effects. To recount the expedition of Espejo in New Mexico and to tell of all the attempted explorations and the many stories and reports of this wonderful land would occupy the space of one book. The entrance of Lomas, and his return to Mexico in chains, after spending the winter in New Andalusia and exploring a score or more of towns, and many other interesting exploits, must be passed by for the more permanent results of the colonization of Oñate. The account given by Espejo and his companions was so flattering that the viceroy of New Spain determined to take immediate control and colonize the country. Espejo enlarged upon the older stories in his representation of populous cities, fertile valleys, and abundance of silver and gold in the mountains. The first mover in this new enterprise of settling New Mexico with Spanish colonists was Juan de Oñate. He made a contract with Louis de Vasco, the viceroy of Mexico, to reconquer and people the new territory. In this petition he pledged

---

[1] See illustration.

himself to take with him two hundred soldier colonists, horses, and cattle, as well as agricultural implements necessary to till the soil. In return for this he was to receive a salary, a noble title for himself and family, large grants of land, and a loan to defray the expenses of the expedition. In addition to this, the Indians were to be subjected; that is, reduced to slavery.[1] The king granted the request of Oñate and confirmed the contract between de Vasco and Oñate by a royal decree under date of July, 1602, after the conquest had been made.

Oñate was very successful in collecting recruits for the expedition. Soon he had the required number; but the delay caused by the almost endless formality of procedure, and by the petty jealousies, and interference of others, caused many of his followers to desert. Again and again he was disappointed and thwarted in his attempts to begin the march. It was not until January, 1598, after two years of preparation and delay, that Oñate was able to start on the long deferred journey. It is difficult to state the exact number that went with Oñate; but the best authorities would seem to indicate that there were one hundred and thirty soldier colonists and a great number of Indians and servants. The colonists and their families were carried in eighty-three wagons, and 7,000 head of cattle were driven before them.

Once in the territory the colonists began to build houses and soon sowed for the first crop. While they were attending to these duties, twelve Franciscan Friars who accompanied the expedition were attempting to convert the natives. The natives received the Spaniards with great kindness and supplied them with food and clothing. As soon as land was located, farms occupied, and all kinds of crops planted, the Spaniards turned their attention to exploring the mountains for mines. The colonies seemed to flourish; as there was a constant increase in the supply of necessaries of life. The missionary work of the

---

[1] Bancroft, *Arizona and New Mexico*, 116.

friars was very successful, for a time at least. The first mission formed was San Gabriel.[1] From this point their work spread throughout the pueblos. In 1608 there were eight padres at work, who had baptized at least eight thousand Indians. Thirty new friars came to the settlements in 1629, and the records of the following year show fifty missionaries in the field ministering to sixty thousand converts, dwelling in ninety pueblos and grouped in twenty-five missions.[2] At first there was good will and harmony between the natives and their conquerors. But as time passed and the Christian religion was pressed more surely upon them to the exclusion of their own religion, which they were forced to give up, except as they continued to worship in secret, the natives became restless. As the mines were opened, they were forced to toil there as well as on the farms of the colonists. It was a great trial for the natives to give up their simple religion, and to be forced to close their council chambers (estufas), and submit to the yoke of bondage which a race of priests was religiously forcing upon them. They finally grew weary of the daily round of penance, toil, and prayer, and planned to get rid of the intruders. These plans ended in the revolt of 1679, by which all of the Spaniards were expelled.

The expulsion of the Spaniards in the revolt led by Popé, in 1680, shows the patriotism of the comparatively docile Pueblo Indian. The organization of the natives was complete. They drove out the Spaniards, rejected their civilization, destroyed their buildings, and returned to their own religion and habits of life. For fifteen years the pueblo rule tried to obliterate all traces of the Spanish civilization. But Vargas, in 1695, reconquered the pueblos and brought them under complete subjection. From that date, the Spanish municipal system, government, and religion prevailed.

The first town was formed near the junction of the Chama and the Rio Grande and was called San Juan de Cabdallero.

---

[1] Bancroft, *Arizona and New Mexico*, 131.   [2] Ibid., 162.

15

This was the centre of the Spanish settlements for a time; but Santa Fé, founded in 1601, became the principal town. It must be confessed that, while the colonists were seldom, if ever, in want of the necessaries of life, the colonial prospects were none of the brightest. There was nothing to relieve the monotony of these inland colonies, and nothing to stimulate trade or industry. They were far removed from the associations of men and the commerce of the world. For seventy-three years they were prosperous enough in some ways; but in all of this time they were an isolated community of settlers, soldiers, Indian neophytes and Franciscan missionaries. The Spaniards with all of their thirst for wealth had to curb their desires within the limits of a bare subsistence. The colonies, though amassing some property, were not self-sustaining. They were too far away to market anything except gold and silver, which, though plentiful in the mountains, was difficult to obtain, as there were but meagre means for reducing it. A small trade was carried on with the outside world. The friars received their salaries, and the colonists their agricultural implements and tools, from Mexico. Added to the other disadvantages of the new settlements were the constant wars with the hostile Indians, the stubborn Moqui, and the fierce Apaches. After the Indian revolt in 1680, there was a period of Indian independence for ten years, when the country was finally reconquered by Vargas.

The conquest of Vargas was thorough and final. The churches which had been destroyed during the rebellion were duly restored, along with the worship of the Christian religion. The pueblos again came under the yoke and submitted to foreign methods of worship and government. From this time on, the life in New Mexico varied but little from century to century. The friars gained in power and pursued their regular parish work among the villagers. Churches were built at the pueblos, and missionary work was begun outside. In civil institutions there was little change. There were a few permanent towns like Santa Fé, which continued to increase

St. Xavier Church.

in Spanish population, and the town governments apparently assumed some regularity. Also, in some of the Indian pueblos, there was a mixture of laws; in others, the pueblo Indians dwelt by themselves, having their own town officers, and the Spanish priest as supervisor of their worship. The mission system differed somewhat from that of California, as the Indians were already living in villages. It only remained to establish the parish church and station the missionaries in their several places, changing the ancient pueblo government to the newly introduced Spanish system. This included a form of municipal organization under the direction of the priest.

The government of New Mexico was similar to that of other Spanish provinces of the time. The religious and civil powers were accorded certain rights and formal privileges, but the true government was military in organization and execution. The chief officer was a military governor appointed by the Viceroy. The local governments were in the form of pueblo governments. Civil pueblos, presidios, and missions, were established here as elsewhere. As early as 1680, a settlement was established at La Canada. After the revolution of 1680, during the Indian rule of 1680–95, seventy-five Mexican families formed the " new villa " of Santa Cruz de la Canada. A pueblo government was established with an *alcalde mayor* and *capitan a guerra*, a sergeant, four corporals, and an alguazil ;[1] that is, with a mayor justice with military authority, a sergeant, four corporals, and a treasurer. This seems to be a peculiar combination of military and civil powers. The town-site was surveyed and the lands were assigned to the citizens.

Santa Fé is said by many to be the oldest town in New Mexico. It is certainly the town of greatest historical interest. It was founded near the site of the ancient capital of the pueblos. There are many who believe that Santa Fé is a continuation of the old Indian pueblo which formerly occupied the same site. Mr. Bancroft holds that there is not sufficient

---

[1] Bancroft, *Arizona and New Mexico*, 158.

evidence to support such an assumption.[1] He also believes that the first town, called Santa Fé de San Francisco, was located at San Juan, and not on the site of the present city of Santa Fé. The Spanish town of Santa Fé was founded at the beginning of the seventeenth century, a few years after the conquest of Oñate. From that time it has been the most important town in New Mexico. The governor's residence was situated at Santa Fé, which was the seat of the garrison. The town increased slowly in population and presumably in civil government. In 1630, the garrison numbered two hundred and fifty, all living at Santa Fé, where a church was built for their accommodation. At this date the number of baptized Indians in New Mexico was 60,000.

The houses of Santa Fé were constructed of adobe, one story high, with thick walls. The town was laid out after the usual manner, around a plaza. The houses were square and block shaped. Lieutenant Pike, who visited Santa Fé in 1806, said, " Its appearance from a distance struck my mind with the same effect as a fleet of flat-boats which are seen in the spring and fall seasons descending the Ohio. On the north side of the town is the square of the soldiers' houses. The public square is in the center of the town, on the north side of which is situated the palace or government house, with the quarters for the guards, etc. The other side of the square is occupied by the clergy and public officers. In general, the houses have a shed before the front, some of which have a flooring of brick; the consequence is that the streets are very narrow, say, in general, twenty-five feet. The supposed population is 4500."[2] The government of the town was on a military basis at this time ; for every citizen was under military duty. But there were the usual town officers whose actions were subject to revision by the military authority.

In 1846, at the time of the military reconnoissance by Lieu-

---

[1] Bancroft, *Arizona and New Mexico*, 158.
[2] Quoted by Prince, *History of Mexico*, 255.

GOVERNOR'S PALACE, SANTA FE.

tenant Emoy and others, the city was spread over a large
territory. With the exception of a few houses built compactly
about the plaza, the houses were scattered and surrounded by
gardens and fields. The Palace then stood much the same as
in 1806, and as it now stands, with its adobe walls and long
portico supported by the trunks of trees. It was noted at that
time as being the only building in Santa Fé with glass windows. Opposite the Palace and facing it was the military
chapel (Capilla de los Soldados), to which the soldiers were
regularly summoned for worship. The private houses are of
the oriental style. " The almost universal style of building,"
says Davis, " both in town and country, is in the form of a
square with a court yard in the center. A large door called
a *zaguan* leads from the street into the *patio* or court-yard into
which the doors of the various rooms open. A portal, or
more properly according to the American understanding of the
same, a porch, runs around the court and serves as a sheltered
communication between different parts of the house." [1] The
flat roof is covered with earth and plastered with mud. Its
appearance is improved slightly by a low parapet around it.
This makes the roof very heavy, sometimes weighing several
tons, and causes a severe strain on the timbers which support
it. In the comparatively dry climate of Santa Fé, the mud
roof, with slight repairs after rains, serves well the purpose of
protection. Along the principal streets, the private houses have
porches outside as well as inside of the court. In 1850 these
principal streets, around the plaza at least, were occupied by
traders who had erected small stores or booths. Now the principal streets are lined with shops, but the appearance of the
town remains to a great extent Mexican. No other town has retained its Spanish characteristics for so long a time. The plaza,
the old adobe buildings, the burros in the streets, the free use of
the Mexican language, the semi-civilized natives, the dress, customs, and manners of many of the people, carry us back to the

[1] Davis, *El Gringo*, 164. (1857.)

early days. Even modern buildings, modern customs, and modern dress fail to obliterate the old Spanish life. Many of the best citizens of the town are descendants of those old Castilian families which obtained wealth and prominence in the early period of New Mexican history.

Several Spanish explorations extended into the present boundaries of Texas, prior to 1682. Immediately there followed the attempts of France to colonize that part of the country from " Fort St. Louis on the Illinois River, into New Biscay." The French failed in their attempt to settle the Mississippi valley and the coast territory, and thus to connect Canada and the Gulf of Mexico. The explorations of La Salle in Texas had the effect of stirring up the Spaniards to renewed activity. Consequently expeditions were sent into Texas for the purpose of apprehending Frenchmen who might be found in this territory. Governor Leon of Coahuila found the deserted French fort. The colony had failed and its inhabitants were scattered. A few captives were made by the Spanish on this and other expeditions. Several attempts were then made to reduce the country, and to make permanent settlements. Two missions were founded in 1691. They were San Francisco and Santa Maria, and were situated between the Trinidad and Neches rivers.[1] The colonizing enterprise was poorly managed. The troops and colonists withdrew and the missionaries became discouraged. The enterprise failed and the missions were abandoned in 1693.

In 1713, the attempts to explore and settle Texas were renewed and resulted more favorably than the previous enterprises. In 1718, the mission and presidio of San Antonio were founded on the St. Anthony river. Other missions were established from time to time. The great object of the Spanish government in settling Texas was to guard against the threatened French occupation. The religious orders desired to found missions for the conversion of the natives.

----

[1] Bancroft, *North Mexican States*, 404.

1. Mission of San Jose.
2. Mission Concepcion.

The San Antonio settlement in due season became permanent and the center of the Spanish operations in Texas. The presidio of San Antonio Bejar, founded in 1718, and the villa of San Fernando, founded in 1730, formed one settlement. In 1785, it contained a garrison of sixty men and about one hundred and forty houses, one-half of which were built of stone. The public buildings were built of stone, but were in a ruinous condition at the above date. Their original cost was $80,000.[1] Ten or twelve other settlements had been formed in this section of Texas; some of them were in a very flourishing condition, others not. From this time on the Spaniards had permanent occupation of the province. Towns sprang up and missions and forts were established. When the province passed under Mexican rule, colonization became more extensive. From that time to 1845 Texas developed more rapidly and showed more thrift than other Mexican frontier states.

The national colonization law of the Mexican Empire, published in 1823, offered liberal inducements to colonists to settle in the provinces or states of the new government. But this law was promptly repealed and replaced by the colonization law of the Mexican Republic, passed in 1824. This was followed by the decree, of April 6, 1830, by the Vice-President of the Mexican Republic. This provided for the appointment of a commission, whose duty it was to aid colonization and see that contracts were properly made and fulfilled by the colonists. The seventh article of this decree provided that Mexican families which desired to become colonists should be conveyed free of expense, supported during the first year, and given a grant of land with the necessary tools for working the same.

Four years thereafter, a circular of the Secretary of relations presented the matter of colonization of the lands of Coahuila

---

[1] Report of Padre Lopez, President of Texas Missions, 1785; Bancroft, *North Mexican States*, 632.

and Texas.   The circular states the reasons why colonization in Texas is desirable.   The government is impressed by the necessity of relieving a multitude of unfortunate persons from their distress, caused "by reason of political errors, the paralyzation of trade, the destruction of fortunes," and all of the attendant evils of a state of constant revolution.   The richness and desirability of the lands in the territory adjoining the boundary line of the Republic are pictured in graphic language. These territories are "open to commerce, unexhausted by cultivation, and fruitful in the extreme, and inviting the robust arms of the Mexican to all kinds of employment which can no where else be so well rewarded and the same facilities afforded, as within their limits."[1]   "The government invites the families that have lost their fortune or their peace to better their condition in the peaceful pursuits of agriculture; this will restore their estates, improve their fortunes, make them forget their errors and wanderings," and convert them into useful citizens. The government stands ready to aid all such.   This general declaration is followed by a colonization law, which is similar to that adopted by the general government of 1824.   The colonists enlist for two years, during which they can not separate from the colony.   To each family there shall be given one-tenth of a *sitio de ganado mayor* of land,[2] "a yoke of cattle and a cow, or their value, two ploughs, and such carpentering and farming tools as the government shall consider necessary."[3]   Each family shall receive a building lot taken from the land which is appropriated for that purpose.   To every person over fifteen years of age, the cattle and carts necessary for transportation shall be given, and they shall be the property of the colonists after they arrive at their destination.   Also each person shall be paid four reals (fifty cents) daily for one year, except those under fifteen years of age, who shall receive two reals.

In spite of all these inducements to colonists, a compara-

---

[1] Rockwell, *Spanish and Mexican law*, 624.
[2] Equal to about 442.8 acres.   [3] Rockwell, 625.

tively small number of Mexicans entered Texas. The pressure of immigration came from the north and the east. To such an extent did foreigners press into Texas that it soon achieved its independence, and as an independent Republic continued to develop rapidly. Then followed the Mexican War and the annexation of Texas to the United States. The institutions of the Spaniards and the Mexicans were about the same in all of the provinces and states of New Spain, so far as general regulations are concerned. The laws of colonization, the establishment of towns with municipal organization, and all of the municipal and central governments, were similar throughout the Spanish-American domain. But each country had its special laws and special officers of administration. Consequently, each state varied somewhat in its particular method of exercising governmental functions.

The most remarkable thing in connection with the settlement of Texas by the Spaniards is the land system and the methods of colonizing. The territory of Texas was formerly included in the same province as that of Coahuila, and represented the same system of government. Texas was settled by the missionaries, and their process of colonizing the natives and building churches was about the same here as elsewhere. Prior to the revolution in Mexico, and while the province of Texas was yet under the dominion of Spain, there was no inducement held out to settlers to occupy the country. Indeed foreigners were forbidden to enter the territory and remain. After the revolution, during which the Spanish yoke was thrown off, a liberal policy was adopted by Mexico in the colonization of Texas.

Texas was one of the provinces of New Spain until the year 1776, when it was joined with the territories of Coahuila, St. Andero, and New Leon, to form the intendencia of San Louis Potosi. This intendencia was in turn under the control of the supreme audiencia of Gaudalajara. After the revolution, Texas and Coahuila were united under a provisional government. While under the Spanish rule, Texas was an insignificant country and did not come into prominence until after it passed under the rule of the Mexican republic. In other words, it was not until people of other nationalities had availed themselves of the liberal colonization laws of Mexico that Texas became of any real importance to the world. Under Spanish dominion the frontier provinces were in a state of neglect. Foreigners were forbidden to settle in them, and their occupation by Mexicans was discouraged; but with the defeat and withdrawal of Spain from her vast dominions in the New World began a new era. There followed almost immediately new colonization laws.

The most important of these laws was in respect to the large grants of land made to contractors who settled the territory. By the national colonization law of Mexico, passed in August, 1824, a colonist could not hold more than eleven square leagues of land, one of which could be suitable for irrigation, four suitable for cultivation but not admitting of irrigation, and six for grazing purposes. All the provinces were subject to this law. Following this came the law of colonization established by the Constituent congress of the free and independent state of Coahuila and Texas for the settlement and regulation of lands within that territory. This law presented explicitly, in forty-eight articles, the various phases of the regulations for colonization. Among the peculiarly narrow provisions of this colonization law is the requirement that the colonist shall take an oath to observe the established Religion of the nation, as provided in the Constitution; this of course being the Roman Catholic. Apart from this consideration, the laws are liberal in the extreme, as far as their letter is concerned. There was a desire on the part of the authorities to people the territory with law abiding citizens and a class of people who would develop the resources of the country. In practice the laws were not always observed; or, if observed, they were accompanied with so much contention and delay as to greatly embarrass settlers. The government was very particular in formulating a law preventing the settlement of the strip of country, twenty leagues wide, bordering on the limits of the United States of the North. Likewise no settlements could be established within ten leagues of the coast of the Gulf of Mexico.

The greatest feature of the Texas laws is found in the contract system. By this a person could plant a colony by contract, provided that he brought a stated number of colonists from a distance. The contractor, or Empresario, agrees to bring one hundred families, all bona fide settlers, into a given territory, within a term of six years. In return for this service he is to receive a stated amount of land. For each hundred families actually settled, to the limit of eight hundred, the contractor is to receive five *sitios* of grazing land and five *labors* of land, one-half of which shall not be suitable for irrigation.[1] This violated the national law, which provided that eleven leagues should be the maximum amount owned by one person. To modify this it was provided that, after twelve years, the excess of eleven leagues should be alienated. If the owner should fail to dispose of it, then the "respective political authority shall sell it and give the proceeds to the owners after deducting expenses of the sale." By this law it was possible for an Empresario to own about 23,000 acres of land, or one township. The families were to be confirmed in the grants of the government by a clear title to the land. Each family was entitled to $177\frac{5}{8}$ acres. For this land the settler was to pay three and one-half dollars, if irrigable, and two and one-half if not. Should he desire to carry on stock-raising, then a *sitio* might be granted him, for which he was to pay thirty dollars, or about two-thirds of a cent per acre. The settler could have six years in which to pay for the land. The funds arising from the sale of land were collected by the ayuntamientos of the respective towns. These laws all applied to

---

[1] *Colonization Laws of the State of Coahuila and Texas*, Art. 12; Rockwell, 643. *Note.*—A *sitio* is one league, equal to 4428 acres; a *labor* is about 135 acres.

foreigners.   Native Mexicans could hold as individuals a maximum of eleven *sitios*, but must pay one hundred, one hundred and fifty, and two hundred and fifty dollars, for the respective grades per *sitio* (4428$\frac{4}{5}$ acres).   If at the end of six years the settlers had not cultivated and occupied the lands, then they were to revert to the government.   Likewise, if any person desired to leave the state, he might sell his land and take his proceeds with him, but might not own the land after he passed out of the state.   Many of the laws determining the privileges and duties of citizens and the functions of government were similar, and in some instances identical with the laws of the Indies for the colonization of New Spain, formulated during the early history of Spanish occupation.   The Indians were to receive and hold land upon the same condition as the other inhabitants of the community.   In the formation of towns, the minute details, as laid down by the old Spanish laws, were re-enacted.   As soon as forty families were in one place they must immediately proceed to form a new town and elect a municipal authority.   To facilitate the granting of lands to the colonists and the formation of new towns, a commission was created by act of September 4, 1827.   In this act the duties of the commissioners were clearly and explicitly defined.   They must, among other things, select the town site, survey it, and designate the places for the public buildings. They must also establish the colonists upon the town lots ; the position of each being determined by lot, the Empresario having his choice of the first two.   As soon as formed, the new town was to elect an ayuntamiento, provided that there were two hundred inhabitants, and provided that there was not another ayuntamiento within eight leagues of the place; otherwise, the new town was to be attached to the ayuntamiento already formed.

Under these liberal laws many settlers came into the territory and obtained much of the richest portions of Texas. Many large haciendas existed which are noted to this day; some maintained by the law and others divided.   One of the most remarkable of the Empresario colonies was that of General Austin. The first grant of privilege was made prior to the Mexican revolution by which the Spanish authority was overthrown. The grant allowed him to take three hundred families to settle in Texas. It was confirmed through the influence of his son, Stephen F. Austin, who went to Mexico, obtained a repetition and confirmation of the grant, and afterwards settled and managed a flourishing colony.

The Empresario could give colonists no right and title to lands, but he could determine who should enter the colony. A contract was made by the government with the Empresario to settle a certain number of families within specified limits. For this service he was granted land which he might use as he pleased. As no person could settle on lands thus set apart for a colony, the contractor had to judge of the suitability of individuals for colonists. Therefore the consent of the Empresario was essential to the acquirement of a title from the government. From this contract policy arose many of the haciendas or large estates in Texas.

The history of Texas during the present century, down to the close of the Mexican war, is full of interest. It is thrilling with adventure and exploit, but its story may not be related here.

CHAPTER XI.

The Social Condition of the Indians.

For a clear understanding of the influence of the Spanish invaders upon the aborigines of the conquered territory, it seems necessary to give a brief sketch of their social life before it was modified to any great extent by contact with the Spanish race, and to follow this by a description of the customs which prevailed among them after the outward forms of social life had been changed by the teachings of the conquerors. To the invaders the Indian question was one of great importance; for there was scarcely a royal decree for centuries, pertaining to the occupation of the soil, to which was not attached a rule for the regulation of the treatment of the natives. The theory that the conquerors and the conquered were to live peaceably on the same soil, each group retaining its own rights, but both mingling in social life under the same political organization, was sufficient in itself to cause endless trouble in the regulation of affairs. The theory was never verified, except in a few cases of infrequent and irregular practice; but it led to the origination of a new race, with a new civilization combining in many instances the poorer elements of the civilization of both races.

But how could there be a social life among savages who had scarcely entered into the upward movement toward modern civilized life? Social institutions were, indeed, fragmentary; but their elements are to be discovered, in such forms as to give unmistakable signs of development. Meagre as this life

238

was in many instances, it is not only an interesting, but also an essential question to the student of sociology who desires to find the outcome of certain existing institutions. The branches of the human race which have attained to a high degree of social development are, in their early life, represented by simple or elemental forms. From these, partly by indigenous growth, or self-evolution, and partly by contact with others, have developed the products of the highest civilization.

The social conditions of the natives of Mexico, New Mexico, and California, at the time of the Spanish occupation of these territories, were widely different. Although full credit may not be given to the extravagant statements of some writers, who have portrayed in high colors the magnificence of the social structure, it must be conceded that the Mexican Indians of the cities were well started on their way toward the development of modern social and political institutions. The chief difficulty in finding out the real status of the Indian prior to his contact with the European races, is that those who have given us records of their institutions have mingled with their description some ideas, which certainly must have been obtained from the invaders.

Cabrillo (1542) was the first to come in contact with the Indians of California; and he reports that they were found in huts along the coast, that they were poorly clad, and of an inferior race. Their food was fish and game, with wild berries and acorns. Venegas, in referring to the general character of the Indians of Lower California, says, " The characteristics of the Californians as well as of all other Indians, are stupidity and insensibility, want of knowledge and reflection, inconstancy, impetuosity and blindness of appetite, an excessive sloth and abhorrence of all labor and fatigue, an incessant love of pleasure and amusement of every kind however trifling or brutal, pusillanimity and relaxity ; and in fine a most wretched want of everything that constitutes the real man and renders him rational, tractable, and useful to himself and to society." [1]

---

[1] Venegas, *Noticias*, Part III, 64.

This is a very discouraging picture of those out of whom the Spanish Government was attempting to build states and make royal subjects. The priest-historian had been in contact with them, and doubtless knew their lives and habits. Father Boscana adds a deeper shade to the picture by asserting that the character of the Indian is diametrically opposed to that of the civilized European. Whatever is falsehood in the European is truth in the Indian, and vice versa. In a moral sense, his positive is our negative. Perhaps this is the reason why Indians seize the evil habits of Americans, deeming these the more virtuous.

The Indians of California have been classed among the lowest grades of the aborigines of America. They are small of stature, light of body, and lacking in mental capacity; yet at times courageous in defense against oppression. The docility of their nature accounts in a great measure for the success of the missionaries in organizing them into missions and teaching them domestic life. Certainly more savage tribes would have required a different process. The Indians of California were not very far advanced in social development. Living as they did a very simple life, their entire energies were devoted to obtaining food and to protecting themselves partially from inclement weather. In New Mexico the houses for protection were more substantial than in California, and the Indians lived in villages in a settled condition. In addition to the common method of obtaining food by means of the chase, they practiced agriculture to a limited degree and made use of irrigation as a means of facilitating cultivation. In the arts, too, they were much farther advanced on the road to modern civilized life. It is not within the scope of this chapter to present a picture of the arts and architecture, the industries and the laws of this race when discovered by Cortés and his followers. But the comparatively high state of civilization and the hoards of wealth discovered in populous cities of the South, furnished the key to northern exploration, as they excited the cupidity of the Spaniards. And in each of the other points of contact, California, New Mexico, and Old Mexico, the natives show evidence of the elements of social and political institutions. Here as elsewhere in the world, religion performs an important part in the organization of society. It is one of the primitive forces of social organization, and the earliest principle of association, except that of consanguinity.

But their religion could be nothing more than unsystematized superstition. When Cabrillo's men landed on one of the Santa Barbara islands, they found a primitive temple of the rudest sort, and in it a god, or rather a place for the object of worship. In the Journal of Cabrillo, it is stated that the natives " have in their villages their large public squares, and they have an inclosure like a circle; around the inclosure they have many blocks of stone fastened in the ground, which issue about three palms, and in the middle of the inclosures they have many sticks of timber driven in the ground like masts, and very thick ; and they have many pictures on these same posts, and we believe that they worship them, for when they dance they go dancing around the inclosure." [1]

When the Indian worshipped, it was with the idea that the spirit of the air met him at this appointed place and received acceptable homage. Boscana describes a temple of the Indians of the mission Capistrano, which is similar to that discovered by Cabrillo. The temple of Vanquech is located near the center of the village or group of villages. It consists of a circular enclosure formed by stakes driven into the ground, and apartments formed in the same manner. Within the inner enclosure is placed on an elevated hurdle the god " Chinigchinich." [2] Here the tribe met to worship. Viscaino discovered a similar temple, and around the seat of the god were

---

[1] *The Voyage of Cabrillo*, Tr. by H. W. Henshaw, *U. S. Geolog. Survey*, Vol. VII, p. 309.

[2] Boscana, *Chinigchinich*, Tr. by Robinson; Robinson's *Life in California*, p. 258.

placed feathers of birds of different colored plumage. These and other examples are sufficient to indicate the status of worship among the natives. Their religion seems to have been a rude spirit worship. It was formulated by the priests, who were also sorcerers and medicine men; consequently the religious belief and mythology varied greatly in the separate tribes, following the interpretations of the individual caciques. According to Boscana, the primitive belief of the Indians of the Mission San Juan Capistrano was founded on a rude cosmogony. They held that before this world there existed two worlds (one above, the other below), and that these were brother and sister. The former signified heaven ; the latter, the earth. But this heaven and earth existed before the present heaven and earth. Heaven came to Earth, bringing the light which was the sun, and said to the Earth that he would take her and make her his wife. But the Earth resisted, reminding him of their relationship. However, they were finally wedded, and their first children were earth and sand. "After which were produced rocks and stones of all kinds, particularly flints, for their arrows ; then, trees and shrubbery ; next, herbs and grass ; and again, animals, principally the kind which they eat."[1] Finally there was born an animated being, Ouiot, who was the *gran capitan* of the first family of beings, which differed very much from the Indians. After the death of Ouiot, there appeared unto the bereaved people, Chinigchinich, who endowed them with power to cause it to rain, to make the dew, to create the acorn and all manner of edible game. The Indian priests, sorcerers, and medicine men, claim to be descendants of this race, and thus wield a power over the people. They manufacture such mythology relative to the obtaining of food as will yield them the best support. By working upon the superstitions of the people they obtain a living without labor, since a part of the products of the chase and of the soil must go to them.

---

[1] *Chinigchinich*, Robinson, 243.

San Juan Capistrano.

Afterwards Chinigchinich created man, both male and female, out of clay. From these the Indians of the present day have descended. They were taught laws and ceremonies by Chinigchinich, and commanded to build a temple for worship. Such are the simple religious ideas of the natives, tinged with the ideas of the priest-historian, but upon the whole the most faithful account given of the beliefs of the natives. Throughout California there were many different tribes with variations of religious practices, but similar in grade of worship. It was this superstitious belief that was to be supplanted by the work of the Spanish missionary. But even under the best influences, it is doubtful if the old superstition was eradicated.

Besides the common plan of worship, there were council chambers belonging to some of the tribes, in which they practiced religious ceremonies. This council chamber seems to have had a variety of uses, but was probably never exempt from religious use. Within it the sacred fire was kept burning from fuel procured by men as a religious ceremony. A fire was built near the centre, sometimes near the door; and the natives, quite naked, stayed in the enclosure until in a profuse perspiration; then they passed out and plunged into a pool of cold water. The building was called the "temescal" or sweat-house. It was also used as a council chamber, sacred to the deliberations of the men who consulted on the government of the tribe. Women were forbidden not only to carry wood for the fire of the council chamber but also to enter the chamber. It has been suggested that much of this custom was founded upon native selfishness; that the air of religious mystery which surrounded it, and the penalty visited on women for daring to enter the council chamber, were instituted for the purpose of keeping the women away from the fire during inclement weather in order that the men might have more room.

The religion of the Indians of New Mexico was of a higher order; but in it may be discovered the same general idea and the same superstition that characterized the natives of California.

Their sedentary life would naturally lead to more definite practices and consequently more symmetrical ideas concerning worship. The Montezuma worship, of which the adoration of the sun is the chief characteristic, was the principal idea in religion. The worship of the sun is celebrated by the Indian dance. There seems to be a variety of dances. The Cachina of the Zuñi Pueblo, although the most noted, is not the most common. It is danced very infrequently and seldom witnessed by outsiders. Perhaps the attempt of the Spaniards to suppress all heathen rites has caused it to occur with less than usual frequency. The Cachina is for the purpose of invoking rain, a bountiful harvest, and other favors of their god. The scene, as described by those who have witnessed it, is truly picturesque. The dance is accompanied with a song and the sound of the drums, and is continued for many hours.[1]

The Pueblo Indians believe in the return of Montezuma at the rising of the sun. Many of them practice the ancient custom of assembling on the housetops, to light the sacred fires before the break of day and to watch for the coming of the sun. Doubtless they worship the sun; at least, Montezuma is a sun god. At Oriabe, the singing for worship begins at sunrise and continues throughout the day. The legend of Montezuma is told with many variations. In general, he is the hero-god of their mythology. From him came all beneficent things, and he will return and restore all things to the Indians. This idea of the return of the god as a benefactor is well-nigh universal among various tribes. They look forward to a time when a messiah shall return to right all wrongs and to reëstablish the lost power of the tribe. The Indians are very religious; they do nothing of importance without connecting with it a religious ceremony. The cacique is present on all public occasions to perform the proper religious ceremony; and the individual Indian is careful to obtain the good will of the gods in every private undertaking. Whether at play, at work,

---

[1] See illustration.

THE CACHINA DANCE.

or engaged in war, the Pueblo Indian shows his devotion. He invokes the spirits for success in war, for a bountiful harvest, for an abundance of game, for success in sports and gaming, and in all times of danger.

In connection with the religious worship of the Pueblo Indians is the estufa, an underground chamber where councils are held for worship, for political organization, and in some instances for health. Estufas are found in nearly all of the ruins of the ancient pueblos and in many of those inhabited at the present time. The estufa corresponds in a measure to the temescal or sweat-house of the California Indians. We find the latter most frequently used as a remedial agent, but also as a place of religious ceremony and political council. The temescal is built of logs and covered with earth. It is wholly or partially sunk below the surface of the ground. There is only one opening, very small but large enough to admit the passage of an Indian. The estufa of the Pueblo Indians is walled up with stone. It has one small opening at the top for the entrance of people and the escape of smoke. One of the main objects of the calling of a council in the estufa was to deliberate on the election of chiefs or leaders.[1] That there was a religious service connected with it is shown by the fact that the inhabitants of Pecos never allowed the sacred fire upon its altars to go out. Tradition said it was started by Montezuma; and they were faithful in keeping it for his return.

Such is the nature of the superstition with which the Spanish *padres* had to contend, a superstition that could not be eradicated so long as the father sought to communicate it to the son through succeeding generations. Question a Pueblo Indian to-day concerning his religion, and he will tell you that he has two gods, Montezuma or the Sun, and the Christian God. This shows that whatever new religious practices were imposed upon the natives, the old religious belief still main-

---

[1] At Zuñi pueblo, there are at present six estufas, all in use by the several clans of the village.

tained its hold upon the Indian nature. In many instances the missionaries allowed the natives to retain many of their old practices, partly because they could not do otherwise, and partly because it was a politic measure for securing better control of the neophytes.

Among the neophytes of the California mission, we find the continuance of the old religious practices. Several hours each day devoted to religious exercises failed to eradicate the old superstition. Such is the evidence given by the missionaries themselves. Churches were built in which the natives were assembled to worship. The bell at sunrise called them to mass. They moved in order under the control of overseers or captains. It must have been an impressive sight to see thousands of Indians bowing in worship to a new God. The religion offered them was a religion of pictures, of images, and of bright promises. It was well calculated to impress the superstitious savages, and it succeeded in winning them to its practice, even though it could not be fully understood by them and though the spirit of the old religion remained in their natures.

While it cannot be affirmed that there was any political society established either among the Californian or the New Mexican Indians, the elements of political life can be clearly discerned. Among the Californians, the unit of government was the small tribe. The New Mexican Indians were organized into clans. In matters of war, politics, and religion, each individual adhered strictly to his clan. Federation was not known, except for temporary warfare or in community of worship. At the head of each tribe was a hereditary chief, or captain as he is called since the advent of the Spaniards. In default of male issue, the kingship reverted to the brother of the king and then to his oldest son. The chief had but little authority except that which came from the reverence paid him by the members of the tribe. The penalty for insulting him was death. Through custom, his powers consisted principally in declaring war against other tribes and making peace with them. All differences of opinion arising between his own and other tribes must be decided by the chief. He also appointed fast-days and days for hunting game and gathering seeds. Every migration was determined by the chief. In some of the tribes there was a council of elders, which had at least advisory power in the decisions regarding peace and war. The council chamber was a universal institution throughout California, and without doubt it was used for determining the policy of the tribe. In New Mexico the *estufa* was used for the same purpose. If it be held that the *estufa* and the council chamber were religious or social institutions, it is still clear that there were political phases of life and a tribal government to be administered, and that the estufa was the meeting place of the tribal council. In early institutions the religious and political customs are closely blended. In fact civil customs frequently spring from religious ones. In all probability the council chamber was first formed to be used as a vapor bath. In the course of time there was attached to it a religious idea, which caused it to be used as a religious assembly and finally for the meeting of the council of old men. Castenada asserts that the villages of Tiguex were governed by a council of old men, and there are more recent instances of the estufa being used for deliberations of a political nature. Here, in secret council, the traditions of the tribe were communicated to the younger generation; here Indians were raised to the rank of chiefs; here war was declared, and the customs of governing the community were considered. The villages were small communes, which held the land and tilled the soil in common, and consequently developed from the tribal or family organization.

The Spaniards, finding the Indians in villages, allowed them to remain, or gathered them into larger towns and systematized their civil government. The estufa or council chamber was still used, as a place of worship where their heathen rites were celebrated, and as a place of political council. There all deliberations on public affairs were held, and the common concerns of the village transacted.   The local government of each pueblo represented a small democracy.   A governor, an alcalde, a constable, and a military leader were elected once a year by the majority of the men of the village.   The governor was called a cacique and carried a silver-headed cane as a badge of office.   The alcalde was the judicial officer of the village, and was usually the most important officer.   He was frequently judge and governor in one, and the principal man of the town.   There was, besides these officers, a council of elders, who advised the governor in regulating the affairs of the town.[1]   It was similar in form to the Spanish ayuntamiento or town council, and was patterned after it; for the old Indian council was doubtless formed of all the warriors. These forms of local government are carried on at present among the Pueblo Indians in their several villages.

The common customs of the Pueblo Indians have changed much less than either their religion or government.   Their houses are similar to those in use in the time of Cortés and Coronado.   Indeed the same houses exist and are occupied just as they were during the time of the Spanish invasion.[2] Their forms are well known; they resemble a series of terraces built one above the other, with no outside window or doors.   The houses are entered by means of ladders, which may be drawn up in time of danger.   The houses are built of adobe brick; the walls are thick and plastered within. The Pueblo Indians are communists.   There is one daily assembly of the tribe for meals, the men and women eating at different times.   Among the most noted pueblos are those of Taos and Zuñi.   The Indian village of Taos lies at the foot of the Sierra de Taos, the town having an altitude of 7,000 feet.   It consists of two large communal houses, in which live about four hundred Indians of all ages.

---

[1] Davis, *El Gringo*, 144.

[2] Morgan, Lewis H., *Houses and House Life of the American Aborigines*, 136 *et seq.*

ZUNI WATER CARRIER.

On the first day of January, the heads of the families assemble to elect their officers. These officers attend to the affairs of the village and control the political organization of the town. As in other villages, there is the secret organization, which controls the religious organization of the clans and attends to the public and private dances. Every year, on the thirtieth of September, the Taos Indians celebrate with a feast the virtues of their patron, St. Jerome. At this time one of the ancient dances is given, and races and games take place.

Taos is full of historic interest. It was first visited by the Spaniards in 1541, and was occupied by Oñate in 1598. At Taos, Popé planned the insurrection of 1680, by which the Spaniards were driven from the territory. After the re-conquest by Vargas, the Taos Indians twice revolted but with little success. After the occupation of New Mexico by the American forces, there was another uprising of the Taos Indians. The Indians fortified themselves and offered a stubborn resistance to the American troops.

The land belonging to each pueblo is held in common by all its inhabitants; but as a matter of convenience, it is apportioned among the several families, who dispose of the fruits of their own labor. The grant, made by the king of Spain, of one square league of land to each pueblo, was confirmed by the United States government, although no titles were given to the Indians in severalty. It was not the custom to grant lands in fee simple. A native could not dispose of his holding to a person outside of his own tribe nor to a Spaniard.

The Pueblo Indians were well advanced in the arts and industries. The tillage of the soil was practiced at an early date, and the method of irrigation was adopted long before Spanish occupation. At present they carry on the same mode of agriculture as formerly. The practice of communal ownership and family holdings is of ancient origin. The Indians were accustomed to clothe themselves in cotton fabrics of their own weaving, and to this day they continue to practice weaving by rude hand looms. Another industry, the making of pottery, was carried to a degree of perfection. The variety and perfection of this pottery, made both for domestic use and for ornament, are a cause of remark by all explorers, and a treasure to the archæologist. Relic hunters to-day find the Indian still engaged in making pottery, to which he not infrequently accords great antiquity.

Upon the whole, the Pueblo Indians were a jovial, happy race, until conquered by the Spaniards. Since that time they have greatly changed. Nevertheless, the free life which they now enjoy under our beneficent laws, enables them to regain something of their old elasticity. Mr. John G. Owens says:[1] " Play finds its best exemplification in the Indian of the Southwest. Living in a mild and genial climate, naturally shiftless and improvident, this true child of nature consumes his exuberant vitality by play instead of work. . . . . This spirit of playfulness remains with the boys, and characterizes their later life. Not so with the girls. These to the age of thirteen are very jolly and playful, but after that they begin to age very rapidly." Mr. Owens describes many of their games, including the rabbit-hunt, the races, and others less imposing. The Pueblo Indians have retained much of their old life since the advent of the Spaniards, although in outward appearance differences may be discovered. Formerly they led a happy life, and worshipped their gods in their own way. The Spaniards became their task-masters, and forced upon them a new religion. They gave the Indians new leaders and a new social system. Freedom was exchanged by the Indians for servitude. But they never fully gave up the old customs of meeting in the estufa, of worshipping their deities, and of practicing their own dances and games whenever opportunity offered. Even now they meet in the council-chamber as of old, celebrate their games and dances, and believe in their ancient superstitions. In his recent book on " The Delight

---

[1] *Some Games of Zuñi*, John G. Owens, *Popular Science Monthly*, May, 1891.

Tuos North Town.

Makers," Mr. Bandelier has given a faithful representation of the life of the Pueblo Indian. Pictures of the religious, social, and political life of the Indians are clearly drawn. They show conclusively the continuity of their institutions in the presence of a higher civilization.

The Indians of California were not so far advanced socially as were the Pueblo Indians of New Mexico. Their social and political organization was less complete, and their products of art were inferior, unless it be in the case of the ancient tribes of Santa Barbara. But the yoke of bondage bore even more heavily upon them. The transformation of their wild and jovial life into one of a steady routine of prayer and toil represents a great contrast, even though we consider the treatment of the missionaries to be mild and humane. Besides the routine of daily duties, the natives had their social hours of enjoyment. Not all the time was spent in prayers, not all in labor. Many spare hours were spent in dancing and playing games of chance, or in associating in idleness. By some their life is pictured as harsh and severe, by others, mild and humane. At best they were unaccustomed to order, system, and confinement, and the transition to the new life was certainly difficult.

The social status of the Indian, even after conversion, was uncertain, and his life unpromising. The attempt of the missionaries, working under the beneficent laws of the country, to make a citizen of him was attended with so many difficulties that it was for the most part a failure. The contact with stronger and more enterprising races, endowed with a mediæval thirst for land, was fatal to all legally obtained rights. The land question is at the foundation of the governmental system respecting the treatment of inferior races. The relation of the Indian to the soil is the one tangible thing that determines his social and political status. Without a permanent right in the soil there is no hope of permanency in other means of civilization. It is customary for those who have a deep sympathy for the Indian races of America to speak of the unjust treatment that the Indians have received from the United States in being robbed of all their lands. However unjust may have been the dealings of the first colonists and the Spanish government with the natives, it may be stated that they held no legal titles to the lands while under the Mexican and Spanish rule. The moral right to the land and the lack of justice in treatment in the case of natives of the United States are another question. Very early in the history of Mexico, the Spanish government began to formulate laws relating to the treatment of the Indians. Charles V. authorized the Viceroys to grant lands to each Indian village. Ten years later the same monarch, by a royal cedula, guaranteed to the Spaniards and the Indians the common use of pastures, woods, and waters adjacent to the village. In 1587, Philip II. decreed that eleven hundred *varas* square of land should be guaranteed to each village, and this amount was afterwards increased to a square league.[1] Subsequent decrees define the titles which the Indians held in these lands as merely possessory. Philip IX., desiring to protect the natives in their rights, decreed, in 1642, that the lands improved by the Pueblo Indians should belong to them ; but that they should have power neither to sell nor to alienate the lands.[2]

Again, in 1781, the decree of the Royal Audiencia of Mexico prohibited the Pueblo Indians from selling, renting, leasing, or otherwise disposing of lands in their possession, without the consent of the Audiencia. It is evident from these and similar regulations that it was the intention of the Spanish government to grant to the Indians only possessory rights in the soil, the real title remaining in the crown of Spain. When the Mexican government attempted to secularize the missions of California, but few legal titles to the land were given ; consequently, in most cases, their rights were recognized as possessory. After the treaty of Guadalupe Hidalgo, the Pueblo Indians of New Mexico were not recognized as citizens

---

[1] Davis, *Conquest of New Mexico*, 416.   [2] *Ibid.*

INDIAN WEAVING.

of the United States or of the Territory. The laws protected them in their persons and property. They had a right, also, to sue in the courts of justice, and were amenable to the criminal laws of the Territory. The United States government gave them assistance in agriculture and provided a reservation of land for their occupation. During the revolution in Mexico, the revolting party declared all persons, whether Europeans, Africans, or Indians, citizens of the republic. The Mexican Congress repeated this doctrine several times during the period of the change of government.[1] But after the national constitution was adopted, the Indians were always considered as wards of the government.

The Indians of the southwest, therefore, continued wards of the government after the close of the Mexican rule; and they will so continue until, placed in possession of a fixed amount of land, they give up their pastoral and nomadic habits and settle down to the pursuit of agriculture and the industrial arts. This must be accompanied with privileges of local self-government, and eventually with the privileges of full citizenship. Even then, their permanent social and political condition will not be assured. The process of changing from their present state to one of independence, thrift, industry, intelligence, permanent ownership of the land, and guaranteed political rights is not only dangerous, but is also difficult and uncertain. Years and years of education, generations of change, the accumulation of property, and the change of desires and tendencies must be brought about before the Indians can hope to enter the lists on an equal footing with the races with which they come in contact. It is feared that before this stage is reached the Indian problem will solve itself. Toil, self-determination, and self-support must characterize the Indians in the future, or they will be crowded to the wall in the struggle for existence. The lands which they occupy must yield their natural produce, the room which they take must yield its proper return of labor

---

[1] Davis, *El Gringo*, 149.

products, or they will certainly reap a swift and sure destiny. If they remain weak, indolent, and irresolute, the protecting care of the government will eventually fail to save them from homelessness and destruction.

The civilization which the Spaniards attempted to force upon the natives was inferior to that which they must face and attempt to adopt at present. The Spaniards led a slow, easy-going life, and the centuries of time occupied in developing the neophyte civilization show what progress may be made if sufficient time be given. Subsequent history proves how quickly these long-developed institutions may be destroyed by a single revolutionary act. With the best efforts, the Indians have never attained a position approaching social or political equality with the whites; they are not even theoretically equal before the law. They show little aptitude for political organization of the modern type, and have less opportunity to practice it. Education and change of pursuits may finally guarantee to a remnant of the race the rights of citizenship and equality before the law, and give them a respectable social position. Some progress has been made in the various Indian schools, and missionaries have done much in a religious way; but it may well be questioned whether the majority of the Indians on our reservations have a better social status than the Pueblo Indians had before the first European entered their territory.

CHAPTER XII.

The character of the people of California differed from that of every other Spanish province. Owing to its isolated position, there was but little communication with the remainder of the Spanish dominion, and there sprung up an independent spirit not observed elsewhere in Spanish America. There was also a larger per cent. of pure Spanish blood in the colonists here than in some of the older provinces of New Spain. In this fact the colonists took great pride, and often spoke of their Castilian descent. Yet with all this independence and pride, there was nothing to be compared to the earnest, vigorous life of the Puritan colonists of New England. The Spanish colonist was not zealous in building up a new government, in developing the resources of the country, or in providing for the education of his children. As a rule, he himself was ignorant and knew little of the culture and refinement that result from educational advantages. Besides, had he desired it, there were no opportunities for education, either from books or from the world. Shut out from contact with other men as well as secluded from their observations, he knew nothing but the easy-going life in a land where bountiful harvests supplied his needs without much exertion.

In the small towns the common settlers were old soldiers who had served out their time and were granted land in payment of past services. The upper class was composed of officials and their families. On the great ranches were frequently men of high rank, in whose veins flowed the best blood

255

of Castile. Here then were mingled two classes of people, the Mexicans and the Spanish, speaking two dialects of the Spanish language. The old Castilian, showing disdain for the Mexican and his language, took great pride in his own language and pedigree. Of this people the majority were kind-hearted and jovial, as is usually the case with people on the frontier who are not too greatly burdened with the cares of life. Their duties were not severe, and the free out-door life kept them in good health and cheerful. There was no necessity for the excessive labor which is generally the lot of the pioneer. The neophytes of the missions did nearly all of the work. The Spaniard lived on horse-back; riding was his only industrial occupation. The Indians did all of the menial work and served the Spaniards as a race of slaves.

At the fort a small town grew up, consisting of soldiers' families and those who settled there for protection. Garrison duty in one of these forts consisted in chasing an occasional stray Indian, disciplining the neophytes of the missions when called upon by the missionaries, and tending the horses and cattle on the king's farm. It was a lazy life at best, and colonists felt no need of exertion to combat cold or hunger, to clear forests, or to subdue the soil. The laws that governed the province were made in Spain or Mexico, and were of such tenor as to credit him with few powers of self-government. There was, therefore, no inducement for him to interest himself greatly in municipal or provincial government. Individually, the colonist was industrially and socially free. There was not much wealth in the country, and as the markets were limited, there was not much inducement to raise surplus crops. Yet there was plenty for all and this without much labor, while a race of servants performed all menial services. It was a land of peace and plenty; a land of sunshine and ease; a land possessed by a light-hearted and happy people. The descriptions of numerous travelers who visited the Pacific coast during the time of Mexican and Spanish dominion, together with old manuscripts, and the recital of the members of the prominent families of the early colonists, have given us glimpses of a social and political life free as in an uncivilized state.

The hospitality of the colonists was unbounded ; they were always glad to entertain strangers. In this the padres of the missions were not excelled by the owners of the haciendas. A person could travel from San Francisco to San Diego and never pay out a shilling. A saddle horse would be furnished him at one mission on which to ride to the next, and there a relay would be furnished. At the missions he would be received with hospitality and be treated to the best food and shelter the place afforded. Among the Spaniards of the better class it was customary to leave in the guest chamber a small heap of silver, covered by a cloth. If he was in need, the guest was expected to uncover this and take such a portion as was sufficient to supply his immediate wants. This custom passed out of use after American and other foreign adventurers came to the coast. Times had changed, and frequently the traveler did not scruple to help himself for prospective need. The spirit of generosity pervading the people is well illustrated by the following incident. A Spanish girl, Amalia Sibrian, relates her experience on a journey from Monterey to Los Angeles in 1829.[1] A young American accompanied her father's party, who insisted on paying for everything he received. " At one house the señora gave him some fruit, whereupon he handed her two *reals* which she let fall on the floor in surprise while the old Don, her husband, fell upon his knees and said in Spanish, ' Give us no money, no money at all ; every thing is free in a gentleman's house!' A young lady who was present exclaimed in great scorn, ' *Los Engleses pagar por todos!* ' (The English pay for every thing.)" Among the American pioneers of a more recent time somewhat of this same hospitality existed. You were welcome, if congenial, to stay a week or a month, to use horses and saddles free of charge, and there was danger of offence in offering to pay for the hospitality.

---

[1] *Century*, XLI, 469.

17

The sources of amusement in this sparsely settled province were not many, yet the people found occasion to exercise their social nature to a considerable extent. Balls and dances were given very frequently. Indeed the guitar and violin were seldom absent from any gathering and had an impartial place in most of the homes. There were numerous feasts and carnivals, at which the people gathered from many miles around and engaged in the festivities of the occasion, always ending in a ball. At the ball there was a variety of dances, including the celebrated fandango. The use of cascarones was commonly practiced at all great entertainments. Cascarones are egg-shells filled with finely-cut gold and silver paper, cologne, or harmless colored water. Sometimes, prior to the formal opening of the carnival, on the journey or at the arrival, cascarones were broken upon one another. Sometimes the sport became so rude that the dresses of the ladies and the faces of the Spanish cavaliers suffered. At the ball this sport was frequently dispensed with ; but it is related by travelers that it was the custom of the dance for the señoritas to break cascarones of cologne water upon the heads of their favorites at the party. It is represented as a challenge to dance or a friendly banter. Besides general *fiestas* there were frequent country dances where the neighborhood beaux and belles congregated for an evening's amusement.[1]

Dana gives the following description of the "fandango" at Santa Barbara which followed the marriage of Doña Anita de la Guerra de Noriega y Carillo, of one of the first families in California. The marriage ceremony was duly celebrated in the morning, and the dance occurred in the evening. "The bride's father's house was the principal one in the place, with a large court in front, in which a tent was built, capable of containing several hundred people. "As we drew near, we heard the accustomed sound of violins and guitars, and saw a great motion of the people within. Going in, we found nearly

---

[1] A Carnival Ball at Monterey in 1829, *Century*, Jan., 1891.

all of the people of the town—men, women, and children—collected and crowded together, leaving barely room for the dancers; for on these occasions no invitations are given, but every one is expected to come, though there is always a private entertainment in the house for particular friends. The old women sat down in rows, clapping their hands to the music, and applauding the young ones. The music was lively and among the tunes we recognized several of our popular airs, which we without doubt have taken from the Spanish. In the dancing I was much disappointed. The women stood upright, with their hands down by their sides, their eyes fixed upon the ground before them, and slided about without any perceptible means of motion; for their feet were invisible, the hem of their dress forming a circle about them, reaching to the ground. They looked as grave as though they were going through some religious ceremony, their faces as little excited as their limbs; and on the whole, instead of the spirited fascinating Spanish dances which I had expected, I found the California fandango, on the part of the women at least, a lifeless affair. The men did better. They danced with grace and spirit, moving in circles around their nearly stationary partners and showing their figures to an advantage." [1] Mr. Dana continues with an animated description of other dances and games which took place at "the fandango."

In all of the provinces of Spain, the national sport of bull-fighting was derived from the mother country. Even to this day it is a customary sport in the Spanish American republics. However, in primitive California it was less cruel than in old Spain or Mexico. The audience having assembled on raised seats and platforms, the bull is let into the ring. He snorts, rushing furiously from side to side as if he would destroy everything in his way. But instead of attacking the horsemen he retires to one side of the arena, where he con-

---

[1] Dana, *Two Years before the Mast*, 281.

tinues to paw the earth and bellow.[1]   Soon a horseman approaches the bull and waves toward him a scarlet cloak or gaudy *serape.* The animal rushes frantically toward the horseman, who skilfully avoids the charge. The excitement now begins; for some on horses and some on foot skilfully endeavor to avoid the infuriated creature. The gay señioritas wave scarfs, handkerchiefs, and shawls to the bold knights of the arena. After one bull is worn out by the struggle, another is let in to undergo the same test as his predecessors. Occasionally a horse is overturned or gored by the animal ; which serves to increase the interest. Thus the popular thirst for sport is satisfied. Other sports are cock-fighting and cock-pulling. The latter consisted in planting the cock in the sand with his head protruding, and the horseman riding at full speed and without dismounting, pulled the fowl from the sand. It took considerable skill to accomplish this feat, for a firm grasp was essential in order to secure the prize. Many other amusements were practiced by this idle, jovial people. As one might expect, gambling was practiced here as in other new countries and occupied much of the time of certain classes. The early colonists did not lack for amusement and apparently had plenty of time to engage in sport.

The dress of the colonists was simple and antique, except on extra occasions, when those who could afford it adorned themselves with such extravagant clothing as the country could furnish. The infrequency of the visits of ships laden with goods and furnishings from Spain or Mexico, rendered the supply extremely limited for those who desired elaborate wardrobes. This fact, coupled with the impoverished condition of the people as to money or exchangeable articles, kept dress within the bounds of simplicity and, in many instances, of poverty. Travelers tell us of the want of the soldiers of the garrisons for respectable clothing. The style of clothing changed at different periods and varied in different localities according to the

---

[1] Robinson's *Life in California,* 208.

contents of the last cargo of finery that arrived on the last ship from Spain. Bancroft cites many authorities of travelers concerning the dress of the inhabitants.[1] Robinson in speaking of the female attire at Santa Barbara about 1829, says, " The dress worn by the middling class of females is a chemise with short embroidered sleeves, richly trimmed with lace, a muslin petticoat flounced with scarlet and secured at the waist by a silk band of the same color, shoes of velvet or blue satin, a cotton *reboso* or scarf, pearl necklace and ear-rings with the hair falling in broad plaits down the back. Others of the higher class dress in the English style, and instead of the *reboso*, substitute a rich and costly shawl of silk or satin. There is something graceful in the management of the *reboso* that the natives can alone impart, and the perfect nonchalance with which it is thrown about them and worn adds greatly to its beauty."[2] The *reboso* is still used in Mexico and Spain as a part of the national dress but has nearly disappeared from the precincts of the United States. At the time when Robinson wrote, a great number of the people adhered to the ancient costumes, a century old. "Short clothes, and jacket trimmed with scarlet, a silk sash about the waist, *botas* of ornamented and embroidered deerskin, secured by colored garters, embroidered shoes, the hair long, braided and fastened behind with ribbons, a black silk handkerchief around the head, surmounted by an oval and broad brimmed hat, is the dress usually worn by the men of California."[3] This description of the dress of the Californians at this period, with some variations, represents the several costumes of old Spain down to the middle of the present century. And these costumes prevailed in America long after their principal features had been abandoned in the old country.

The best representations of the social life of the Spaniards on the Pacific coast are to be obtained from the writings of

---

[1] Bancroft, *California Pastoral*, 360 *et seq.*
[2] Robinson, *Life in California*, 46. [3] *Ibid.*, 47.

travelers who visited California, or else from the stories of the survivors of early times. Richard Henry Dana, who visited California in 1834–5, gives some graphic descriptions of the customs and habits of the people. "The Californians," he says, "are an idle, thriftless people, and can make nothing for themselves. The country abounds in grapes, yet they buy, at a great price, bad wine made in Boston and brought around by us and retail it among themselves at a real (12½ cents) by the small wine-glass. Their hides, too, which they value at two dollars in money, they barter for something that costs seventy-five cents in Boston; and buy shoes (as like as not made of their own hides, which have been carried twice around Cape Horn) at three and four dollars, and 'chicken skin boots' at fifteen dollars a pair. Things sell on an average, at an advance of three hundred per cent. upon Boston prices."[1] The dress of the people of Monterey at this time was similar to that worn in old Spain. The officers at the presidio dressed according to the custom of the country. Mr. Dana gives the following description of their picturesque style. They wore a "broad-brimmed hat, usually of a black or dark brown color, with a gilt or figured band around the crown, and lined under the rim with silk; a short jacket of silk or figured calico (the European skirted body-coat is never worn); the shirt open in the neck; rich waistcoat, if any; pantaloons open at the sides below the knee, laced with gilt, usually of velveteen or broadcloth; or else breeches and white stockings."[2] Their shoes are made of deerskin, much ornamented. In place of suspenders they always wore a red sash around the waist which varied in quality according to the wealth of the owner. In addition to this, the *serapa* or the *poncho*, and the costume was complete. The better class of people wore cloaks of black broadcloth, with abundant trimmings. The middle classes wore the *poncho*, a large square cloth with a

---

[1] Dana, *Two Years Before the Mast*, 85.
[2] Dana, 83.

hole in the centre for the head. The lower classes and Indians wear the blanket. So the *serapa* in its different forms determined the rank of the wearer. Among the Californians there were no working classes, the Indians performing all menial services. Therefore the poorer classes of Spaniards appear as if in holiday attire, "and, every rich man looks like a grandee, and every poor scamp like a broken down gentleman. I have often seen a man with a fine figure and courteous manners, dressed in broadcloth and velvet, with a noble horse completely covered with trappings, without a *real* in his pockets, and absolutely suffering for something to eat." [1]

The women wore gowns of silk, satin, or calico, made after European patterns, except that they had short sleeves and wore no corsets. Their shoes were of satin or kid and, like the men, they wore bright colored sashes. They had no bonnets and their hair was usually worn long, either loose or in braids. If it were necessary to protect the head, the Spanish woman covered it with a mantle, which is worn on most occasions. The love of dress and display is characteristic of both men and women. The better class of Spaniards take great pride in their purity of blood. The families of this class were mostly composed of the officials either in active service or those having settled in the vicinity after the expiration of their term of office. These are careful never to intermarry with lower classes of people and thus are able to keep their so-called Castilian blood free from the contamination of the base born. Bartlett, who visited Monterey in 1852, says that " Monterey has always been noted for its excellent society ; and although the Americans have monopolized every other town in the State, it still preserves much of its original character." [2] He says further, that "the old Californian or Castilian families are still in the ascendancy, but the young Americans and other foreigners are making terrible inroads upon them, and

---

[1] Dana, 84.
[2] Bartlett, *Personal Narrative*, II, 73.

carrying off their fair daughters." He speaks of the grace and beauty of the Spanish ladies and of the superiority of the inhabitants of California over those of Mexico, which he attributes to purity of blood and a superior climate.

The Spanish people were always extremely polite, even to superficiality in ceremony. It was customary for each member of the family to meet and embrace an acquaintance as he entered the room. This cordiality was given to strangers as soon as the people of the household whose guest he was recognized his genuine character. This ease and grace of character extended to all classes of people. The Mexicans of New Mexico are well described by Mr. Davis in " El Gringo." "They are distinguished for their politeness and suavity." It matters not how evil his character, the poorest wretch of the country often exhibits a refinement that would become a prince. This address and courtesy is practiced towards each other as well as toward strangers. " In their houses they are particularly courteous, and in appearance even outdo the most refined code of politeness." As you enter their house they assure you that you are at home and that they are entirely at your disposal. Should you happen to admire an article in the house, "the owner immediately says to you, ' *Tomele Vmd., Señor es suyo* ' (take it, sir, it is yours). But in these flattering expressions the stranger must bear in mind that the owner has not the most remote idea that he will take him at his word—that he will either command his household, lay his personal services under contribution, or carry off whatever pleases his fancy."

The society at the centers of population was peculiarly marked by the surroundings of the pioneer life. A portion of the time was devoted to the enjoyment of such pleasures as the country afforded. The homes in which the colonists dwelt, whether in the towns or on the ranches, were of the rudest structure. They were neither beautiful, artistic, convenient, nor comfortable. But the scanty means for improving buildings made any sort of a protection desirable in a new country.

In addition, the mild climate and the constant out-of-door life diminished the inducements to build substantially, even were the means present. The people lived out of doors, and returned to the house for sleeping and eating. Nearly all of the pioneer houses were of adobe with coarse timbers for the framework and the universal tile roof. Sometimes these one-story adobes were whitewashed without, plastered within, and had board floors; but frequently they were without any of these marks of comfortable appearance. Very little attempt was made at adornment of yards and gardens with flowers, and little attention was given to surrounding appearances. The interior of the buildings was rude in the extreme. The only furniture consisted of a bench along the wall and possibly a few chairs plaited with thongs of raw-hide. The rooms were seldom floored, much less carpeted. In an alcove, or at one side, was the bed, separated from the main room by curtains or board partitions. The floor was usually of hard earth. Although the majority of these houses have gone to ruin, the writer has visited houses of this description, occupied by rancheros and their families in the rural parts of California. There was a better class of houses of a block shape with small inner courts where flowers bloomed and possibly fountains played. This type is after the fashion of the houses in the villages of Spain and prevails to a great extent in some of the Spanish towns of New Mexico. All around the inner court was a gallery or corridor upon which opened the rooms of the house. These houses were frequently well supplied with im-ported furniture. The beds of the poorer houses were gener-ally formed of raw-hide stretched across head and foot pieces, or else common boards fastened to the sides of the house at one or both ends for support. Sometimes the outside door was formed by a frame covered with raw-hide. The houses sel-dom had chimneys or fireplaces, for the climate was sufficiently warm to render the trouble unnecessary. The kitchen was separated from the sleeping apartment. Homely as were these accommodations, they were occupied by a cheerful and

happy people whose only great aim in life was that of existing.
These homely apartments, if in town, were presided over by a
fair señorita, who directed the affairs of the household and
commanded the numerous Indian servants who performed all
the menial service.[1]

Of the state of society in the colonial period much may be
inferred from what has already been said. As the towns gradually developed, home products increased, and foreign trade
improved. There were greater marks of a settled state of society
and of civilization in general. By 1830, San José contained
about one hundred houses, besides a court-house and Jail.
Many of the houses were surrounded by a garden and fruit
trees, while a wider vista disclosed extensive fields of wheat and
corn.   Irrigation was carried on to a considerable extent and
the stream that furnished the water also lent its power to run
a respectable grist mill.   A well known writer of the period
describes the men as "indolent and addicted to many vices,
caring little for their children, who like themselves grew up
unworthy members of society."—The same writer praises the
female members of the community as chaste, industrious, and
of correct deportment.   This condition of affairs he applies to
the country in general.   Society was in a state of confusion.
At a later period and in the wealthier communities there was
greater distinction of classes ; especially was this true of Mexico.   In that country, even to the present time, the Indian,
the Mexican and the Spanish of pure blood form a series of
classes almost as distinct as the castes of India.   Among all
Spanish inhabitants there was extreme veneration for the
missionary priests and a faithful adherence to the practices of
the Catholic church.   The superiority of the friar in intelli-

---

[1] In the *Century* for Jan., 1891, will be found two cuts of famous Spanish
houses; the one of General Vallejo at Sonoma, and the other of the Camu-
los Ranch rendered prominent by Helen Hunt Jackson's "Ramona."   In
the same contribution, by Chas. Howard Shinn, is a picture of the Guerra
Mansion, illustrating a home of another style.

gence and general knowledge of the world, placed him in a station far above the average status of the community; therefore he wielded great influence.

Throughout California the ancient usages of the mother country survived in the attempt to suppress immorality by civil law. The institutions of Sola, in 1816, declared that "harmony and good morals must be maintained and particular precautions must be taken to prevent adultery, gambling and drunkenness.[1] It was also stated that religious duties should be enforced by the stocks and there should be no intercourse maintained between the citizens and the Indians. Notwithstanding the power and the influence of the friars, who stood for the church, there seems to have been but little interest in the progress of civil society except as it tended to forward the interests of the neophytes of the missions. Perhaps the dealings of the Spaniards with the natives had taught the padres to protect their own interests and to defend the Indians. At least the friars always assumed a great deal of power which they sometimes wielded without authority.

The friars were opposed to popular education, and as there was a lack of funds in the treasury and few teachers, all of poor qualifications, education did not flourish.[2] The attendance in the primary schools established was very small, and the actual good accomplished of doubtful significance. At San Diego, in 1829, there was a primary school of eighteen scholars; the teacher Menendez was paid from fifteen to twenty dollars per month, out of the municipal funds.[3] At an earlier period, Sola founded a school at Monterey, and took a great interest in the education of the children; this subject having been much neglected before this time. "Children were taught religion, reading, writing, and reckoning," four r's instead of the three characteristic of the primitive school of the eastern

---

[1] Bancroft, *California*, II, 390.
[2] Bancroft, *California*, II, 679.   [3] Bancroft, *California*, II, 548.

colonies. Thus, between the formal rites of the church on one side and a life given over to the pleasures of the hour on the other, with enforced idleness on account of the services of the neophytes and preparation for life by way of education, grew up a race of people not able, in educational and industrial zeal, to cope with the Anglo Saxons. A time came when the careless, indolent, unprogressive life was insufficient to maintain the civilization, which had been established, against the rude encounter of a superior race. The gay, jovial life, full of good fellowship and hospitality, soon found no opportunity for its exercise.

The industries of the Spanish population consisted chiefly in the rearing of cattle for the commerce of the hides and tallow, and a small agriculture. To the missions is to be credited the immense crops of grain produced in these early times. In the towns small tracts of land were apportioned to the settlers for tillage, but their chief property consisted of the flocks and herds that wandered beyond the precincts of the town into the great pasture fields. Yet some attention was paid to crops and to the introduction of different agricultural plants. Olives were introduced by the padres at an early date, and, in 1801, these were utilized in the manufacture of oil. An unsuccessful attempt was made to raise cotton, in 1808, and hemp culture continued to receive attention from the government from time to time. The soil was imperfectly tilled, but bountiful harvests were secured. It is reported that grain yielded a hundred fold from a single sowing. The plow that was used down to the middle of this century was of primitive make; it consisted of a crooked branch of a tree sharpened at the end and then shod with an iron point. A long pole extended to the yoke of the oxen, where it was fastened with a wooden pin. The ox-yoke rested upon the back of the oxen's heads and was tied to the horns. The driver took the handle of the plow in one hand and the ox goad in the other and thus the soil was stirred and nature smiled on the rude effort.[1] It was a common practice for the Spaniards to employ Indians to till the soil. The former remained idle, giving from one-half to one-third of the crops to the latter for cultivating the soil.[2] A crop of wheat or corn could be produced with little labor, and fruit of all kinds became plentiful with little effort on the part of those who would take the trouble to plant trees. The vine was early introduced and yielded bountifully. Some wine was made and occasionally a little brandy. There was no market for fruit beyond the amount demanded for home consumption. In all domestic trade a tithe had to be paid on every transaction.

On the great ranches cattle and sheep ranged with little attention. Sometimes they became so plentiful that they were slaughtered to lessen their number, there being no market. At San Fernando the sheep became so numerous that the "friars complained that they must all be killed as there was no place for them."[3] Many instances of the slaughter of cattle to decrease their number are recorded by Bancroft. A general council was formed at San José in 1806, by order of the Governor, to decide how many horses should be killed and how many preserved. It was finally decided that twenty-five horses should be allowed to each family and the remainder destroyed. Within a month 7500 horses had been killed.[4] The slaughter was continued at other places. Here as elsewhere the domesticated Indians did most of the work. Sometimes they worked for a plain support, sometimes they received wages for services rendered. The missionaries were the first toilers among the colonists of California. With the aid of the soldiers, they took and held possession of the territory. But

---

[1] Plows of this sort are still used in some parts of Mexico. They are no improvement on those with which the Egyptian stirred the fertile soil of the Nile valley, five thousand years ago.

[2] Bancroft, *California*, II, 415.

[3] Bancroft, *California*, II, 358.   [4] Bancroft, *California*, II, 182.

there were not wanting from the beginning artisans to labor. From time to time, skilled workmen in the industrial arts were found in every town and at every mission. So, too, came tradesmen, and stores were opened from which the colonists secured their supplies. But manufactures were limited to the needs of a simple life, as were also the articles of commerce; consequently there could be but little of either commerce or manufacturing.

As to the political life, there was comparatively little interest in self-government. The colonists belonged to a race who were jealous of their liberty, but centuries of rule by princes and potentates who seldom consulted the wishes of the people, in legislation or administration, had accustomed them to the dictates of a central authority. They performed their duties perfunctorily and with some occasional signs of zeal, but, as a usual thing, they had but little liberty, except to carry out the decrees of higher powers. In the towns there was a show of local self-government in the election of the alcaldes and other councilmen, but anything like national life or nationality seemed to be wanting. Having no independence and no close bond of union with the mother country there was but little opportunity to develop either a national or a colonial spirit of any power.

There are still survivals of this colonial life in the modern state of California. There are the Indian neophytes, dispersed and diminished in numbers; there are the Mexicans, who have dwindled in power and number. Besides these, thirty of the old Castilian families still have surviving members engaged in the industries of the state.

Even after the end of Spanish rule in California, the Mexicans changed their method of government but little. There was still a wide separation in life and sympathy between the people of California and of Mexico. The exercise of independent political power was very slight. The apathy that characterized other things existed also in political affairs. The town officers endeavored to discharge their duties perfunc-

ORAIBE, EASTERN COURT.

torily; the commandant of the presidio attended to his; but the townspeople desired their ease and pleasure and cared little about politics. There were plenty of laws and a detailed system of administration, but in execution, in actual government, the people were quite indifferent. There was considerable show of a spirit of local independence in the revolution that occurred in 1836, but it soon subsided. Many of the officials were appointed in Mexico and sent out to California, consequently the aspirations for office could not be cultivated with much surety of reward. The selection of a few local officers, from time to time, for the proper government of the town, represented their chief exercise of political rights. Their laws were already made and their chief officers appointed; so that there was nothing to be done.

Among all institutions, language is the first to be recognized in the contact of one race with another, and one of the most enduring in its effects in the decadence of a system of institutions. Law, government, and even religion may be replaced with greater ease than language. The Spanish language has had an extended use in America for nearly four centuries, and is now the common speech in the Spanish-American republics. In many of the towns and hamlets of our own republic its musical flow is still to be heard. In the region of the southwest, where the English civilization has not overpowered and nearly obliterated the Spanish civilization, the use of the Spanish language has had a decided influence on the English tongue, and has added not a few words to our common speech. Here two dialects of the Spanish language have been spoken, and consequently the influence on our own language has arisen from two sources. The first source is the old Castilian language, still used by the few remaining aristocratic families of pure blood. I say *old* Castilian, for several centuries of use in the provinces have changed it but little from the form in which it was introduced into the colonies from the continental Spanish. Even now it differs but little from modern continental Spanish, for the

Spanish language, as compared with other modern languages, changes but little from century to century. Indeed we are told that the language spoken by the people in the rural districts of Old Spain is retained through its constant use in the commercial contact of these people with the better classes of the towns. However, it seems that the literary language of Old Spain has changed far more than the language of the provinces, and in an entirely different way. But this only illustrates a well-known law, that old forms of speech are retained in the colonies and remote parts of a nation, while more rapid changes are to be noted in the intelligent and progressive centres.

Thus we find in the provinces that the *ll*-sound loses its force and is used as a long *i*-sound, or, more properly, as a long *i*-sound with a slight breaking. Also, that the *ñ*-sound so prominent in continental speech is in the provinces suppressed to a smothered *n*-sound. Likewise the *b* is used interchangeably with *v*, with a tendency to substitute the *v* for the *b*. (It has been maintained that these changes are noticeable in a comparison of the language of the rural districts of Spain with those of the centres of intelligence). The old Castilian families using this speech are rapidly disappearing from the country : their great estates have passed into the hands of others, and their prominent position in society is gone.

It is chiefly through the second source, the Mexican dialect, that words have found their way into the common speech of our country. It is through the language of the common people, through the Spanish language clipped and degraded by the commingling of unlettered Spaniards with an inferior race, that words find their way into English. It was the policy of Spain to amalgamate conqueror and conquered into one homogeneous nationality, and the results of this attempt are plainly visible in the nature of the language produced. The Mexican dialect is quite extensively used in New Mexico and California by the great majority of the people of Spanish blood and their native converts to Christianity. This language is also quite commonly used as a matter of convenience by those associated in business with the Mexican race. But what concerns us most in the consideration of this topic is the fact that this dialect is furnishing the English language with words, some of which are to be used for the sake of convenience for a time, and others to be permanently incorporated into our common speech. I will mention a few of the latter class, which seem to admit of universal use, and appear indispensable to an intelligent expression of thought; afterwards I shall refer to others in common use in certain sections of country by certain classes of people.

Adobe. Prominent in the first class is the word *adobe*, meaning sun-dried brick. The greater number of the primitive houses and public buildings of the Spanish colonists were constructed of this material. It is not uncommon to see these buildings, some of them at present over a hundred years old. By those familiar with this style of architecture, the word *adobe* is used without question as the only term that will exactly describe it. It is frequently used as a substantive, as " an old *adobe*."

Cañon. No other word will express just what the word *cañon* does, so long as the mountains on the western half of the continent retain their present structure. It is indispensable; for the words gulch, valley, gorge, fail to convey the exact meaning. It is of universal use as applied to a channel with high walls, formed by an upheaval or by the erosion of water, or probably by both. Its specific meaning is apparent to one familiar with western mountains. In common speech it is frequently applied indiscriminately to a valley or gorge of any kind.

Tules. This is a common expression for a rush or water-reed that grows along the bays and rivers of California. The word was in common use by the Spanish population, and has continued to be about the only designation for this species of rush. Bret Harte in his 'An Apostle of the Tules' speaks of the " ague-haunted *tules*."

18

Bonanza. It is difficult to determine whether this much-used word will obtain a permanent place in our language. It found a ready use in mining times as an expression of good fortune in the discovery of a rich mine. Originally it meant "fair weather at sea;" but now it is applied indiscriminately to a treasure of any sort. Its specific application to the great silver mines of Nevada has tended to give it prominence.

Vara is the old Spanish yard, adopted by the Mexican government as the standard for linear measurements. It had its origin in the Castilian *vara* of the mark of Burgos. It is equal to about thirty-three and one-third inches of English measure, thus representing a short yard. The word is still found in deeds and specifications, especially of titles of village lots. It is not uncommon to hear an old-time settler speak of a "twenty-vara lot," or of a "fifty-vara lot." Occasionally we find the lots advertised in *vara* measurements.

Fandango. This word has long been used in America. It is the name of a dance brought into the West Indies by the negroes of Guinea. It has frequently been used to designate any sort of dance of a low order, but should be applied to a dance of the common people written in three-eighths time. The dance is practiced to such an extent by the Spanish-Americans that it has been nationalized.

As the Spanish and English-speaking people mingled at a time when the tending of flocks and herds was the chief occupation, many of the new words adopted refer to this industry. A few of this class will be mentioned.

Corral. This word originally meant a circular yard formed by setting posts in the ground and fastening them together with thongs of raw-hide. The *corral* is essential to the herder as a place where his stock may be collected for the purpose of protection or for successful handling. If the *ranchero* wishes to capture a certain horse to ride, the whole band is driven into the *corral* and the *vacquero lassoes* the one desired with his *lariat*. The *corral* is one of the first structures built by the herder on his arrival in a new territory. The farmer of the far west never says " cow-pen," " barn-yard," or " farm-yard," he says *corral*. The word is applied indiscriminately to any small enclosure for stock.

Vacquero, according to its strict etymology, means " cow herder" or, in more common English, "cow-boy." However, this is not its better use, although it is frequently so applied. The *vacquero* is pre-eminently a horseman or a horse trainer. He is frequently employed to tend stock, but his chief business is to manage wild horses or to tame *broncos*. The horses of a *ranchero* frequently run at will, unfettered by bit, bridle, or even halter, until they are desired for use. Here is the difficult work of the *vacquero*. He drives the band into a corral, captures the one to be ridden, succeeds in putting a bridle or *jácquima* on his head, blindfolds the animal, puts the saddle on, mounts for the ride, and then removes the blind. Then begins a series of antics on the part of the animal, and the rider is fortunate if he keeps his seat through them all. This process must be repeated from day to day until the animal is domesticated. Sometimes the *vacquero* finds steady employment at a single *rancho*, and sometimes he goes from one to the other, plying his trade as there is need.

Ranch is from the word *rancho*, and was first used in connection with the land-grants to the Spaniards in the Indies. It is of Spanish American origin. The word ranch needs no comment. It sounds a trifle inelegant in contrast with the long accustomed word 'farm;' but it has succeeded in entirely replacing this word in many parts of the west. It is doubtful if it will retain this prominence as the large ranches are broken up into small farms and a diversity of agriculture is introduced.

Rodeo. It is in connection with the rearing of stock that this word is commonly used. In pastoral territories all stock runs somewhat at large ; consequently the property of different individuals is widely scattered and commingled. To sort the stock and accredit each owner with his property, the annual or semi-annual *rodeo* or "round up" is held. Each owner sends one or more representatives to the *rodeo*. The cattle are "bunched" in the open field, and the *vacqueros* proceed to separate from the band each owner's stock. This requires great skill of the horsemen. In the olden time a judge (*huez de campo*) presided over the field-assembly and judged of the rights of each according to customary law. The word *rodeo* comes from the Spanish *rodear*, 'to surround, to compass.' Its vulgar pronunciation is "rodeer."

Loco is a good old Spanish word meaning insane, crazy, or crack-brained. It is specifically applied to horses and cattle afflicted with a strange disease, accompanied with variations of insane and idiotic symptoms. It is a common belief that the disease is caused by eating a plant called "loco-weed," of the family *Leguminosae*, genus *Astragalus*. But this has not been proved, and there are many different theories concerning it ; some attributing the cause to the use of bad water, some to poor food, and others to too much food. The animal afflicted with the disease stops, trembles, staring all the while in an insane manner, snorts, and springs suddenly to one side as if dodging a blow. It apparently sees things that are not, and is a victim to strange hallucinations. Becoming useless, it is turned out to take the chances of partial recovery or final death. The term has a wide application in common use. A person not quite sound in mind or rational in thought is said to be *locoed*, or is "loco," as the term is frequently applied. It is quite curious that the plant is also called "rattle-weed" from its peculiar properties, and that the term "rattled" is derived from the idea of its effect on animals. Consequently the word "rattled" designates a mild form of locoism.

Burros. Throughout the west, and especially in New Mexico, the term burro is applied to a small breed of the donkey or Mexican ass. This homely but useful creature was brought from Spain at an early date and is now much used in the Spanish-American states. It is the same creature that carries the burdens in the streets of the towns in old Spain, or bears the traveler over the mountains of Asturias. In the towns and mountains of America, it is found performing the same respective services. Wherever this patient, durable, and useful creature goes he is known by the name of *burro* and by none other.

Bronco is the name applied to a wild or untamed animal, as a *bronco* colt or a *bronco* horse. Sometimes it is applied colloquially to an unruly boy.

To pass to the words of the second class, those which are used by persons of certain sections or by special classes, there is a multitude. I will mention a few : *sombrero* 'hat,' *lariat* 'raw-hide rope,' *jácquima* 'head-stall' or 'halter,' *reata* 'raw-hide rope,' *hacienda* 'estate,' *compañero* 'companion,' *vara* 'a Spanish yard-stick,' etc.

There are many short phrases in common speech which are temporary in use, such as *mucho frio, mucho caliente, poco tiempo, muchas gracias, si Señor,* etc. Their chief influence is exercised in detracting from the use of good English. But to the student of institutions nothing is more interesting than the names of places, which so copiously illustrate the former domination of another race. As the Roman, Saxon, Dane, and Norman have left their monuments in England, so we find in the names of the mountains, rivers, towns, and political divisions of the land, evidences of a preceding civilization. In most cases the names have been carefully selected, and doubtless will remain unchanged. The country is still full of the names of the saints, patrons of early expeditions and enterprises. Santa Barbara, Santa Fe, San Diego, San Francisco, Los Angeles, and Sacramento bring vividly before us the labors of the religious orders and of the *padres* who attempted to establish a civilization in a new land. Pioneers they were who broke the virgin soil and settled a new state. So too in *Alameda* 'the grove,' *Fresno* 'the alder,' *Alcatraz* 'the pelican,' *Lobos* 'the wolves,' and in a thousand other words, we have evidences of a Spanish nomenclature without a Spanish civilization. Likewise *Puebla* reminds of the village common, and *alcalde* of the chief officer of the town. We need not omit from this medley of words "Monte del Diablo" and the legend of the appearance of the wearer of the cloven hoof, with the tradition of strange sights accompanied by the noise of clanking chains.

In literature nothing of any note was done, unless it be the historical epic of the conquest of Oñate, written by Captain Gaspar de Villagrá. According to Bancroft, this poem is a correct account of the conquest. It is written in a smooth flowing style. "Of all the territories of America—or of the world, so far as my knowledge goes—New Mexico alone may point to a poem as the original authority for its early annals."[1]

Bancroft gives a long quotation from this ancient document. The poet begins by translating the first line of Virgil, and continues by narrating the events of the expedition as they occurred, not failing to praise the heroes of the invasion. The argument of the first canto is as follows:

> "*First Canto,*
>
> "Which makes known the argument
> of the history, and the situation of New Mexico and
> knowledge had of it from ancient monuments
> of the Indians and of the departure
> and origin of the
> Mexicans."

The first canto begins as follows:

> "Of arms I sing and of the man heroic
> (*Las armas y el varon heroico canto*)
> The living, valor, prudence and high effort,
> Of him whose endless, never tiring patience,
> Over an ocean of annoyance stretching, etc."

Aside from its historical representation, this poem, though of no great literary merit, has about it a picturesqueness quite unique. Recounting the long, hard marches, hardships, fatigues, and encounters with the Indians, it could scarcely

---

[1] Bancroft, *Arizona and New Mexico*, 115.

reach any great height as a work of poetic art. Nevertheless, it is the only attempt to describe the conquest and settlement of America in an epic poem. There were other attempts at poetry, and some very fair verses were written in the Spanish colonial days, though they were chiefly the products of Mexico. The pastoral life in California had its poetical phases, but there was a dearth of poets.

Upon the whole, the social and political phases of Spanish colonial life are full of interest. The subject borders on the romantic. The people were free from the dangers that usually threaten colonies, though afflicted by their peculiar evils. The people were happy, jovial, and hospitable. Their life was one of ease and idleness. They were contented with little. They were not ambitious for wealth or political power, and apparently thought little of the development of the country. Recent writers have given us graphic pictures of society as it now exists in Mexico, resembling to some extent the society in California, three-quarters of a century ago. This easy-going, simple life, free from care and anxiety, has its charms, but cannot be compared with the active existence of the great state of California.

CHAPTER XIII.

POLITICAL AND JUDICIAL POWERS.

In the government and administration of the Spanish provinces, there are to be found traces of the old feudal régime. The establishment in Spain of a strong central government, administered by officers appointed by the crown, failed to eradicate the ancient feudal forms. Not only did these forms re-appear in local government, but the colonies were treated as feudatories of the crown, governed by the king's special agents. It never occurred to the king that the colonies were to be treated otherwise than as his special property, existing for the sole purpose of yielding revenue and performing service. Therefore to the crown and to the royal officers it appeared that the colonists had no civil rights other than those contingent upon the king's will and pleasure.

During the whole of the Spanish rule the colonists were treated according to the foregoing principles. The local officer reported to the provincial governor, the provincial governor to the viceroy, and the viceroy to the king; and the king and boards of royal officers made laws for the government of all.

After the Mexican Revolution of 1821, the same laws, principles of government, and forms of administration continued, except as they were modified by the Republican administration which was engrafted upon existing forms and institutions. Therefore if we seek the municipal practice, the civil government, and the powers of officers held during the early part of the Mexican rule, we shall find the old Spanish usage that had hitherto prevailed continuing with the exception of a change

280

in the supreme authority. The administration of the Spanish colonial possessions was carried on chiefly by a system of chambers or boards. The supreme authority in administration rested in the Council of the Indies, in perpetual session at Madrid. All departments of government were under its control. Under its authority the territory was divided into viceroyalties, provinces, audiences, and many minor divisions. The government continued to expand and the territorial divisions to multiply, until toward the close of the eighteenth century there were four viceroyalties; Peru, New Spain, New Grenada, Buenos Ayres. The viceroyalty of New Spain, which is the only one that concerns us at present, was divided into Provincias Internas and New Spain proper. Of the former there were two internal provinces depending directly upon the Viceroy, and five subject to the governor of Chihuahua. In the latter group are found the provinces of New Mexico and Texas. New Spain proper was divided (1804) into twelve intendencies, which had taken the place of the former gubernatorial provinces in 1786. Two of these divisions were represented by Old California and New California respectively. The viceroy was the head of the governmental system in America. He received his office by appointment and stood for the king in all things. In the viceregal authority, all powers of administration were concentrated. The local affairs of different provinces were referred to the viceroy, who in turn reported to the king through the Council of the Indies. The royal provinces were revenue districts whose heads were appointed by the king. These officers were subject to the supervision of the viceroy and governors. The governors were captains-general of their districts, and acted as presidents of the audiences.[1]

After the gubernatorial districts were changed into intendencies, the chief officer in each intendency had financial, judicial, political, and military control of the district, though assisted

[1] Bancroft, *Mexico*, III, 520.

by the assessor. The intendants were all appointed by the king. In the cities, sub-delegates also were appointed by the king, and exercised functions similar to those of the intendants, but in a lesser degree.[1] These latter officers replaced the town officers by taking charge of the political and commercial supervision of the town. As each set of rulers was appointed by the king, they were so arranged as to watch one another in administration. As new abuses developed, new officers were created for the purpose of espionage, and the official list became greatly extended. The number of officials and the amount of governing exercised in Spain, far exceeded that of any other nation on record. Large numbers of persons came from Old Spain chiefly to hold office ; for it was a policy of the government that only Spaniards of the mother country should fill the offices of New Spain. With the numerous departments, the details of each, and the distance from the seat of the central government, it frequently took years to settle some small question of administration which should have been settled by an alcalde or a provincial governor.

After Mexican rule, the supreme authority rested in a congress, and each state had its provincial assembly. The two houses of congress had their especial legislative restrictions, but together represented the legislative assembly of the Republic. The Californias were ruled by governors, prefects, and sub-prefects representing the central administration. The military authorities continued to exercise great control. Thus the governor of the province was called military commander of all of the forces within the province, and the commandant of the presidio on the frontier was in reality the chief officer within the surrounding territory.

The governor of the Department was appointed by the central authority at Mexico, and he had the power of appointing the prefect and of confirming the sub-prefects within his jurisdiction. The governor presided at the meetings of the

---

[1] Bancroft, *Mexico*, III, 520.

Departmental legislature, and had charge of public order throughout the department. His appointing power extended to all other officers not otherwise provided for by special legislation. With the consent of the departmental legislature, he had the power to suspend the ayuntamientos of the department, and to suspend the officers of the department for a term of not more than three months. It was made one of the important duties of the Departmental governor to publish and execute or cause to be executed the laws of Congress. The prefects were official inspectors of the affairs of the department. As such, they supervised the administration by reporting to the governor many things concerning the actions of officers and the complaints of the people. It was their duty to see that the laws were carefully enforced and to report any delinquents. They had to report on the economic conditions of the country, and its political and economic needs. The prefects appointed the sub-prefects, subject to the approval of the Governor.

The Departmental legislature, as composed by the Mexican law of 1837, consisted of seven persons. The law provided that it should be convened every four years. Among other duties it belonged to the Departmental legislature, " To pass laws relative to taxes, public education, industry, trade, and municipal administration." [1] Thus we have in the provincial system of government, one that was closely united with the central administration, and that extended down to the municipality, having power to make laws relative to municipal administration. In this respect it did not differ from the administration of the provinces while under Spanish rule.

The local government of New Spain was a very complete and formal affair as far as the law was concerned, but in practice it was very irregular and subjected to the domineering power of the royal or provincial officers. The municipal governments were represented by alcaldes, regidores, and

---

[1] Section III, article 5.

syndicos. In most towns there were alcaldes. In large towns there were twelve regidores or councilmen, and in small towns six. "In minor places," says Bancroft, "many of these offices remained vacant, partly owing to the interference of governors and their lieutenants, who wished to retain the sole control. In other places, the alcaldes were mere figure-heads."[1] During the Spanish rule the municipal officers were at first usually elected for one year; but later the office of regidor was commonly sold to such persons as had gained the favor of the royal officers. However, in the regulations of 1779–81 for the government of California, it was provided that the governor should appoint alcaldes and other town officials for the first two years, and afterwards the citizens of the town should elect some one from their midst, subject to the approval of the Governor.[2] The powers of these municipal officers were to administer justice in small cases, control the police, supervise public works and the distribution of water privileges. The duty of the alcalde, as prescribed by law, was to try civil and criminal cases "of first instance." Appeals could be made to the city council (ayuntamiento), the governor, or the supreme audiencia. It was the duty of the alcalde to preside over the town council in the absence of the governor, his lieutenant, or of an alcalde mayor. The alcalde, associated with one or more regidores of the council, could fix the licenses to shops and taverns in towns where no governor resided; otherwise that duty belonged to the governor. There were other officers not essential to the town government, but frequently chosen in the larger towns, especially toward the close of the eighteenth century. These were the *alferez real* or banner carrier, the procurador-sindicos (city attorneys), who represented the council in legal matters and made collections, and the treasury officers.[3] In addition to these, there was sometimes elected the alguazil, mayor or sheriff, who had

---

[1] Bancroft, *Mexico*, III, 521.
[2] Title 14, sec. 18; Rockwell, 450.   [3] Bancroft, *Mexico*, III, 522.

numerous duties, chiefly limited to carrying out the orders of the governor; and the alcaldes of the municipalities. It is evident that the Spanish town lacked neither officers nor a sufficient code of municipal laws to insure a model administration, had the system been successfully carried out. There were two remarkable offices filled at each municipal election. The citizens chose two alcaldes de mesta,[1] whose duty it was to preside at the semi-annual " round up " held by stock owners. They were given certain duties in the town relative to stock inspection.

The municipal revenue was raised primarily from public lands set apart for this purpose at the founding of the town. It is not supposable that this amounted to a great sum ; for to carry on special public improvements or extraordinary judicial processes, the magistrate levied contributions to a certain amount, which could be extended by the audiencias to a limit of two hundred pesos.[2] In addition to these methods of raising revenue, certain fines were paid into the city treasury. In the management of the public lands, they were rented by auction to the highest bidder. These funds were in charge of officers called depositarios. The drafts for ordering expenses were issued by magistrates and council. A city was divided into eight wards, five of which were administered by the five criminal judges representing the audiencia, and the other three were represented by the ordinary alcaldes and regidores. Later subordinate alcaldes were created in each district.

After the Mexican revolution, the main principles of local government continued. In 1823, the Mexican congress passed an elaborate set of rules for the government of town councils for the Province of California. Mr. Bancroft gives, in fifty-two articles, a summary of the rules for the government

---

[1] The mesta was a term applied to the collective owners of black cattle and sheep. Membership was limited to those owning three hundred head of small stock and twenty mares or colts.

[2] Bancroft, *Mexico*, III, 523.

of the ayuntamientos of the towns.[1]   These ordinances provide
that the pueblo shall have a house for the council, necessary
offices, place for storing public property, and barracks for the
national guard where organized.   They provide names for the
house and its apartments, appoint minor officers, and designate the duty of each.   The ordinances provide for times of
meeting, procedure at meetings, official duties, and give rules
for the entire procedure of each member and of the whole
body collectively.   Rule number eleven of these ordinances
reads as follows : "Should a member arrive after a sitting be
opened, he is to be received by the others standing, and the
secretary must inform him of what business has been done."
So, for the whole order of business, the most punctilious rules
are given.   The formal procedure of the local officers, the tedious processes necessary to be endured in the accomplishment
of a little business, are sufficient to bring pain to the reader of
the *ordinanzas.*   But here as elsewhere in Spanish administration, the simple informal practice under the best attempts
of the officials to be ceremonious, contrasted strikingly with
the formal grandeur of the laws and rules of procedure.

In the Spanish municipal government, the ayuntamiento or
town council is the most important organ of administration.
It was differently organized in different towns, varying according to the number of the respective officers that composed it.
However, the ayuntamiento was always created after the same
general plan, and existed according to specified conditions.   It
was a time-honored institution, and has changed but little in
fundamental characteristics since its first establishment in
Spain.   It was provided that every pueblo of five hundred
inhabitants was entitled to an ayuntamiento composed of one
alcalde, two councilmen, and one procurador-syndico.   The
alcalde acted as president of the council, and in conjunction
with the other members (regidores) had control of the political
and economic affairs of the town.   Aside from this, the alcalde

---

[1] Bancroft, *California Pastoral,* 540.

had special functions as police judge, which will be explained later. The syndico acted as city attorney in legal cases and disputes, and frequently as treasurer. The authority of the ayuntamiento was limited by the laws of the province or the state, and it could act only within well-defined limits. It was responsible to central authority, and was the organ through which the provincial governor or viceroy made known the will of the government to the people. In the simplest form of government, the alcalde and one regidor were elected every year, while the syndico and one regidor served two years.

In 1837, the law for the regulation of the territory of California relates, among other things, to the management of the ayuntamientos or town councils. Article first defines what towns may have town councils; and article third states that "The number of Alcaldes, Regidores, and Syndicos will be fixed by the Departmental legislature in concert with the governor, but the first must not exceed six, the second, twelve, and the third, two." The members of the ayuntamiento are elected by the citizens of the town, the alcalde is elected every year, half of the councilmen the same, and when there are two syndicos, one must be elected each year. Persons may hold office repeatedly, and no one may refuse to serve without a just cause. To illustrate the minute provisions for the control of the town councils, a few of the forty articles of the Mexican law relating to the powers and duties of ayuntamientos will be given. It may be seen that the central government has given but little latitude for the exercise of self-government by the town councils.

Art. 10. The ayuntamientos, under subjection to the Sub-Prefects, and through them to the Prefects and Governor, will have charge of the police, health, comfort, ornament, order and security of their respective jurisdictions.

Art. 11. They will consequently take care of the cleanliness of the streets, market places and public squares.

Art. 12. They will see that in each town there be one or more burying grounds conveniently located.

Art. 13.   They will watch over the quality of all kinds of liquors and provisions, in order that nothing unsound or corrupted be sold.

Art. 14.   They will take care that in the apothecary shops, no rancid or adulterated drugs be sold, to which end they may appoint intelligent persons of the faculty to examine them.

Art. 15.   They will see that marshes be drained, and that stagnant and unhealthy waters be made to run off, and that everything which tends to injure the health of men or cattle be removed.

Art. 16.   They will likewise take care of prisons, hospitals, and establishments of public beneficence which are not of private foundations.

Art. 17.   The moment that any prevailing sickness makes its appearance in the district of the municipality, the Ayuntamiento will inform the Sub-Prefect, or should there be no Sub-Prefect, the Prefect, in order that through his means, the necessary assistance may be administered; but this will not prevent the Ayuntamiento from taking in the meantime the necessary steps to cut off or restrain the evil in its commencement.

Art. 18.   With this laudable object, they will name a committee of charity, composed of a Regidor or alcalde, a Syndico, a Physician should there be one in the place, and two residents or more, should the Ayuntamiento think it necessary, according to the extent of the place and the duties to be performed.

Art. 19.   The Ayuntamiento will remit semi-annually, to the Sub-Prefect, or in default of him to the Prefect, that he may forward it to the Governor, an account of the births, marriages, and deaths in each of these periods, which must embrace all its district, and mention the sex, age, and diseases of which they may have died, keeping in its records a copy of this document.

Art. 20.   In order to obtain these data, they may ask them of the parish curates, the Justices of the Peace, the municipality, or any other persons or corporation capable of furnishing them.

Art. 21. In order to attend to the ornament and comfort of the towns, they will see that the market places be well distributed and that every obstacle, tending to hinder them from being sufficiently provided, be removed.

Art. 22. They will take care of the preservation of the public fountains, and see that there be abundance of water for men and cattle.

Art. 23. They will otherwise endeavor, as far as possible, to have the streets straight, paved, and lighted, and to provide public walks and abundant plantations, for the beauty and health of the towns.

Art. 24. It belongs to them to procure the construction and repairing of bridges, causeways, and roads, and to encourage agriculture, industry, trade, and whatever they may consider useful to the inhabitants.

Art. 25. At the junction of different roads, they will place inscriptions pointing out the different directions and distances to the nearest towns.

Art. 26. It belongs to the Ayuntamientos to make contract for all kinds of diversions, license having been previously obtained from the first local political authority.

Art. 27. The products from these contracts must be paid into the municipal funds.

Art. 28. If the regulations of police and good government should not embrace all the measures which the Ayuntamiento may consider necessary for the preservation of order and the security of persons and property, they may propose to the Governor whatsoever others they may deem convenient, in order that those which appear just may be adopted.

Art. 29. They will see that in every town there is a safe and commodious prison, that in said prisons different departments be found for persons arrested and for prisoners, and they will take care that the latter be usefully employed.

19

Art. 30.   They will pay careful attention to the establishment of common schools in every town, the masters and mistresses of which must be paid out of the municipal fund, and they will be careful not only to appoint proper persons, but to see that at all times they continue to be of good conduct and sound morals.

Art. 31.   They will distribute with all possible impartiality, the municipal duties imposed upon the citizens, guiding themselves by the existing laws, or by such as may hereafter be made.

Art. 32.   They will watch over the arrangement of the weights and measures, agreeably to the laws on the subject.

The alcalde is an historic officer.   He dates from the early annals of Spain, and was the most important personage in the Spanish municipality.   In the town of the Spanish provinces he was reckoned the first officer in importance.   His functions were not always clearly defined ; he might do almost everything that would conduce to the welfare of the town.   As president of the ayuntamiento, he performed duties similar to those of a member of a modern town council ; in settling disputes by arbitration or application of the law, he acted like a modern police judge ; in apprehending persons for misdemeanors, he represented the modern constable or policeman. In inquiring into the occupations of the citizens and reprimanding the idle and vagrant, he exercised a paternal oversight of the affairs of the town.   In addition to this, the chief alcalde performed the service usually falling to the mayor of a modern city.

As a sign of office, the alcalde carried a silver-headed cane, which served as a means of summoning persons to court. When the alcalde was detained from appearing in person at any place, he could be represented by sending his cane.   When the American columns entered the towns of New Mexico, they were met by the alcalde with his cane, who gave them the rights of the town or else stipulated on what terms they were to be received.

The actual judicial practice of the alcalde in the towns of Spanish-America was of a very informal nature. It usually consisted in sending for the offending parties, and by conciliatory means effecting a settlement, or by an informal process arriving at a judgment and fine. In the towns in which the governor resided, all judicial functions, great and small, were absorbed by that officer. In the trial of minor cases, it was the alcalde's business to summon the witnesses and arrange for the trial, and frequently to appoint an arbiter for the case. There were no courts of law competent to try cases of any magnitude. The alcaldes were usually ignorant of the law, and could not administer it either in civil or in criminal cases. They frequently acknowledged this in their reports. There were no law codes to assist them as at present. Bryant, who visited the coast in 1847, found no written statute, and the only law books were *The Laws of Spain and the Indies,* published about a century before,[1] in connection with which was issued a small book defining the powers of the various judicial officers of the Mexican government. "In cases of capital offences, the alcalde had simply power to examine, testimony being taken down in writing and transmitted to the *juez de primera instancia,* or first judge of district before whom the case was tried."[2] The trial by jury was practiced when the prisoner demanded it; but the jury seldom consisted of more than three or five members.

The alcaldes of the ayuntamientos and the justices of the peace had the exclusive power to exercise the office of conciliators in towns having one thousand or more inhabitants. These trials of "conciliation" are carefully explained in the Mexican laws of 1837. The Alcalde summons the accused and the accuser, and has each tell his own story in the presence of an appointed arbiter. After the parties retire, the alcalde or justice pronounces the sentence. Then, if the parties agree to the decision, the trial is at an end, and a satisfactory conclu-

---

[1] Bancroft, *California Pastoral,* 575.　　[2] *Ibid.*

sion has been reached.   In the law of 1837, twenty articles are devoted to giving minute details concerning the management of these trials.   But here, as elsewhere in Spanish administration, the practice of the law did not approach its formal letter.

The administration of justice in the Mexican States and provinces was in a very lax condition.   The authorities took great care to issue instructions to alcaldes for the purpose of insuring a better judicial usage, but with no good effect. Even the court of the first instance was in no better condition, as it was presided over by the alcaldes.   In 1824, minute instructions were given to alcaldes concerning procedure in apprehending criminals, obtaining evidence, and the minutest details of the trial.[1]   These extended and artificial rules contrast very greatly with the loose and careless method of administering justice which usually prevailed.

"As an instance of the way civil cases are disposed of in this strangest of strange places, I may cite the example of a Mr. Stokes, who summoned a farmer before the alcalde, to compel the payment of a debt which had been two years outstanding, contrary to the previous stipulation between the parties.   The justice, instead of meeting the case, referred it to arbitration. The case was going against the farmer, who entreated for a further indulgence, as, if compelled to pay that moment, he would be compelled to sell his cattle at a heavy sacrifice. 'Well,' says the justice, 'how long do you ask?' 'Why,' says the farmer, 'I promise to make the first installment in twelve months hence.'   'Very well,' replied the justice, with the utmost indifference, 'that will do;' and the case was dismissed without further procedings."[2]

All cases of a serious nature were referred to the prefect of the district, who reported them to the governor.   It might be necessary for the governor to report a case to the central

---

[1] Bancroft, *California Pastoral,* 576.
[2] Journal of Douglas.   Quoted by Bancroft in *California Pastoral,* 581.

authorities at Mexico and thus the case would be continued indefinitely, while the accused was lying in prison without a trial. In all probability, when the decision did come from Mexico, the case would be dismissed or the accused sentenced and punished without trial. The jails, in cases where they existed at all, were of the poorer class of prison pens; and innocent persons might languish in them without just cause, while waiting for a decision from unscrupulous or careless authorities. Yet with this loose system of judicial procedure the number of criminal cases seemed to multiply during the latter days of the Spanish and Mexican régime.

Towns at or near the presidios were subject to a more rigorous discipline in judicial affairs. They were overshadowed by military authority, and the functions of the civil authorities were reduced to a minimum. But the decisions upon cases were very inconsistent; sometimes they were severe, sometimes lax, and in many cases unjust. Upon the whole, judicial affairs were administered according to the whims of the officers in power. Theoretically, the trial of all civil cases was to be referred first to the alcalde, second to the commandant, and third to the governor. But all civilians residing at the presidios had to apply to the commandant for redress of grievances, and all criminal cases had to be referred to the military for trial by court martial without any appeal.[1] This finally threw the greater part of the judicial procedure into the hands of the military powers, to be directed by the governor or the commandant.

The classification of crimes and the application of penalties show ignorance and gross carelessness on the part of many officials. Severe punishments were frequently given for what would now be considered slight offences, and again, flagrant crimes were allowed to go unpunished. There were many attempts to govern society by establishing for the conduct of individuals, a multitude of restrictions, which succeeded in

[1] Bancroft, *California*, II, 512.

irritating the people and not infrequently inciting to wrong-doing. For instance, at Monterey no person could be out of his house after the hours "of *la queda*," except in case of urgent necessity, under penalty of eight days' imprisonment. The hour of *la queda*, or retirement, was proclaimed by the sound of the bell or the beat of the drum. No person could have company in his house after the hour of *la queda* without the previous consent of the Ayuntamiento. Strict attendance on church was imperatively enjoined, and persons were forbidden to leave the church after service had commenced, under penalty of a fine. These and many other rules are found on the records of the municipal ordinances of Monterey.[1] Gaming, either in public or private, was forbidden; there were fines for drunkenness and for the sale of intoxicating liquors at specified times. There was an attempt to discourage the free use of horses irrespective of ownership, a custom which had long prevailed in California. If a person desired a change of horses, he caught the first desirable one that he saw, changed his saddle, turned his old horse loose, mounted the fresh one, and continued his journey. In early times, when there were plenty of horses and everybody adopted the same custom, there was nothing wrong in this practice; but as society became more settled, the lines of distinction between the property of individuals became more prominent. The act was finally regarded as a misdemeanor, a theft; and the penalty attached to the act of taking another's horse without the owner's consent was a fine of six dollars. In January, 1824, Argüello decreed that no person should leave town, presidio, or ranch, without a passport from the civil authority; and soon after forbade the buying and selling of cattle without notice to the administrator of revenues. No person could make a transfer of produce without the consent of the alcalde. In each case, the penalty for disobeying the ordinance was fine and confiscation of property. To illlustrate

[1] Ordinanzes Municipales; Bancroft, *Cal.*, II, 612.

the vagaries of judicial procedure, the proclamation of Argüello will suffice. He declared the death penalty for all
thefts exceeding twenty-five dollars; and, where force or false
keys were used, that the body of the accused should be quar-
tered.[1] The severe attempts made to lessen crime were failures; for they did not inspire people with a sense of the
majesty of the law. The whole procedure of justice was
erratic in the extreme. There was an abundance of laws
enacted, and minute rules of procedure were not wanting;
but in practice the system was irregular and impolitic.

Upon the whole the central government exercised the
major part of administration, and left but little for the local
authorities to do. Yet the distance from the seat of central
government made it possible for men of determination to exercise great authority for a time. The organization was complete enough. With president, congress, territorial legislature,
territorial diputacion, prefects and sub-prefects, supreme and
secondary courts, alcaldes and ayuntamientos, there was sufficient machinery of government to have given the people a
wise and just administration. As it was, the whole subject is
a picturesque representation of the attempt of a class of careless, ignorant, or inefficient officers to use a great system of
law and administration. Many of the laws were wise and
humane; but they were apt to prove otherwise in their application. There were many conscientious and well-informed
officials; but the conditions of the country forbade any show of
their intelligence. Should one man undertake a reform, his
sub-officers were slow in assisting him to carry it out. Yet
it may be said in general that the people were happy under
this rule, at least until they learned that a better government
was possible.

---

[1] Bancroft, *California*, II, 513.

CHAPTER XIV.

Trade and Commerce.

The chief object that impelled the nations of Europe to plant colonies and extend civilization to barbarous countries was the promotion of commerce. Whatever other motives have from time to time prompted nations to enter into the process of colonization, to make a market for home productions and to stimulate home industries have always been uppermost in the plans of monarchs and statesmen. Nor did colonization rest wholly upon the schemes for gratifying personal or national ambition for conquest, although this must be considered ; but it was rather a movement incident upon modern industrial progress and especially competition in trade. As has already been stated, the mother country sought to control colonial trade for the sole benefit of the home government.

In attempting to do this, nations have varied in their methods as well as in the degree of success attending such arbitrary usage. But for a pronounced attempt at direct and complete control of colonial trade, the Spanish monarchs represent a unique type of absolutism. For the purpose of regulating trade, there was created in Spain, in the year 1501, the Casa de Contratacion, or House of Trade, which combined the powers of a board of trade and a supreme court of adjudication. Its authority was final in all matters pertaining to trade and commerce, with the exception that it was formally amenable to the Council of the Indies as a supreme governing body. Through this board, Spain sought to control commerce for her own benefit by competing with other nations

296

in making the best possible use of her colonies. In order to place all commerce more completely under the control of the government, it was ordered that all colonial trade should pass through the town of Seville. Consequently, for many years not a vessel could unload a cargo except at this port, nor could the out-bound ship receive goods except as they passed through Seville. At a later date, Cadiz became the favored city in place of Seville. All commerce had to be carried on in Spanish ships, and all colonial trade had to pass, not to other nations, but through a single town in Spain. Even a carrying trade between one colony and another was forbidden. Instead of placing trade in the hands of monopolies, the Spanish government became a monopoly for the purpose of manipulating colonial trade. Yet the custom of passing all trade through one town necessarily threw it into the hands of a few business houses, and created a monopoly without a special grant.

In the colonies this oppressive policy was even more arbitrary; for the home government, in its passion to secure an exclusive trade, endeavored to keep foreigners from the coast by force of law. No foreigner could enter the colonies without express permission, and no vessel could enter their harbors. To prevent colonists from trading with foreigners, the penalty fixed was death and forfeiture of property. To strengthen further the trade policy, Spain forbade the cultivation in the colonies of such raw products as came into direct competition with the home industries. The culture of saffron, hemp, tobacco, olives, grapes in vineyards, and many other products was strictly forbidden. These laws were enacted at different times, and it is astonishing to observe to what extent the Spanish government succeeded for many years in maintaining a trade monopoly. Yet there could be but one result of such a pernicious policy, that of final collapse and failure.

In consequence of these arbitrary measures, smuggling was carried on to a great extent, not only by foreigners but by the Spaniards themselves; and there were organized at this time in the West Indies bands of pirates whose descendants still ply the dark trade.   Other nations made the arbitrary measures of the Spanish monopoly an excuse for preying upon the Spanish commerce, and many a galleon loaded with treasure fell into the hands of the English and Dutch free-booters.

On the Pacific coast a continuous intercourse was kept up between New Spain and the Philippine Islands.   In 1564, Philip II. succeeded in planting a colony in these islands, and established the capital of Manilla.[1]   From this point, active commerce with China sprang up, and trade was opened with America by a long route to Callao and afterwards to Acapulco on the coast of New Spain.   There were only one or two ships each year that plied their trade on this famous route between these distant points; but they were laden with silver products of American mines on their outward course, and with spices, clothes, and the products of the Orient on their return.   Their cargoes were valuable, and the inhabitants of New Spain had their wants supplied from the other side of the Pacific in exchange for the products of their mines.   It is a remarkable event that the monopoly of this trade was secured to a single part of New Spain; that other provinces, such as Peru, were forbidden to barter even for a part of the ship's cargo.   It is a single instance of a mother country granting a monopoly for the benefit of her colonies; and those who discovered this fact tried in vain to repeal the laws granting such great privileges, which they claimed would encourage the independence of the colonists.   But the Manilla galleons still pursued their lonely course across the wide Pacific, unmolested, except by the Dutch and English free-booters.   In order to control the trade between the New and the Old World, every ship's cargo had to be inspected by the Board of Trade, and in order to secure these ships against free-booters, the trading vessels sailed in squadrons with means of defense.   The squadrons of the Galeons and the Flota each sailed annually from Seville. The former landed at Panama, where it was met by the mer-

---

[1] Robertson, *History of America*, II, 427.

chants of Peru, Chili, and the South, and in a short time after its arrival the native wealth of the New World was exchanged for the finished products of the Old. Within the space of forty days there was carried on the most extensive trade of the world. The Flota landed its cargo at Vera Cruz, where a similar traffic was carried on. For over two centuries, Spain supplied with a meagre hand the wants of her American colonists, and brought to the home government the riches of the mines and the products of the fertile soil and tropical climate of the New World. But notwithstanding the great precaution assumed, the trade declined; and the mother country failed to reap the benefits of an industry so jealously guarded. In the first place, as the industries of the home government declined, the finished products were furnished by the surrounding nations; consequently, Spain became but a shipping station, from which European goods were forwarded to America, and through which returned the silver of the mines of Peru and Mexico on its way to repay the nations who furnished the supplies. Another great difficulty was the practice of smuggling, carried on alike by foreigners and the officers of the Spanish government. In every possible way the government tried to suppress it, but without marked success. The trade was continually absorbed more and more by foreign ships. To prevent this, Spain passed laws forbidding foreigners to trade with the colonies, and finally established a coast guard to protect the trade and to apprehend and arrest smugglers. On account of the increase of contraband traffic, Spain finally granted through the council of the Indies the privilege of private commerce by means of registered ships. The owners paid a high license for the privilege of this trade. This process led to the abolishment of the Galleons by a fuero of 1748. Thus the trade policy of Spain broke down by reason of its own defects, and was not revived until the middle of the eighteenth century. This exclusive trade policy, which forbade the commercial intercourse of two adjacent provinces, prevented the development of commerce. Indeed there could be no trade until a reform was made. It was not until the time of Carlos III. that commercial intercourse was established among the colonies, and then it did not exist without certain arbitrary restrictions. The revival of commerce under Carlos III. has been described elsewhere. It was before the settlement of California, in the year 1765, that the king of Spain relaxed the stringent trade restrictions which had been in vogue for more than two centuries. The monarch saw that neither Spain nor the colonies prospered under the excessive prohibitions. The reform was begun by opening up several of the maritime towns of Spain to the trade of the colonies, instead of forcing all trade through one port. In 1799, during the war of England with Spain, the latter allowed neutral vessels to share the carrying trade between the mother country and the colonies. But there were still sufficient restrictions to bear heavily upon commerce. Under Mexican rule many of the trade restrictions were continued, and when trade between California and the other countries and nations began to increase, the people, the traders, and the government officials attempted to evade the rigorous laws.

A royal order of 1786 permitted free trade between the province of California and San Blas.[1] In 1785, the government attempted commerce with China, a trade of peltries for quicksilver; but the trade was restricted to the government through an authorized agent, and private individuals were forbidden to indulge in trade or to purchase furs. The government officials collected a considerable quantity of furs, and after the usual delay sent them to China. But the attempt of the government to realize the benefits of a fur monopoly failed, although legal restrictions were imposed upon the rights of individual enterprise. In this, as in many other things, the government failed to execute the laws; and the result was that trade and commerce gradually made inroads upon the provinces. The Russians at an early date made excursions south-

[1] Bancroft, *California Pastoral*, 459.

WALPI, A MOQUI TOWN.

ward along the coast in search of the otter, and established a trading post near Bodega Bay. They even entered the harbor of San Francisco to take the otter and for purposes of trade. Their ships secured supplies from the missions and water from the coast. Their presence led to a great deal of uneasiness on the part of the Spanish government, although the people of the province were little concerned. The early trade of California consisted essentially in the exchange of hides and tallow for goods or for money. This along with the supplying of the ships with grain, beef, and other domestic produce, represented the total amount of business of the country. First upon California coast for the purpose of trade were Boston trading ships. The missions of California had furnished supplies hitherto to such expeditions as that of Vancouver and La Perouse, and there was occasional barter with lesser explorers and hunters, but the first trade opened up to the towns and villages of California was conducted by the Boston merchants. Prior to their arrival, the colonists depended upon the Spanish packet boats to bring from Mexico such supplies as they used. The Boston ships carried all kinds of goods, which they traded for hides and tallow, then almost the sole exports of the country. It was one of these trading ships that Dana accompanied in the two years' voyage, which he has so graphically described. His vessel went from port to port, and most of the trading was done in the ship, while riding at anchor in the bay. Mr. Dana gives the following description of their trade at Monterey: " The next day, the cargo having been entered in due form, we began trading. The trade-room was fitted up in the steerage, and furnished with the lighter goods, and with specimens of the rest of the cargo; and Mellus, a young man who came out from Boston with us before the mast, was taken out of the forecastle and made supercargo's clerk. He was well qualified for this business, having been clerk in a counting house in Boston; but he had been troubled for some time with rheumatism, which unfitted him for the wet and exposed duty of a sailor on the coast. For a week or ten days all was life on board. The people came off to look and to buy, men, women, and children; and we were continually going in the boats, carrying goods and passengers, for they have no boats of their own. Everything must dress itself and come aboard and see the new vessel, if it were only to buy a paper of pins. The agent and his clerk managed the sales, while we were busy in the hold or in the boats. Our cargo was an assorted one; that is, it consisted of everything under the sun. We had spirits of all kinds (sold by the cask), teas, coffee, sugars, spices, raisins, molasses, hardware, crockeryware, tinware, cutlery, clothing of all sorts, boots and shoes from Lynn, calicoes and cottons from Lowell, crapes, silks; also shawls, scarfs, necklaces, jewelry, and combs for the women; furniture; and in fact, everything that can be imagined, from Chinese fireworks to English cart-wheels, of which we had a dozen pairs with their iron tires on." These were the articles that the Californians desired in exchange for their silver and for hides and tallow. The prices were high and the profits great.

In the early period a foreign vessel in the harbor was a rare sight, but after the Mexican revolution, the vessels appeared with greater frequency. In 1831, nineteen vessels, chiefly from Boston, anchored in Californian harbors.[1] They brought the usual supplies in exchange for hides and tallow. In 1832, the number was increased to twenty-four, seven of which were whalers. During the period from 1831 to 1835, there were, according to Bancroft, ninety-nine vessels on the coast, composed chiefly of traders, whalers, and vessels seeking supplies.[2] The trade in hides and tallow was quite brisk during this period. The larger number of the trading vessels floated the American flag. The customs duties collected for 1834 and 1835 amounted to about $50,000 per annum. At this time Governor Victoria made strenuous efforts for a more

---

[1] Bancroft, *California*, III, 363.
[2] Bancroft, *California*, III, 380. A list of vessels is given.

Old Custom House, Monterey, Cal.

rigid enforcement of the revenue laws. He declared Monterey to be the only legal port, and that a vessel could not discharge its cargo elsewhere without a certificate from the revenue officer that the duties had been paid at that place. Rule after rule was declared by the Governor, and also by the Mexican congress, much to the dissatisfaction of the people and of some of the local officers. For the people desired to see vessels coming to port and trade increased. The severe restrictive measures had the effect of driving the vessels to Honolulu, and led to the practice of smuggling. Nearly all of the fur trade was contraband, as well as much of the regular import trade. The heavy duties imposed upon domestic and coast trade were very detrimental to all progress. A distinguished traveler stated in 1838, "If the laws now in existence on paper were rigidly enforced, there would not at this moment be a single coasting vessel on all of the Mexican coast of the Pacific."[1] The following quotations from Bancroft illustrate the situation in 1826: "In June, Herrera, following instructions from his superior in Sonora, ordered that no vessel be allowed to load or unload in any other port than Monterey. He admitted that such a rule was ruinous to the territorial commerce, and said he had protested against it, but could not disobey orders. Echeandía, however, countermanded the rule provisionally, and it did not go into effect, but at the same time an *internacion* duty of fifteen per cent. and an *averia* duty of two and a half per cent. were added to the former import duty of twenty-five per cent., making a total of $42\frac{1}{2}$ per cent., besides an anchorage tax of $10 for each vessel, and a tonnage rate of $2.50 per ton. Naturally these exactions displeased both the traders and the consumers of foreign goods; but they sought relief, not in written petitions, but in various smuggling expedients, in which they were rarely detected, and which therefore, for this year at

---

[1] Forbes, *California*, 298.

least, find no place in the records."[1]   The officers nearly
always made a show of trying to execute the revenue and
commerce laws, but they failed as often as they succeeded.
Occasionally a contraband ship was taken, and its goods
were confiscated or sent to Mexico for adjudication.   Some
officers claimed that it was impossible to enforce the laws.
Although under the Mexican rule, the ports of California
were opened to foreign trade, it was still the policy of
the government to continue to make laws and restrictions
after the manner of the Spanish government, and to hedge
up the way of progress by a multiplicity of regulations
and a system of espionage.   Under the old régime the
product of one country could not be sent to another
without the payment of a heavy duty (*alcavala*); neither
could it be removed from one town to another without repay-
ing the odious duty.   Add to this the intrigues and the petty
policy of the government officers and the multiplicity of laws
and regulations, and there is no wonder to be excited by the
failure of domestic commerce to flourish.   What could have
prompted the Spanish government thus to cripple the domestic commerce of her subjects and at the same time injure her
own interests, is an unsolved problem ; unless it was a revival of
an ancient policy, adopted for the purpose of keeping the provinces from developing unity, strength, and finally independence.   Certainly *divide et impera* was the result of the well-
worn policy.   As the people were in great need of foreign
products, and the tax on imports was so high that few traders
could pay it with any degree of advantage, smuggling was common, and was encouraged by the people, who desired goods, and
by the officers, who were in sympathy with the people.   Governor Argüello said in 1824, "I see not why we should prevent
it, since our people are the gainers."[1]   The trade restrictions
were so great that merchants could not conduct their business
on an honest basis ; therefore they joined with the contraband

---

[1] Bancroft, *California*, III, 117.

parties for the purpose of obtaining free goods. In 1849, smuggling became so common that the country was flooded with cheap goods, which greatly interfered with trade. Officials became rich by means of bribes paid them to allow goods to be admitted free of duty. The Mexican administration was not powerful enough to protect the laws which had been enacted. Had they been rigidly enforced, California would have suffered great loss.

In the general trade between the mother country and her colonies, restrictions were also very oppressive. Orders were given as to the time of departure of vessels, the route to be pursued, and the due inspection of each vessel by the commandant of the port from which it sailed. Papers duly certified could be readily obtained by bribes, and the custom prevailed to such an extent that it was difficult to obtain the certificates without bribes. When the vessel arrived in an American port, the captain had to deliver up to the commandant the ship's papers, and he and his crew were subject to marine military law while in the port. In other words, they were liable to be tried for all offences by the naval officers of the port.

After the separation of the provinces from Spain, trade did not improve much for a long time; partly owing to the fact that there were few products to exchange, and partly to the fact that Mexico, though opening the ports to foreign trade, still persisted in following the line of restrictions adopted by Spain. The result was that the merchants became a set of smugglers, and were frequently aided by the local officers.[1] Even the friars were forbidden by law to trade and barter; but they were always ready for an exchange of any sort; and frequently set the law aside in order not to spoil a good bargain. But the results of this narrow policy were more widely extended; for all the commerce was carried on by foreign nations, and their vessels continued to encroach more and more upon the restriction laws. Of the ninety-nine vessels hitherto referred

---

[1] Forbes, *California*, 298.

to which touched on the coast from 1831 to 1835, only thirteen carried the Mexican flag.

It was early in the thirties that the overland immigration of trappers and traders assumed prominence. Prior to this, trappers and traders had frequented New Mexico, and it was from this locality that the first important expedition was fitted out in 1830.[1] During the four years prior to this, persons had made the trip across the continent. As early as 1826, Jedidiah S. Smith made the first overland entry into California. He started from a port of the fur company established at Great Salt Lake.[2] Other expeditions followed for various purposes; but little trade or profit developed from these early expeditions. They represent the opening of the territory from the east by the overland route, and prepared the way for that voluminous stream of emigration which was to follow after 1849.

At quite an early date, trade sprang up between the Sandwich Islands and the California coast. This continued its rapid development during the latter part of the Mexican and the early American rule. The islands were a rendezvous for vessels engaged in smuggling fur and other products. A large number of vessels from the Sandwich islands became regular visitors to the coast. They laid the foundation of what afterwards became a substantial trade with California. The shipment of live stock to the Islands began about 1830, while California was still under Mexican rule.

One can not approach any part of the western history of the United States without coming across the pioneer work of the fur traders. Through trackless forests and over rugged mountains they have carried the news of civilization to the lone trapper and to the Indian tribes, and have acquainted the older settlements with the nature of the undeveloped portions of the country. They have been a means of intercommunication between isolated communities and the civilized world.

---

[1] Bancroft, *California*, III, 385.   [2] Bancroft, *California*, III, 152.

Professor Frederick J. Turner of the University of Wisconsin, in an address before the State Historical Society of Wisconsin at its annual meeting, January 3, 1889, on "The character and influence of the trade in Wisconsin," has touched an important phase of history, showing the era previous to real settlement, when the wilderness is becoming the sparsely settled community. What may be said of one part of the country relative to the influence of the fur traders on its development, may be said in general of every part. On the Pacific Slope, at an early date, we find the zealous hunters and trappers trying for the otter and other wild game. Some of them collected furs and pelts, and prepared to sell to the first out-bound vessel. The Russians came down the northwest coast, exploring and searching for game. They formed a settlement at Bodega Bay and, with this point as headquarters, scoured the surrounding country for the otter. They came into the bay of San Francisco, while the country was in the possession of the Spanish and Mexicans. The otter and seal hunting and trading brought many parties to the coast, and stirred up considerable interest in the country. Seals and otter were plentiful along the coast and the trade was lucrative. The Spaniards tried to monopolize this industry by severe restrictive measures; but the laws were a failure, and the capture of otter and seals was continued by those who, keeping a wary eye upon the government, were willing to run the risk. When La Perouse visited California in 1786, the Spanish authorities were attempting to secure a monopoly of the fur trade. A commissary had been appointed by the government, and stationed at Monterey to collect the peltries from the missions as property of the government. He had already collected 20,000, which number might have been increased to 30,000. La Perouse thought that 50,000 could easily be procured annually. But from this time the trade declined, and was chiefly carried on by foreigners, who secured most of the otter pelts by contraband methods.

Foreign commerce is one of the greatest means to a nation's prosperity, and the government that militates against it without receiving a proper compensation for restrictive measures will eventually experience the unfavorable results of such an unwise policy. In most instances the Spanish laws reacted against the national prosperity. They arose from a misconception of the proper relation that the colonies should sustain to the mother country. To use the colonies merely as a garden spot to furnish the table of the royal household, and to insist that none but the royal family should reap the benefit of the garden, were principles that could not but react against the nation that tried to enforce them. The colonists were prevented from exercising a free intercourse in trade, much to their injury. The intercommunication of the different parts of New Spain ought to have been encouraged rather than suppressed. The Spanish regulation of foreign and domestic trade served not a little to hasten the downfall of her supremacy in America. By the many exactions, antiquated prohibitions, exorbitant duties, the hordes of officials, and the unreasonable laws, the domestic trade was destroyed, foreign commerce suppressed, the treasury of the nation bankrupted, and the amount of the customs duties collected reduced to a trifle.

CHAPTER XV.

The Land Question.

One of the most interesting as well as the most important of all the questions that concern the development of a state, is the method adopted for the disposal of the land. The land question was prominent in early Grecian history; it was the great cause of social strife in Rome, and the fundamental idea in the development of the feudal system. Two-thirds of the wars in Europe have arisen over disputed territory. The desire for land was the force that impelled the movement of the barbarians into the boundaries of the Roman Empire. The desire for land has marked the long struggles of the rising modern nations, and the later diplomatic strifes of the great powers of Europe. But the land once obtained by a nation from whatsoever source had to be distributed among the governed and the governors, and the policy of disposing of the public domain and controlling private property, characterized by different methods at different stages in the progress of nations, has been a political influence in advancing or retarding the interests of the state. For centuries after the dissolution of the Western Empire, the feudal tenure of land arising from Roman law and Teutonic custom prevailed almost universally among the young nations of Europe. Feudalism rested upon a land basis, and feudalism was everywhere the system of government. Feudal tenure was therefore the land tenure of the middle ages, and its forms prevailed almost universally down to the close of the last century; in some cases, to the middle of the present century. The first formal renunciation of all forms

and effects of feudal tenure is to be credited to the United
States in the land system established in 1785–87.

While feudalism prevailed in Spain, the law of real property
in vogue at the time of the discovery and settlement of
America, followed very closely after the Roman. The laws of
ownership, usufruct, emphyteusis, dower, prædial and urban
servitudes were taken almost bodily from the Roman laws.
Likewise, occupancy, contracts, and obligations were determined by the same principles as those that governed the
Roman customs. Feudal tenure prevailed only in the accession and disposal of large tracts of land, and it was manifested
in the disposal of land in the colonies. As has been previously stated, the monarchs of Spain regarded all newly discovered land in America as their peculiar possession, to be
disposed of at will, since they had secured it as a special fief of
the Pope. While this was true in theory, and the possession
of land came through grants from the king, yet the civil law of
Spain prevailed in the colonies. The disposal of property in
fee simple followed the laws of Spain which had arisen after
feudal tenure began to decline.

The monarchs of Spain disposed of the land of the New
World with great liberality, in accordance with a desire to
reap an advantage thereby. It was necessary to reward explorers and all of those persons who had rendered the king
special service, and there was no easier way to pay the debt
than to grant a few square miles of land to the royal servants.
Again, it was necessary that the new territory be peopled with
colonists and laborers, so that the products of America might
enrich Spain. Therefore, the Spanish government held out
extraordinary inducements for settlers to occupy the new
possessions. Colonists were offered free passage, the loan of
money or stock, free lands and free homes, gifts of stock and
farming implements, and exemption from taxation and tithes,
if they would comply with the conditions of the prescribed
contract to settle on the land. This extreme liberality was
fully offset by the rules, restrictions, and burdens laid upon

the colonists after they were permanently located on the soil. The sole object of all this generosity on the part of the crown of Spain was to bring about a condition which should make the new possessions yield the greatest possible income to the owners. This was the idea always uppermost in the minds of the Spanish rulers, and it led frequently to oppression, taxation, and abuse. Like the ancient feudal lord, the Spanish sovereign aimed to take all that the soil would yield above a bare subsistence for the tenants.

The methods by which the monarchs of Spain early sought to establish towns and colonies in New Spain, have already been presented.[1] From time to time the Spanish government established new laws for the purpose of increasing their interests in the New World. The government, though generous in the giving of land to encourage colonization, was not slow in imposing upon those who had accepted it the severest restrictions. Among the last of the laws enacted by Spain on account of the land policy in America was the decree of the Cortes of March 12, 1811. The object of the decree was " to furnish the inhabitants of the extensive provinces in America all the means necessary to promote and secure their real happiness." To secure this, it was deemed wise to issue the decree " with the interesting object of encouraging in those countries the advancement and improvement of agriculture and industry, and to diminish, as far as practicable, the impediments and obstructions which at present retard their progress, to the great injury of the state." [2] The main articles of the decree relate to the reduction of taxes and the removal of restrictions. The reduction of taxes was accompanied by a request to purchase securities to help pay for a loan of twenty millions of dollars then recently opened in Spain. But the reduction in the taxes was for the purpose of pleasing the people of America, and of relieving, in a measure, their burdens.

---

[1] See Chapters IV. and VIII.
[2] Rockwell, *Spanish and Mexican Law*, 397.

This law was followed by a decree of September 27, 1820, abolishing all kinds of entails. One of the celebrated methods of disposing of land was known as the *mayorazgo*, which is defined as "the right to the enjoyment of certain aggregate property, left with the conditions therein imposed, that they are to pass in their integrity perpetually, successively, to the eldest son."[1] The property of the *mayorazgo* was "indivisible even to the enjoyment of its fruits." It could not "be alienated, hypothecated, given in emphyteusis, encumbered with servitudes, nor disposed of by compromise."[2] Nearly all of the lands granted to colonists, and indeed many of the large estates granted to individuals, were more or less entangled in this form of grant. By a decree of the Cortes, referred to above, the possessor of an entailed estate was granted power to sell half of the property, and the other half descending to the rightful heir could be disposed of at the will of the possessor.

In the following year (1821), the Cortes passed another decree explaining the law of 1820, that it might be executed without confusion. The Mexican congress, by an act of August 7, 1823, passed a law abolishing entails, which was almost identical with the law of the Cortes of 1820. The Mexican law declared all property, held in the form of mayorazgos prior to 1820, free; and prohibited the creation of mayorazgos in the future. This was a great step forward toward free trade in land. It was the last blow to the mediaeval forms of land tenure. The above laws applied to all Spanish or Mexican territory, including California and New Mexico. Under the government of Iturbide as Emperor of Mexico, the national colonization law of 1823 was passed. The law was explicit and liberal in all matters of colonization; but as it was suspended soon afterwards, it does not merit attention here. The following law was recognized in California down to the time of the occupation of the United States. A general

---

[1] Schmidt, *Law of Spain and Mexico.* Title II, Art. 273.
[2] *Ibid*, Arts. 274, 275.

colonization law of the Mexican congress, dated August 18, 1824, opened up the Mexican possessions to foreign settlers. It guaranteed protection to the rights, property, and persons of foreigners who came into the territory of Mexico to settle. Public lands not belonging to towns might be occupied by new settlers according to contract or as should afterwards be provided by special regulations. As an inducement to settlers, no tax could be imposed for the space of four years on foreigners who entered the nation for the first time for the purpose of settling. The law guaranteed all contracts with empresarios, or contractors, for the establishment of the colonies. It was also provided that no one who acquired property by virtue of this act could retain it, if he resided out of the territory of the Republic.[1] No person could obtain the ownership of more than one league square, or five thousand varas square, of irrigable land, four square leagues of land dependent upon the seasons, and six for the purpose of rearing cattle. That is, the maximum amount of land that one person was permitted to own was not far from seventy-five square miles.

In 1828, general rules were made for explaining and enforcing the national colonization law of 1824. By these regulations, the governors of the territories were empowered to grant vacant lands in their respective territories to individuals, families, and contractors. Applications for land were to be drawn up in due form and addressed to the governor, giving information concerning the number and character of the persons petitioning. If the petition and information accorded with the law of 1824, the governor might make the grant, provided that the grants to families should receive the sanction of the territorial deputation, and the contracts with the expresarios should receive the consent of the supreme government. The minimum amount of land given to one person for colonization, if irrigable, was two hundred varas square ; the minimum of land dependent upon the seasons (de temporal) was eight hundred

---

[1] Rockwell, 451; Schmidt, 341.

varas square; and the minimum for pasturage was twelve hundred varas square.[1]   This applied to the colonist, and was not intended to abrogate the law of 1824, which permitted the special grant of larger amounts to a single person.   The colonists were obliged to prove after a certain length of time that they had lived on the lands and cultivated them according to contract, before they could obtain a title to the lands.   When there was a union of families into a town, it was governed according to the municipal regulations of the country, and was subject to the interior government and policy.

A law of 1828, "in relation to passports and the mode of acquiring property by foreigners," was very important to those desiring to enter and pass through Mexican territory or to settle within its borders.   It was declared that "naturalized foreigners may purchase and colonize individual property; but in such a case they must obtain special permission of the General Congress if the land lies in the territories, and of the State Legislatures, if the land lie within a state."[2]   Should the State Legislatures grant permission to colonize under this act, the contract was subject to the following stipulations: "That one-fourth of the colonists must be Mexicans; that within seven years the land shall be divided into small lots of such dimensions as the Legislature requires; that a non-naturalized Empresario cannot reserve for himself a tract of land exceeding sixteen square leagues, which must be sold within twenty years, counting from the period of the acquisition of the property."

The general rules for naturalization were a peculiar commingling of liberal and narrow provisions.   The person desiring to be naturalized must declare his intentions of establishing himself in the country and present a petition with such declaration to the ayuntamiento one year prior to the date

---

[1] This would give to each colonist an aggregate of four hundred and ninety acres.

[2] Article 9; Schmidt, 349.

of naturalization. He must prove that he is a member of the "Roman Apostolic and Catholic Church" and "that he has some trade, profession, or income, sufficient for his maintainance." These propositions must be proved by witnesses before the district or circuit judge nearest his place of residence. This having been done in accordance with the law, the candidate for naturalization takes an oath of allegiance and renounces allegiance and obedience to all foreign nations, and all titles and favors granted by them. An empresario who effects a contract with the government for the settlement of a colony, becomes naturalized by taking an oath to support the constitution. Colonists are considered naturalized after a residence of one year from the date of their settlement. Thus bona fide settlers were favored by lenient naturalization laws.

The growth of the United States, and the gradual influx of immigrants from that country into the Mexican territory, caused the government of the latter country to enact a law restricting the former liberal inducements to foreigners. Article eleven of a decree issued by the Vice-President of the Mexican Republic, April 6, 1830, contains the following prohibitory measure: "In the exercise of the rights reserved to the general congress by the 7th article of the law of the 18th of August, 1824, the citizens of foreign countries lying adjacent to the Mexican territory are prohibited from settling as colonists in the states or territories of the republic adjoining such countries. Those contracts of colonization, the terms of which are opposed to the present article, and which are not yet complied with, shall consequently be suspended." Three years after the passage of this article, it was "repealed in all its parts." After the declaration of independence was proclaimed by Texas, the law as quoted above was reinstated by a decree dated April 4, 1837. In this is observed the revival of the old exclusive policy of Spain in the attempt to keep foreigners from entering the territory. It was suicidal to the interests of Mexico.

The decree of 1830 contained several remarkable provisions, among which was that the government should cause the convicts destined for Vera Cruz and other places, to be removed to the colonies. They were at first to work out their term of sentence on roads, fortifications, and public buildings. At the expiration of their term of sentence, they were to receive grants of land, if they desired to become colonists. This is an illustration of the method of disposal of convicts during the Spanish and the Mexican dominations. Another important act established a commission to inspect and control Mexican and foreign colonization within the territories. The commission had power to purchase of the territorial legislatures lands suitable for colonization, to enter into arrangements for the security of the republic, to enquire into the validity of the land contracts and affairs of similar nature. It was further provided in the decree that, " Mexican families who may voluntarily desire to become colonists " should be conveyed free of expense, supported during the first year, and given a grant of land and the necessary implements to till the soil. The decree prohibited the further importation of slaves, while it declared that no change would be made in respect to the colonies which already had slaves. The government was authorized to spend five hundred thousand dollars in aiding colonists in public improvements, in premiums to agriculturists in the colonies, and to encourage cotton manufactories by purchasing looms and machines and granting subsidies. The money was to be raised by a loan. Mexico realized the commercial and industrial supremacy of the United States even as she feared her political supremacy. Nearly every political law or decree issued by the government from this time had reference to the security of the colonies in the territories and states. The government seemed to feel that the only way to secure its great possessions was to fill the territory with people of Mexican blood.

A law, dated April 4, 1837, was enacted by the Mexican congress, which provided " for rendering effective the colonization of the lands which are or should be the property of the Republic." The lands were to be disposed of by sale, emphyteusis, or mortgage, and the amount thus derived was to be applied to the payment of the public debt. The best lands should be held at not over ten reals per acre, and sufficient land should be reserved for the payment of obligations to old soldiers, Indians, and those who aided in the restoration of Texas.

Immediately following this, a decree of the supreme government provided for the consolidation of the national debt. Stock certificates, bearing five per cent. interest, were to be issued for the whole amount. All outstanding debts were to be paid; one-half in the bonds in the consolidated stock, and one-half in the public land scrip in the departments of Texas, Chihuahua, New Mexico, Sonora, and the Californias, at the rate of four acres to one pound sterling. The land scrip was negotiable paper bearing five per cent. interest. It could pass from person to person by endorsements. No scrip was to be issued for less than four hundred acres nor for more than ten thousand. The government reserved land to the amount of one hundred million acres, as a guarantee of the payment of the scrip. All foreigners who purchased scrip and came to the Republic to establish themselves in the new estates, acquired the title of colonists and were entitled to all of the privileges of naturalized citizens. It was provided, in accordance with a previous law, that one person could not hold over one square league of irrigable land, four of land dependent upon the seasons, and six for grazing purposes. The law was published the following month, May 17, 1837.

After Mexico had lost Texas, and just as she was about to lose her control of New Mexico and the Californias, the government became fully aroused to the fact that one of the most urgent and necessary measures for the security of the Republic was to "promote foreign immigration, in order to people our immense lands, which are at this time the object of foreign cupidity." So said his excellency, Mariano de Salas, on November 27, 1846, and he immediately proceeded to resuscitate the board of colonization and give it new powers. In the following month, December 8, he issued regulations to the number of fifty-six for the specific action of the board of colonization. The regulations included methods of surveying lands, contracts, sales, prices of lands, inducements to colonists, and indeed a complete category of all laws and regulations concerning colonization. In conformity with previous decrees, the new colonists were to be exempt from active military service for twenty years, except in case of foreign aggression. They were to be exempt from all taxes except municipal, for the same term, and exempt from all duties on articles of subsistence for a term of ten years. Agricultural implements and supplies were free from duty, and the vessels that carried full cargoes of goods for colonists were free from tonnage. But the elaborate law never went into effect in the northern provinces, for they soon passed under the control of another government.

The special laws of the free state of Coahuila and Texas were very favorable to colonization. They have been discussed under the subject of Texas, in chapter ten, and will be only casually alluded to here. The liberal laws of colonization invited in foreigners, and soon a majority of the settlers were not in sympathy with the Mexican government. On the first occasion, the state of Texas revolted, declared her independence, became an independent state, and finally a member of the United States. The colonies were formed mostly by contract. The colony of Mr. Austin was the most important one, containing more inhabitants at the time of the declaration of independence than all of Texas besides. By 1832, much of the area of Texas had been parceled out into separate grants to empresarios for founding colonies. The country was organized into four jurisdictions or subordinate departments, each comprising a number of grants. These were the department of Nacogdoches comprising five grants, the department of Brazos comprising three grants, the first and second Austin grants and the Austin and Williams grant, the department of Bexar comprising three grants, and the department of the Northwest comprising at least three grants. Under the policy of colonization by agents, the population continued to increase until in 1835 there were twenty thousand Anglo-Americans in Texas, and only about three thousand Mexicans. Of the former over thirteen thousand were in General Austin's colony, while the majority of the latter lived near Bexar or San Antonio.[1]

Not all of the lands of New Spain were disposed of by the process of colonization. As the monarch was proprietor of all conquered territory, he might dispose of it as he chose. The lands of the colonial possessions of the New World were disposed of in several ways. First, certain lands were conceded to the support of pueblos and for the citizens of the same; second, some were granted by the king to his vassals who had been instrumental in conquest; third, there were lands that were sold to individuals for the purpose of swelling the royal treasury; and, finally, certain lands were retained under the title of "common lands," "vacant lands," and "royal lands." The use of the last mentioned class of lands was granted by the king to his vassals under the declaration of laws and decrees issued from time to time relating to the grants. These lands were granted for occupation and use, and usually for a specified time. The amounts varied according to the needs of the individuals. These grants, for the first two hundred years of Spanish occupation, had to secure the approval of the king before they became valid. But during the period between 1754 and 1786, the royal audiencias granted the lands to settlers and occupants. From the latter date until the Mexican revolution, the governors of the provinces granted the lands, subject to the sanction of the supreme council of estates at Mexico.

Owing to the routine of administration, the confusion made by its frequent changes, and the failure of the officials

---

[1] Monette, *History of the Valley of the Mississippi*, II, 573.

to proceed legally, the land titles of Mexico and adjacent provinces have been in an atmosphere of doubt. Lands were granted by persons without supreme authority, and the grantees thought they had a clear title to the land. Others were content to occupy the lands tentatively, without taking the trouble to secure a sure title; and the delay caused them great trouble. After the revolution, affairs under Mexican supremacy went on almost in the same way as under Spanish rule. The disposal of the royal lands then belonged to the authority of the Mexican government, where formerly it belonged to the crown. The Mexican colonization law of 1824, as defined by the regulations of 1828, permitted the governor of provinces to grant lands to colonists, families, and empresarios, but the grants, the presarios, for colonies or pueblos were not valid until approved by the supreme government. The grants to families were not valid until sanctioned by the territorial deputation. However, if the latter failed to accede to the grant, the governor might appeal to the supreme government.

The grants to individuals outside of colonies were very few in the province of California under Spanish rule. As early as 1775, a grant of land was made to Manuel Buitron. In 1784, Governor Fages allowed several men to occupy certain lands; and, in 1786, he was authorized to grant tracts not exceeding three leagues in extent. The grant was not to encroach upon any pueblo or mission.[1] During the entire Spanish period, the only ranchos granted as real property to holders, "were those of the Nietos, Verdugos, Dominguez, the Maligo of Bartolo Tapia, and probably also la Ballona of the Zúñingas."[2] At least five were in private possession in 1795. Governor Fages granted the Nietos tract, embracing all of the land between the Santa Ana and San Gabriel rivers, and extending from the sea to the hill land on the northern

[1] Bancroft, *California Pastoral*, 257.
[2] Bancroft, *California Pastoral*, 539.

ZUNI PUEBLO.

frontier, to Manuel Nieto.[1]   In October of the same year, the San Rafael tract, lying on the left bank of the Los Angeles river and extending to the Arroyo Seca, was granted by Pedro Fages to Jose Maria Verdugo.   It is also known as the La Zanja.   The Santa Ana tract, lying along the east side of the Santa Ana river, was granted to Antonio Yorba in 1810. The famous San Pedro rancho was granted to Juan Jose Dominguez during the last century, and confirmed by Sola in 1822. The Encino rancho was granted to Francisco Reyes, where he kept his stock and the stock of Cornelia Avila and others. Between 1795 and 1800, there were granted the San José de Gracia de Simi to Javier, Patricio, and Pico; and El Fugio to Captain Ortega or his sons, a year or two later.   All of these described were of the southern district and near Los Angeles.   The great majority of the ranchos and haciendas were granted under Mexican rule.

Some of the ranchos were like the old feudal estates.   The ranchero lived like a lord.   He had his retainers and servants, his flocks and herds, as well as great landed estates.   The land owned was great in extent, and it was not uncommon for a ranchero to have several thousand horses, ten to fifteen thousand cattle, and from fifteen to twenty thousand sheep.   The great Vallejo rancho of Sonomo contained thirty-three leagues, or about 146,000 acres.   There was, of stock on the farm, 12,000 to 15,000 head of cattle; 8,000 head of horses; and 2,000 to 3,000 sheep.   There were three hundred men at work on the rancho, besides women and children.   The land of these vast estates was frequently re-granted to others.   Sometimes papers were made out and a survey was effected; but it as frequently happened that the gift was made as simply as a man would make a present of a horse or a cow, without legal formality.   Frequently there was an understanding with *los Americanos* to occupy the land for a short time; but they subsequently laid claim to it.

---

[1] Bancroft, *California*, I, 662.

21

In 1851, the 31st congress of the United States passed an
act, "To ascertain and settle the private land claims in the
state of California." This act provided for a commission of
three persons, appointed for the purpose of hearing testimony
and settling all claims to lands granted prior to the accession
of California to the United States. This commission was empowered to investigate all claims of grants by the Mexican
and Spanish authorities. They were empowered to sit at
different places and listen to claims, hear testimony, and give
decisions. The district attorney was empowered to appeal
from the decisions to the Supreme Court. In Santa Clara
county alone, the commission settled more than fifty claims.
These claims ranged from a few acres to six square leagues.[1]
Among the grants are some of the most noted in California;
such as Las Animas, Laguna, Las Llagas, Las Uvas, and
others. The private grants during the latter part of Mexican
rule were very frequent. In the northern district of California,
including San Francisco, San José, and Santa Cruz, there were
not less than eighty grants made under Spanish and Mexican
authority prior to 1840.[2] A large number of these ranchos
were registered by the United States Land Commissioner.

The occupation of California as a colonization scheme has
been described elsewhere in this volume. The private grants
occurring after 1786 give an entirely different phase of the
land question. Mr. Bancroft, acknowledging that the governor
had power to grant lands after 1786, holds that no *bona fide*
titles were confirmed prior to 1800. The fifteen or twenty
ranchos said to be granted within this period were held provisionally by their occupants. This may be true, but it was
owing to some informality of the law; for the grantors gave
and the grantees accepted the grant in good faith, and never
considered it otherwise than genuine, unless so specified. The
carelessness in making records and in the final execution of the
law, rendered the grants technically, and perhaps legally,

---

[1] Hall, *San José*, 484.   [2] Bancroft, *California*, III, 711.

defective. The greater number of grants was made during Mexican rule, particularly between 1833 and 1846.[1] At the latter date, the total number of grants was nearly eight hundred, the most of which varied from one league to five leagues in extent. As each league contained something over 4428 acres, it is easily seen to what an extent the fertile valleys of the coast of California were occupied. The ease with which some of these grants were obtained shows with what lavish hands the Mexican authorities disposed of the public domain. Any citizen might petition the governor for a grant of land. His petition had to be accompanied with at least a rude sketch of the proposed grant. The only limit placed upon the amount was determined by the law of 1824, which divided lands into three classes. As has been stated in a preceding chapter, of the first or irrigable land, the grant could not exceed one square league ; of the second or non-irrigable arable land, four square leagues; and of the third or pasture land, six square leagues. Thus no person could receive more than eleven square leagues (about 48,709 acres) of land. The governor frequently referred the petition of the person desiring a grant to the local alcalde, with instructions to investigate the case and report in favor of the grant or against it. If the alcalde returned a favorable report and the governor was satisfied as to the character and needs of the applicant, he endorsed the application and turned it over to the secretary of state, who wrote a formal grant of the land. This the governor signed and referred to the departmental assembly for approval. If the assembly disapproved, the governor then forwarded the case to the authorities at Mexico. As soon as the grant was approved, the alcalde placed the grantee in actual and legal possession of the soil. This last act was accompanied by a rude survey, and a location of boundaries with rude monuments. The grant usually included an obligation on the part of the grantee to erect buildings, and to stock the farm within a year after occupation.

---

[1] Bancroft, *California,* IV, 530.

As land was plentiful, there was great carelessness in regard to specifications of boundary, and the surveys were very general in their nature. In the early period this lack of exactness was not felt; but as grants multiplied and contentions arose as to lands, endless confusion followed on the track of former slackness.

By the treaty of 1848 between Mexico and the United States, all private rights and titles were secured to individuals, and this rendered a valid title under the Mexican government just as valid under United States law. When the latter government obtained control of California, nearly all of the good lands along the water courses had been taken up by the Mexican grants. Some of these lands were merely occupied, others were held by complete titles, and others still were of doubtful ownership. As immigrants poured in from other nations, particularly the United States, there was precipitated immediately strife for the land, which led to increased confusion. Matters continued to grow worse until 1851; when Congress, after much delay and discussion, created a land commission to adjust the difficulties. The commission was furnished with a secretary well versed in the Spanish language, and was authorized to hear cases and make investigations, to administer oaths, and to take testimony in the proof of titles. Each person holding a title under the Mexican or Spanish laws was obliged to file his claim within two years, with such evidence as he was able to summon. Many of the titles apparently valid were subject to long and tedious litigation, chiefly because of contentious parties who had laid claim to them. Others were settled with little difficulty, while some have not been settled at all. The dearth of reliable witnesses, the incompleteness of records, imperfect surveys, and contentious lawyers working in somebody's interest, all combined to render the proper adjustment of affairs very difficult.

The law of 1851 declared that all towns in existence on July 7, 1846, should be considered as entitled to their pueblo lands, according to the ancient law which guaranteed four square leagues of land to each pueblo. Therefore all claims had to be presented to the commissioners in the name of the town, and not in the name of the owners of the lots situated within the town. San José received by direct grant in the courts a tract much larger than four square leagues; but the various exceptions of private grants within the pueblo made the real amount much less than the stipulations of the grant would seem to indicate. The claims of San Francisco were confirmed in 1854, but there has been much subsequent legislation. The claim of San Diego was acknowledged in 1870, and the claims of Monterey and Santa Barbara in 1856 and 1861 respectively.

The land titles within a pueblo were to be referred to the pueblo authorities for settlement. The pueblos never received any direct official title to their lands; they held them under a law which secured to them the several classes of lands belonging to all pueblos. The founding of a pueblo according to this law, and the placement of individuals in possession, was a guaranteed title to the land. The residents of the pueblo received their lands through the pueblo as an intermediary between them and the general government. Therefore, in the settlement of titles on pueblo lands, the owner looked to the pueblo for a title, and thus answered the demands of the commission.

In regard to the mission lands, there were, with two exceptions, no legal titles given.[1] The priests had no titles to the lands, and the neophytes owned no property, except where a few had settled in severalty on the land and had received a title from the government. The church could not claim a foot of soil under the general fact of occupation of the mission lands. The lands had been reserved to the missions simply for convenience and use, but no legal enactment granted the lands. The personal property and the improvements attending

---

[1] Santa Inés College Ranch and La Laguna in San Louis Obispo were secured to the church by formal grants. Bancroft, *Cal.*, IV, 565.

the establishment of missions doubtless belonged to the church, or the religious orders as agents of the church. But in the final settlement the government gave to the church the missions and the lands immediately adjacent, declaring the so-called mission lands, upon which the mission herds were wont to roam, public domain. This merely followed the Mexican and Spanish law, and was no injustice to anybody except to the credulous neophytes, who had been allowed to live so many years under the fiction that they had a right to the lands upon which they dwelt.

New Mexico had long been settled by the Spaniards when it passed under the control of the United States. Three centuries of occupation had enabled the colonists and officials to secure for themselves the most fertile portions of the lands of the valleys, lying along the streams. Besides the grants to pueblos and towns, many private ranchos were granted to those in favor with the authorities. In the Spanish and Mexican grants there was great carelessness in regard to titles and surveys. The subdividing and re-granting of ranchos had added to the confusion, and the public archives were very imperfect in their information. In July, 1854, Congress provided for the appointment of a surveyor-general to survey the lands of New Mexico. The work proceeded very slowly. There was great confusion of titles and claims to lands owing to the early grants. The Surveyor-general was authorized to investigate private and town land claims and report them to Congress for approval.[1] He searched the records and asked claimants to present titles. After investigating about two thousand documents, he discovered about two hundred titles. There were many claims filed, some of which were examined and approved by the Surveyor-general. By 1863, over sixty claims had been filed and at least thirty examined, most of which were approved. But Congress would have shown greater wisdom had it appointed a land commission, as in the case of Cali-

---

[1] Bancroft, *Arizona and Mexico,* 648.

fornia, and examined claims, taken evidence, and confirmed or rejected titles. As it was, the land question was allowed to drift on through contention and almost endless litigation. The whole number of land claims filed in the Surveyor-general's office down to 1886 was two hundred and five. These were exclusive of the pueblo Indian claims which were approved at an earlier date.[1] Of the claims referred to, thirteen were rejected and one hundred and forty-one approved. Of those approved, Congress had confirmed forty-six leaving ninety-five still in controversy. The earliest of these grants was given in 1700, several followed in the eighteenth century, but the majority were either made or re-granted under Mexican rule.

The settlement of the Mexican land titles was an extremely intricate question. Complications arose on every hand. The settlement of town lands, mission property, and public and private grants included many grievous questions of titles, of surveys, and of false claims. The whole subject was one of dire confusion both to commissioners and to settlers. Under such circumstances it would be almost impossible entirely to avoid injustice to some one. And, although forty years have passed since the formation of the land commission, many questions are still unsettled. "In 1880," says Bancroft, "twenty-nine years after the land act had become a law, there were four claims still pending in the courts on a question of title; in case of ten others no survey had been made; 48 surveys had not been fully settled; 27 were in the hands of the general land office, presumably pending ready for patent; and 527 had been patented in 1856-80."[1] Thus does justice drag its slow length along in this age of steam and electricity. The original holders of lands have lost most of their holdings either through the mis-judgments of the courts and commissions, or else by the wily intrigues of the Anglo-Americans, espe-

---

[1] Bancroft, *Arizona and New Mexico*, 757. See a carefully compiled table of New Mexican grants on page 758, of *Arizona and New Mexico*.

cially the latter. The Mexican has been no match for the invader in business thrift and property cunning.

The laws of colonization in Mexico have always been of a very liberal character. The laws now in vogue, enacted in 1876, offer excellent inducements to settlers. The colonists are assisted to enter the state; their transportation is advanced to them, and they are furnished subsistence for one year after settlement. All colonists are freed from the payment of poll and capitation taxes, and other contributions, for a term of ten years after settlement. The colonists are, for the same length of time, free from national guard service, road taxes, and all local taxation, from real and personal property taxes, as well as taxes on property invested in commercial enterprises. All products that the colonists export are free from taxes, and all goods imported for their consumption are free from duty for the term of ten years. Under these circumstances, settlers acquire definite tracts of land for use. There are still public lands to be acquired in Mexico by the payment of a small sum. These public lands (terrenos baldios) are divided into three categories, according to fertility and situation, and the prices are fixed every two years by the minister of public works for each state and territory of the Republic. For 1887 and 1888, the prices of the first class in the different states ranged from one dollar and seventy-five cents to four dollars and fifty cents per acre; those of the second class from one dollar and ten cents to three dollars; those of the third class from seventy-five cents to two dollars. Lands may be acquired in other ways; either by purchase from private owners or by rent. Large tracts of land are still owned by the municipalities of the Pacific slope, and are laid out in plantations and rented or leased to responsible persons.

CHAPTER XVI.

DIPLOMATIC RELATIONS.

The diplomatic warfare through which Spain attempted to make good her extravagant claims to the greater part of North America against the encroachments of other nations, is not less interesting than is her struggle to secure territory by the establishment of colonies. The whole history of this subject, from the days of Columbus to the treaty of Gaudalupe Hidalgo, is a graphic illustration of the principle of what constitutes the title to the land of newly discovered countries. It clearly demonstrates that mere discovery, with a few occasional visits to an unsettled territory, does not stand against the facts of actual possession and use. In the international usage of the past, the real right of ownership has rested chiefly in the power with which a nation could possess and hold lands either by diplomacy or by the force of arms. In all diplomatic controversies respecting the ownership of land, the nation in actual possession by settlement had a vast advantage over one that held the title by mere theory of discovery and conquest. International law generally gave the land in dispute to the former, and if backed by military power, the possessory title was always sure.

The unfortunate attitude of Spain in respect to the territory of America arose chiefly through the pretentious power of the Pope, who assumed to hold the universe as a fief granted to him through a higher power. All lands not yet discovered by European nations were his to dispose of at will; indeed, the powers of Europe occupied the lands either by usurpation

or by his free consent. When Alexander VI. granted to
Spain all of the lands that might be discovered by the Spaniards in the New World, the monarch of Spain accepted the
grant and assumed that it was a bona fide title to the lands.
All that was necessary to clear the title was to catch a glimpse
of a distant shore, or perchance land for a few hours in order
to replenish fuel and water. Therefore, when Balboa unfurled
the Spanish flag on the shore of the Pacific Ocean, it gave the
Spaniards a just claim to all lands yet to be discovered in its
waters, and gave them control of all commerce and explorations therein. On the Atlantic ocean, the Spaniards claimed
the whole territory as far north as Labrador, which, according
to Spanish geography, was the northern boundary of Florida.
But on the other hand, Russia, England, France, and the
Netherlands did not accept this indefinite title as valid.
England began very early to protest against this assumption of
ownership, and her attitude is well represented in the reply
given to Spanish demands made on account of the treasures
which Sir Francis Drake had taken from the Spanish galleons.
On his return from a voyage around the world, during which he
had despoiled Spanish shipping, the Spanish nation demanded
immediate reparation. The English government responded,
"That they could not acknowledge the Spanish right to all of
the country, either by donation from the Pope or from their
having touched here and there upon those coasts, built cot-
tages, and given names to a few places; that this, by the law
of nations could not hinder other provinces from freely navi-
gating those seas, and transporting colonies to those parts where
the Spaniards do now inhabit; that prescription without possession availed nothing."[1] On this principle was carried on
the warfare for supremacy in North America.

In 1578, Sir Francis Drake landed at Bodega Bay, north of
San Francisco, on land claimed by Spain, and raised the
English flag, claiming the entire country in the name of the

---

[1] Brown, *The Genesis of the United States*, I, 9.

English sovereign and giving to it the name New Albion. No settlement was made and therefore no title was acquired. In 1607, Spain beheld with dismay the encroachments of the English companies upon her territory on the Atlantic seaboard. Powerless she looked on, while a new nation was being founded within her own borders. Diplomatic correspondence and protests were unavailing; the English took possession, settled and developed the country, and decided the question of ownership.

At the time of the treaty of Ryswick in 1697, the northern boundary of Spanish claims on the Atlantic seaboard was fixed by a line drawn through Cape Romaine, a point a few miles above Charlestown, and extending westward to the Mississippi. In the lower Mississippi valley the Spaniards still held the country; but the encroachments of the French by way of the Great Lakes had already begun. In the interior, west of the Mississippi, the Spanish claims extended to the headwaters of the Arkansas river in the interior of Colorado. Although the treaty of Ryswick had diminished their pretended possessions on the Atlantic coast, they had not yet lost territory in the southwest. In order to hold territory, the Spanish government adopted an exclusive system of trade. All foreign vessels were forbidden to enter Spanish waters for "traffick and trade." Not contented with this, Spain went a step further, and opposed as far as it was possible the near approach of any nation to the boundaries of her territory. To meet this difficulty, other nations granted licenses to privateers, ostensibly to explore and to make discoveries, but really to prey upon the commerce of Spain and to engage in trade against the laws of the latter. Hawkins and Drake are examples of these voyagers who played the part of sea-pirates toward the nation that was acting selfishly and unjustly in claiming more of the earth than belonged to her. In turn, the viceroys of New Spain began, as early as 1598, to study how to meet the open depredations upon Spanish commerce. Paper *cedulas* had no effect in the protection of the Spanish domain and seas.   The Spaniards attempted to guard the coasts and to send with each merchantman an armed fleet for protection.   The Dutch began their predatory warfare early in the seventeenth century, and France likewise had some sea-rovers in the Spanish main.   This irregular warfare continued until the commerce between Spain and the American colonies had about ceased.   Then, to thwart England and the Netherlands and relieve her commerce, Spain granted France liberal privileges in the carrying trade between the Indies and Spain. This was so favorable to the colonists that Spain was again obliged to interfere, to prevent an entire separation of the colonies from the mother country.   The treaty of Utrecht brought relief.   This treaty, occurring in 1713, gave great advantages to the French in the South American trade, and made contracts with England by what is known as the Asiento Treaty.[1]   By the latter, England was permitted to land slaves at Porto Bello, and to engage in commerce at that port.   England, having obtained a foothold, carried out the natural instincts of trade, and soon interfered greatly with Spanish commerce.   Trouble with the Spanish coast guards led to the war of 1739.   This war resulted in the changing of the contracts with England, and the Spanish ships were allowed to have a greater carrying trade.

The French continued to enlarge their territory in the Mississippi valley until the Spanish were practically crowded out.   They yielded the land reluctantly and with protest, but prescription had no influence on the people already in possession of the country.   In 1762, by a secret treaty, France conveyed to Spain all of Louisiana.   This gave to Spain Florida and the whole territory of the Mississippi valley west of the river and extending to the Pacific; the entire country west of the Mississippi river, with the exception of Oregon.   By the treaty of Paris in 1763, Spain ceded the Floridas to England, but regained them in 1783.   At this time Spanish territory

---

[1] Winsor, VIII, 307.

Map of
SPANISH
POSSESSIONS
in the UNITED
STATES
IN 1783

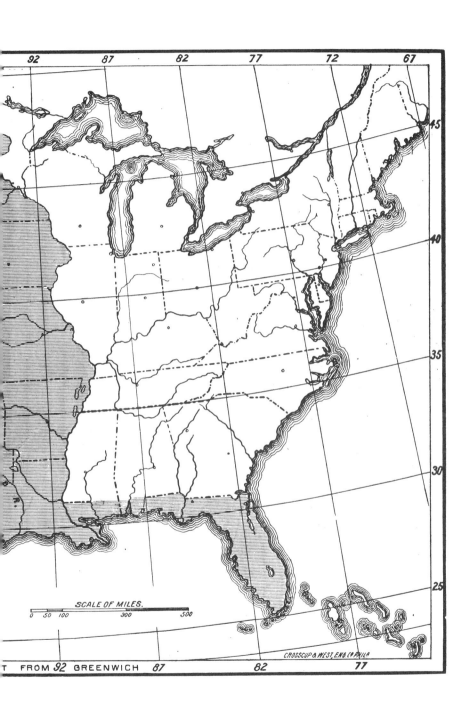

SCALE OF MILES.

0 50 100   300   500

CROSSCUP & WEST, ENG CO PHILA

FROM 92 GREENWICH 87   82   77

reached its maximum in North America.[1] Over two-thirds of the present territory of the United States was in the hands of Spain; and Mexico, the West Indies, and much of South America besides. It was a magnificent empire, but not long to be ruled by one power. In 1800, Spain ceded Louisiana to France, but retained for herself all of the interior country north of Mexico, including Texas, New Mexico, and the greater part of Colorado. Contrary to the expectations of Spain, the United States purchased Louisiana from France, and thus the territory of the restless young nation bordered on that of the Spanish possessions. The rich valley of the Mississippi, even to the headwaters of the Yellowstone, passed from the possession of Spain.

On the Pacific coast, the shrinkage of territory had already begun before the cession of Louisiana. The Nootka controversy began in 1789. At this time Spain claimed all territory from Panama to Prince William's Sound, on the basis of priority of discovery. Spanish explorers were the first to discover this part of the coast, but no permanent settlement had been effected north of San Francisco. England now sought, on the strength of Cook's explorations, to make settlements on the northwest coast for the purpose of carrying on the fur trade. Also the Russians were pressing down the coast, and the Spanish government endeavored to establish Prince William's Sound as the northern limit of its territory. Spain and England were the first nations to come into controversy concerning the northwest coast, and the point under dispute was Nootka Sound.

It seems that England and Spain each tried to establish a settlement at Nootka in 1789, and that Spain was the first in the field. At this period there were many trading vessels, mostly English and American, coming and going in the region, engaged in the fur trade. A Spanish expedition to the north, returning in 1788, brought news of the situation, and

---

[1] See Map of Spanish Possessions in the United States in 1783.

of the rapid encroachments of the Russians. To secure the territory for Spain, Viceroy Flores despatched the Princess and San Carlos, under their respective commanders, Martinez and Haro, with orders to make a settlement at Nootka. They sailed from San Blas on February 17, 1789, with instructions "to conciliate the natives, for whose conversion friars were sent; to erect buildings for the colony, and fortifications for its defence, as well as an indication of the Spanish sovereignty in that region; if Russian or English vessels appeared, to receive them with courtesy, but with a manifestation of the right of Spain, by virtue of discovery, to this establishment and others that were to be founded; and after the foundation, to send the San Carlos on an exploring tour to the coast between 50° and 55°."[1] The vessels arrived at their destination in May, and the commander, Martinez, proceeded to take formal possession of the port. He erected barracks for his men, and established a fort at the entrance to the sound. The Spanish commander seized the Iphigenia, an English trader of the Hudson Bay Company, flying the Portuguese flag. The commander was under the impression that the ship carried instructions hostile to the Spaniards; therefore the ship was seized, but was afterwards released, a better understanding having been reached. Other difficulties arose, and several vessels were seized, under the supposition that they had orders to make settlements at Nootka. This led to a diplomatic controversy which threatened war. The Spanish government claimed that by priority of discovery and settlement and by former treaties, it had a just right to the territory. According to the Spanish version, during the controversy Russia declared in favor of the rights of Spain, by prohibiting Russians from settling in Spanish territory and by requesting the Spanish sovereign to apprehend and punish all offenders against the law. Without doubt, Spain had legitimate claims to the territory of the northwest, but they did not figure in the present contro-

---

[1] Bancroft, *History of the Northwest Coast*, 213.

versy ; it was an immediate struggle, out of which the nation strongest in diplomacy and war must come off conqueror. England claimed damages for the seizure of British ships, and demanded the privileges of trade in the waters and on the coasts of the North Pacific.

While war was threatening, the convention of Nootka in 1790 settled the question between Spain and England. The treaty was signed October 28, which, though it did not relinquish the rights of Spain, practically excluded her from colonization on the northwest coast. By the terms of the treaty, Spain agreed to restore the buildings and lands taken from the British in the preceding year. Each party was to make just reparation to the other for all acts of violence or hostility which might have been committed subsequent to April, 1789. England secured the right of commerce, navigation, and settlement on the Pacific coast above San Francisco, and the same rights were secured to Spain. " Each nation was to have free access to the establishments of the other in the same territory above San Francisco. England pledged herself to prevent illicit trade at the Spanish ports, and to refrain from approaching within ten leagues of Spanish settlements."[1] The terms of the treaty were very fair to both parties, yet it was in reality a triumph for England and a humiliation to Spain ; for the latter practically renounced all sovereignty on the North Pacific coast, and the former was placed in a position to contest for supremacy after the manner of Englishmen.

Notwithstanding the fact that Spain had an acknowledged permanent settlement at Nootka, her forces were withdrawn from there five years after the signing of the Nootka treaty, quietly, and without relinquishing her right to the territory. Subsequently she fixed the limits of her territory at the northern boundary of California. This ended the struggle on the part of Spain for supremacy in the Northwest. The only desire that Spain had in securing these lands was to protect her other

---

[1] For condensed copy of the treaty see Bancroft, *Northwest Coast*, 234.

interests by keeping foreign powers several hundred miles from her own establishments, and perhaps to maintain as a matter of pride the ancient claims to territory. But these were not sufficient causes for war with England, and the case demanded either war or withdrawal.

In 1794, a permanent settlement of the difficulties was effected. By the agreement at this time, no permanent settlement was to be made at Nootka, though temporary buildings might be erected there for trading purposes. It is very difficult to tell whether Spain withdrew from Nootka by force of agreement due to the power of Great Britain, or whether the withdrawal was voluntary on account of the expense of keeping up an establishment that now yielded but a faint shadow of the old time glory of exclusive dominion. It is to be noticed that the advice of the viceroy, Revilla Gigedo, given in a report dated April 12, 1793, favored the abandonment of Nootka. He thought it not advisable to keep up the expensive port of Nootka for the sole purpose of keeping out foreigners. In his opinion the fur trade would soon decline, and it was therefore considered unwise to advise Spanish traders to compete with the English in Nootka waters. But he advocated the strengthening of presidios in California, the occupation of the port of Bodega, and if it could be found, the fortification of one other port north of this.[1] In regard to Nootka, he says, " I am then of the opinion that we should cede to the English wholly and generously our establishment at Nootka, since, so far as the way of thinking of the English commander, Vancouver, and his emissary, Broughton, could be ascertained, it seems that they desire and aspire to wave the English flag over that port without recognizing that of Spain, moved rather by the idea or vain-glory of sustaining what by reason of opposition they have made a point of honor, than by motives of interest or advantages which are truly problematic in connection with the fur trade."[1] Another significant point is

---

[1] Bancroft, *Northwest Coast*, I, 291.

that though the treaty limited the territory under controversy to that already occupied by the Spaniards, or, as is generally stated, that north of the port of San Francisco, the Spanish government set up a claim to the northern boundary of California as a limit of its possessions, a point within the disputed territory. This northern boundary of California was maintained by the Spanish and Mexican government as the limit of their possessions, down to the American conquest of California in 1848. These two significant facts would seem to indicate that Spain withdrew, not by formal agreement, but on account of the supposed advantage to her own affairs. Had the advice of Gigedo, namely, to contract her boundaries and strengthen her fortifications, been the general policy of Spain, it would have been a thousand times in her favor in conducting her policy in America. Unfortunately the policy of Spain was to enlarge boundaries, and thereby necessarily weaken defenses.

After the loss of Oregon in 1795, and Louisiana in 1800, Spain was next forced to part with Florida in 1819. The only pretence to the occupation of Florida in 1818, consisted of two garrisons, one at Pensacola and the other at St. Augustine.[1] Spanish authority had become nearly extinct, so much so that a buccaneering band of not more than one hundred and fifty men held Amelia Island against the power of the governor. One short futile attempt was made to dislodge the pirates, and that was all. There were many reasons why our government desired to be rid of the imperfect government of Ferdinand VII., who despised free institutions and feigned a contempt for the nation advocating them. The lawless misrule of Florida was a continual trial to the United States, and the treaty of 1819 brought great relief. The Spanish government would not regulate her own territory, and the United States was obliged to do so in her own behalf. General Wilkinson moved upon Mobile in 1813; General Jackson drove the British out of Pensacola in 1814; four years later

---

[1] Schouler, *History of the United States*, III, 31.

the same general defeated the Seminole Indians within Spanish territory, captured Pensacola, and hanged two British subjects who had been instrumental in inciting the war against him. The United States government did not sanction these movements. Spain was helpless, and the treaty was signed as a necessity on her part. The United States paid \$5,000,000 for Florida, but the sum was to be paid to American citizens who had claims against Spain.[1]

The revolt of the Spanish-American republics in 1821 resulted in the overthrow of Spanish dominion, and the creation of the United States of Mexico. The overthrow was attended with great humiliations on the part of Spain; for by it she relinquished her claims to the whole of North America. All controversies then in vogue or to be in vogue in the future, respecting the territory of the United States, devolved upon Mexico to settle. Mexico, by the treaty with Spain, obtained the whole territory that hitherto belonged to Spain, extending to the forty-second parallel on the northwest, and to the Sabine river on the southeast. The causes of the Mexican revolution are to be found in the evils of the Spanish system. It is true the tide of revolution that began in 1776 had at last reached Mexico. The growing differences between the people or Mexicans and the rulers or Spaniards brought great discontent. The people of Mexico knew not what they wanted, but they were certainly weary of the Spanish government. The extra demand on the people for taxes to meet the wars against Napoleon increased the discontent. Spaniards born in America were excluded from rights enjoyed by the Spanish-born, and the revolution sought to remedy this injustice. As the spirit of freedom and equality stirred, it became necessary to use force to suppress it, and this hastened the outbreak of the revolution.

Texas was the next empire to be carved out of the old Spanish dominions. Long controversies ensued after the treaty of

[1] Winsor, VII, 546.

Paris in 1763, and subsequently after the Louisiana purchase, concerning the boundaries of Texas and Louisiana; the latter then being a remote province of New Spain. At the time of the Louisiana purchase, France and Spain had joint claims to the land lying west of the Sabine river.[1] France based her claims upon the exploration of La Salle, and Spain based hers upon her assumed general title to all lands discovered in America. Spain then had settlements in Texas, but they were in the west and remote from the boundary marked by the Sabine; though some Spaniards had traversed the eastern part of the country. Under the conditions of the purchase, the United States succeeded to the rights of France west of the Sabine river. The question of settlement was left open until 1819, when the United States, in her treaty with Spain, abandoned all claims beyond the Sabine. This line was affirmed in a treaty with Mexico in 1828, and a treaty with the Republic of Texas ten years thereafter.

Attempts were made by the United States government in 1827 and in 1829 to purchase Texas from Mexico, but without avail. The state of Texas was a remote province of New Spain and therefore poorly governed. With the absence of independent power of self-government, the remote territories were too far away to receive the beneficial influences of the central government. But though afflicted with the evil of too little administration, they were free from the terror of too much government that intimidated some of the provinces of Spain. But Texas soon became peopled with Anglo-American immigrants; and these showed a far different spirit from the Spanish colonists, who had received a long training in over-government and subjection. They came principally from the southern States; but nearly every state in the Union contributed its quota to the colonists who believed in self-government. For some time Texas was united with the State of Coahuila under the name of the Free State of Coahuila and Texas. But the

---

[1] Winsor, Justin, *Narrative and Critical History of America*, VII, 550.

first movement toward revolution was seen in the separation of Texas from Coahuila, giving the former an independent government. This separation was brought about in part by the patriots of Texas. General Santa Ana was shrewd enough to see what this meant for the liberty-loving people of this remote province, and he therefore endeavored to reduce the government of Texas to a more direct subordination to the central government. To force a liberty-loving people to a more complete dependence upon a weak, revolutionary, and wretchedly administered government was not an easy task. The result of the attempt was a revolt, and a declaration of independence by the Republic of Texas. This declaration, which was made in 1836, led to the entire separation of Texas from the United States of Mexico. After this Mexico indulged in a great deal of talk about the recovery of Texas, and did not a little fighting; but it was of no avail. The question was to be settled finally by a greater power than the young republic of Texas. The whole aspect of affairs was changed by the annexation of Texas to the United States. The result was war, which ended in the treaty of Gaudalupe Hidalgo signed in 1848. This was about the last struggle of the Spanish American power to maintain itself within the present boundary of the United States. With the exception of the Gadsden purchase, by which a part of Arizona was obtained, the treaty of Hidalgo gave us all of New Mexico, Texas, California, Arizona, and the greater part of Colorado. It was the last final triumph of the Anglo-Americans over the Spanish-Americans.

Prior to the Mexican war there were several powers that looked with some anxiety toward the possible possession of California. These were France, England, Russia, and the United States. It is not easy to say to what extent France and England had designs on California. Probably nothing definite was ever planned, although without doubt they were looking to a possible occupation. The United States made her desire known by attempts to purchase the territory. Russia early declined the struggle. In 1812 the Russians obtained permission of the Spanish governor to establish a trading station at Bodega Bay. Their ostensible purpose was to obtain supplies for their northern posts and stations. In a few years they had grown so strong in numbers and in fortifications that the Spanish authorities asked them to depart from the coast. The Russians boldly informed the Spaniards that they intended to remain, and verified their determination by erecting another fort in 1820, about forty miles north of Bodega. Russia now made pretentious claims to the northwest coast, which were denied by England and America. She claimed a right to the territory north of the parallel of forty-five degrees and fifty minutes. After much controversy, the boundary line was fixed at 54° 40′, the Russians agreeing to remain north of that, and the United States agreeing to remain on this side. The Russians still continued at Ross and Bodega; and the English complained that they were violating treaty stipulations, and asked the Mexicans to drive them out. Mexico was not able to do this, but asked the intercession of the United States; and at the request of the latter nation the Russians withdrew. This ended their struggle for California.

The explorers and writers for many years had been representing the desirability of California. They had spoken of the fine climate, fertile soil, and especially of its advantageous position; and had created a general desire among nations for occupancy. France had sent La Perouse, and later De Mofras, who had given faithful descriptions of the country. Forbes, representing English interests, inquired carefully into the situation. The United States depended somewhat upon the explorations of John Wilkes. It was supposed that both France and England had agents who were ready to inform the government of the opportune time for conquest and occupation. This was greatly exaggerated, although it must be held that each of the nations desired California, and would not lose a favorable opportunity of obtaining possession.

The Mexican government owed France a large sum of money, but would not pay it when demanded; therefore

France with her army and fleet took Vera Cruz, and thus forced the government to pay the loan. Mexico also owed England, and it was suggested that the territory of California would about cancel the debt, in the event of a separation of California from Mexico. France seemed greatly interested in California. Without doubt she thought her services might be useful to the Californians, should a crisis appear. Her claim to a probable protectorate was based upon the idea of a common religion, a common race as opposed to the Teutonic, and a common sympathy in dislike for the aggressive Anglo-Saxon. The British government had on the Pacific coast a fleet of four vessels, the French had a fleet of eight vessels, and the United States sent Commodore Jones with a fleet of five ships, to look out for her interests in the Pacific. Commodore Jones raised the American flag at Monterey, an act for which the government afterwards apologized. No doubt it was the understanding that the American flag was to be raised, but Commodore Jones was too hasty. This was not a diplomatic contest for supremacy in California, but rather a shrewd watchfulness to take advantage of occasions as they arose. Of the three powers, the United States had two points in her favor. First, the stream of emigrants that began to pour into the province would soon Americanize it, if not hindered; and second, the territory would fall naturally to the United States as an addition to her national territory. As soon as hostilities had begun on the Rio Grande, the occupation of California was a simple matter.

But the writer will forbear attempting to describe a very interesting epoch of history, as condensation into a few paragraphs would spoil the story. The raising of the Bear Flag; the influence of Thos. Larkin; the action of Commodore Sloat, in raising the American Flag at Monterey; the action taken by Generals Kearney and Fremont; the work of Commodore Stockton; the feeble resistance of the Californians;—this and much more is familiar to the majority of readers. The result of it all was that the United States obtained the most interesting portion of old Spanish territory in America, and indeed that which has proved of greatest benefit to the race in furnishing products of the mines and the soil, and happy homes for millions who rejoice in a free and intelligent government. The method by which California was won to the United States has been clearly set forth by Mr. Bancroft, in his fifth volume of the History of California,[1] and the story of the Secret Mission of Bear Flag has been admirably told by Mr. Royce, in his "California." [2] Interesting and inviting as the subject is, the writer of the present volume has nothing new to offer. Besides, want of space would necessitate a curtailed account; and this I consider worthless in this connection. The whole story should be told with a complete analysis of motives and plans, to render the presentation creditable.

Thus we have seen how the great assumptions of Spain have ended in humiliation and defeat and resulted in her entire withdrawal from the soil of America because of inability to cope with other powers in the struggle for territory. We have seen how in diplomacy and war, in civilization and progress, Spain has fallen behind in the race of nations. But the problem of the decline and fall of Spain was solved before the writer entered upon the subject of the last chapter. The nature of Spanish institutions as previously presented in this volume, the laws, the government, the administration, and the conditions under which the nation worked, all point to the secret causes of retrogression. The institutions were too stereotyped and inflexible to be adapted to the requirements of a new country. Beyond a few leaders, the colonists were lacking in vigor, enterprise, and the power of developing institutions. The commercial policy of Spain was immediately and continuously ruinous to the colonists, and detrimental to Spanish enterprise. Trade that would have sprung up spontaneously was stifled in its attempts by burdensome restrictions and

---

[1] Bancroft, H. H., *History of California*, Vol. V, Chaps. III-XVII.
[2] Royce, Josiah, *California, American Commonwealths*, Chapter II.

laws. Again, Spain had attempted to compass and settle lands of too great extent, and therefore could not defend them, much less develop them. Declining power, manifested in the decrease of wealth, commerce, and diplomatic prowess, caused Spain to yield her vast possessions to more vigorous nations, that were willing and able to develop the natural wealth of the land, and to give to the inhabitants an enlightened and free government untainted with mediaeval wrongs. Yet with all of this and more to be said, Spain has rendered great service in opening up undiscovered tracts of land to the world, and in performing pioneer work in much of the vast territory of America.

INDEX.

A.

Acapulco, trade of, 298.
Adobe, defined, 273.
Agricola, founds colonies, 21.
Alameda, the grove, 277.
Alaric, code of, 25.
Alcalde, 67, 115, 277; duties of, 191, 290–293.
Alcatraz, 277.
Alexander VI, and Spain, 2, 54, 330.
Alferez real, 284.
Alfonso the Wise, 28.
Alfonso X, formulates Siete Partidas, 159.
Alguazil, 67, 284.
Alhambra, 129.
Alonzo XI, 28, 32.
Alta California, settlement of, 84, 88–111.
Amadis of Gaul, 91.
Amazons, 218.
Amelia Island, buccaneers on, 337.
" An Apostle of the Tules," 273.
Anian, strait of, 75.
Arab-Moors, architecture of, 127.
Architecture, of Moors, Spaniards, Romans, etc., 127 ff.
Argüello, and San José, 182; decree of, 294 ff.; quoted, 304.
Arizona, Spaniards in, 8, 220–223.
" Arizuma," 220.
Arrillaga, 203; and Guerra, 186.
Asiento Treaty, 332.
Astralagus, 276.
Atlantic Monthly, quoted, 91.
Audiencia, of Mexico, 252.
Augustus, and Spain, 16; and colonization, 18.
Austin, *Gen.*, colony of, 237, 318, 319.
Austin, S. F., and Texas, 237.
Austin and Williams' grant, 319.

Authorities consulted, xxi.
Autos acordados, defined, 61, note.
Alvarado, *Gov.*, proclamation of, 137.
Averia, 303.
Avila, Cornelia, 321.
Ayuntamientos, established, 135; described, 286–290, 294.

B.

Bac, mission of, 221 ff.
Baja California, 92, 93; missions of, 82.
Balboa, and the Pacific, 330.
Ballona of the Zúñingas, 320.
Bancroft, Hubert Howe, cited, vi, 221, 222, 227, 261, 269, 285, 302, 322, 343; quoted, 72, 73, 81, 109, 203, 212, 214, 278, 284, 303, 327.
Bandelier, on the Pueblo Indians, 251.
Bartolo Tapio, Maligo of, 320.
Bartlett, quoted, 263.
Bear flag, raising of the, 342, 343.
Beechy, cited, 150.
Bellamy, 118.
Benedictines, come to Mexico, 72.
Bexar, department of, 319.
Blackmar, Frank W., vii.
Bodega Bay, Drake at, 330; Russians at, 301, 307, 340 ff.
Bonanza, defined, 274.
Borica, *Gov.*, 196; and land grants, 204; report of, 214.
Boscana, and California Indians, 241 ff.
Botas, defined, 261.
Branciforte (Santa Cruz), founding of, 184 ff.
Brazos, department of, 318.
Breviarium, 25.
Bronco, defined, 277.
Broughton, and Vancouver, 336.

345

Index.

57334